DEATH AS A LIVING

Doyle Burke and Lou Grieco

Published by Inkshares, Inc., Oakland, California
www.inkshares.com

Edited by Delia Davis and Kaitlin Severini
Cover design by Tim Barber
Formatted by Kevin G. Summers

ISBN 9781950301034
e-ISBN 9781950301041
LCCN 2019936610

First edition

Printed in the United States of America

This book takes you behind the police tape. Some of the crimes, and descriptions of the crime scenes and victims, may be disturbing to some. The graphic descriptions of the scenes are not dwelled upon, but are essential to adequately tell this story. Even so, reader discretion is advised.

DEDICATION

I would like to dedicate this book to both of my families.

Yes, both families.

First, my personal family. My loving wife, Nicole; son, James; daughters, Michelle and Katie; and seven grandchildren. Especially Katie, who was the first person to actually read this book. Without them, my work means nothing.

This career requires you to drop whatever you're doing and leave your happy home at a moment's notice. You then race to a gruesome crime scene, do your job, and return home. Once home, you have to forget what you've seen and be Daddy instead of Detective. If only it were that simple. It's difficult—if not impossible—to forget the things we've seen, but we try. The family of a homicide detective is a tough job itself. My family always understood, and that was important. Likewise, I tried to be at every school conference, game, and party, physically if not mentally.

I would also like to dedicate this book to my other family.

The men and women of law enforcement, the thin blue line. Especially those who have served, and are still serving, on the Dayton Police Department. And yes, those of us in law enforcement are brothers and sisters, and together we are strong. I worked with unbelievably strong men and women whose courage is often unheralded and most times not fully appreciated.

To the families of those officers who gave their lives, I admire you. I've stood at many memorial services and wondered how you must feel. The death of a police officer is major news, for a while. Everyone talks about it and wants to help, for a while. Eventually, the public forgets and moves on. We never move on; we can't.

To the families of the homicide victims, I hope you know—solved or unsolved—I gave it my all. While I can't bring your loved ones back, I tried to at least bring a sense of closure to you.

I must give a special thank-you to my wife, Nicole. Without her, this book would not be possible. While it seemed a simple undertaking at first, this book, while a labor of love, took an enormous amount of time. Time away from my family. But my wife encouraged me. "This is a book that needs to be written," she would say. When I completed a chapter, I would take it to my wife like a little child bringing Mommy their homework. I was proud of my work, but then reality hit. My wife would read it and hand it back to me. "Now, don't get mad, but it makes no sense," she would say. What? *This is a masterpiece*, I thought, then she walked me through it. Three of the hardest words for me to say are: She was right. With her help, my random thoughts became the chapters that became this book. I can't thank her enough, and I love her even more for telling me the truth and making this book better. Even the strongest detective needs a strong home, and I have been blessed in that respect.

PREFACE

ON AUGUST 4, 2019, the national nightmare came to Dayton. A gunman in the Oregon District, the city's premier entertainment destination, opened fire in front of Ned Peppers Bar. Connor Betts fired 41 rounds into a crowd in less than 30 seconds, killing nine people.

Within twenty seconds of the first shot, local police were already engaging with Betts. Thirty-two seconds after his first shot, Betts was dead. Police had used deadly force, legitimately, and stopped a fatal threat. While the deaths of nine bystanders is unbelievably tragic, and many more people were injured or traumatized by the events, the quick response of the officers undoubtedly prevented further deaths. Those officers were considered national heroes, and rightly so.

In the wake of the May 25, 2020, death of George Floyd, at the hands of Minneapolis police, many cities were convulsed with anti-police protests. I had to visit the Miami Valley Regional Crime Laboratory in downtown Dayton. I found many officers facing down angry protestors. The first officers I saw? The very squad that stopped Connor Betts's fatal assault.

"And to think you guys were national heroes less than a year ago," I said to them.

The events of 2020 left me angry and sad. On the one hand, we had an officer causing the death of a man in his custody. This was not in any way a justified use of force. This was a crime. Even worse, there had been three other officers present who had not intervened in any way. I can understand public anger about these events, which are profoundly disturbing and have harmed the profession of policing immeasurably.

Yet, at the same time, we had protests demanding that we "defund the police," which struck me as lunacy. Protestors held signs that said, "ACAB," meaning "All Cops Are Bastards." This was completely unfair to the vast majority of police officers, who were, I can assure you, horrified by George Floyd's death.

I wrote this book to reflect on my own career as a police officer and a homicide detective, to show readers what this job is really like and how it is really done. It's a job that has evolved over the forty-three years that I've been in law enforcement, and must continue to evolve. We were in what we thought were the final edits for this book when George Floyd died. Those events caused us to pause, to think, to edit again. But they did not change my mission, which was to illuminate what policing and detective work is like, and what it looks like when it's done well.

This is critical. I fear that we've lost the ability to communicate with each other in this country, to have rational discussions about issues, to disagree peacefully without burning the bridges we need to survive. Anyone who is holding a sign that claims all cops are bastards is not interested in any kind of rational debate.

But we police officers can be our own enemies. A few paragraphs earlier, I noted that most police officers were horrified by George Floyd's death. I know this because we talk to each other. But the things we say to each other, we're often reluctant to discuss with people outside the profession. This is for a number of reasons: we're afraid of being used politically; we worry that laypeople won't understand what we go through; and we believe that policing is, in a sense, a family. While you might be willing to argue with your brother or sister, sometimes even bitterly, you generally don't take sides against them publicly.

This book is, for me, a leap of faith. I know that some veteran officers will read this book and I hope they enjoy it, but I'm probably not going to reveal anything they don't already know. I wrote this book thinking of two other audiences.

The first is the general public. I want to take you behind the thin blue line and the yellow crime scene tape to help you better understand the world I come from, which is not perfect, but does more than its share of good.

The second audience is future police officers. We need to draw good people, from all backgrounds, into policing. And if policing is a family, it's natural for family members to wish for better things for the next generation.

If we're going to have honest, open dialogue about law enforcement issues, we've got to talk, freely and openly and respectfully. In this book, you'll see that I believe open dialogue between police and community leaders has prevented riots over the past five decades. We need a larger conversation like that, nationwide. I hope this book can be part of the start of that conversation.

Sincerely,

Doyle Burke

1.
WHO YOU GONNA CALL?

IT LOOKED LIKE any other homicide. Bright yellow tape with the warning POLICE LINE DO NOT CROSS surrounded the area around the house. Outside the tape were scores of people, including the usual types: concerned neighbors, rubberneckers, news media. Uniformed officers kept everyone back and held the scene securely. After seven years of police experience, I'd seen death scenes numerous times. But this was only my second homicide as a detective.

Death is always different. Rapes were horrible. Robberies left terrified victims. But death was final, and as I was already learning, it wore you down as an investigator.

We already knew this would be atypical. Most homicides involve one body. But shortly before midnight on November 1, 1985, we got the call. "Homicide at 35 South Ardmore with multiple victims," the dispatcher said.

As I approached the scene, a veteran officer looked at me and said, "It's bad."

His warning resonated. Work as a police officer for any length of time and you'll get used to seeing some pretty nasty stuff. To survive, you adapt, shrugging off the ordinary horrors that would traumatize the average civilian. But every so often, you will see things that no officer, no matter how seasoned, can ever get used to.

If this veteran officer thought it was bad, I knew it had to be horrible. But I didn't understand until I stepped inside.

The house itself looked like something out of a horror movie. An old two-story structure, it had dirty windows and a leaky roof. Every floor was damp and as you walked through the house, your shoes sank into the filth. Roaches were everywhere. These were "Dayton roaches," as we called them. In most houses, the roaches would scurry away if you turned on the lights. Not Dayton roaches. They ran toward you.

To add to our misery, there was no power in the house except what was supplied by an extension cord strung between neighboring houses. The "borrowed" electricity powered a small television on the first floor. There was nothing on the TV but static and it cast an eerie, dim glow into the room.

The only uninjured victim was four-year-old Daniel Talbott, found wandering among the dead on the first floor. In the darkness he had somehow gone unnoticed by the murderer.

Using flashlights, we began assessing the scene. Through the limited range of our lights, the home looked more like a haunted house than a crime scene. You would walk through the moldy filth, shaking roaches from your pant legs, until your light spotted a victim. Then you would stop, jot down your observations, and move on. The scene was immense. There was blood everywhere, seeping into the already damp floor. Sometimes there would be a pool of blood but no victim. There were numerous victims, and most were children. Due to the conditions, it would take us considerable time to tally the true numbers. The officer outside was right. This was a bad one, maybe one of the worst.

Each victim was diagramed and photographed. We took measurements to show where each one was found. We collected blood samples, and anything of interest was photographed and collected. We took long-range photos to show where that victim or item of evidence had been found. A close-up photo of a shell casing on the floor meant nothing without a long-range photo to show where it was in the house as well as where it was in relation to the victims.

Our victims ranged in age from two to forty-six. In total, there were nine victims: three who survived their injuries, five who died, and one lucky four-year-old.

Glenna Green was the household matriarch. Her daughter Tia Talbott came home that night from the grocery store to discover her family had been massacred. Tia's twenty-three-year-old sister, Lana Green, was the first victim we encountered. Lana was on the first floor leaning against a chair. Well-dressed in a black dress and bright white shoes, Lana had been shot in the head. Blood emanated from the wound and seeped into the dress. Her eyes and mouth were open and looking upward at us, as if to ask, "What happened?"

I wish I knew, I thought.

Lana's six-year-old daughter, Violana Green, lay near her. She, too, had been shot in the head. As the girl lay on the floor, the blood seemed to disappear. It appeared as though she were taking a nap near her mother's feet. She was so small and so young.

What could she have possibly done to deserve this? I would ask myself variations of this question several more times that night.

In a bedroom upstairs, we spotted a pool of blood next to the wall. Paramedics had found Tia's son, seven-year-old Daytrin Talbott, there. Despite intense efforts to save him, Daytrin died at a nearby hospital. The blood here was different, though. At the time, blood-pattern interpretation was rarely used and none of us were trained to do so. But even without formal training, it was obvious. In the center of the blood was an absence, a round area where there was no blood. And the blood splattered up the side of the wall, away from that absence.

Picture a melon lying on a floor next to a wall. Now take the butt of a rifle and smash the melon. The juice fans out and goes up the wall. But the area where the melon sits is shielded by the melon itself. This prevents the juice from getting on the floor beneath it. That is the absence in the pattern. But this was no melon. This was the child's head. He had been beaten to death.

In the same room, another of Tia's sons, six-year-old Datwan Talbott, lay on his back on the filthy floor, roaches crawling over his body. A bloody cloth covered his face. He had been shot in the head. I don't recall who placed the cloth on his face and at the time I didn't care. The boy looked peaceful, since you couldn't see where the bullet had ripped through his head. I welcomed that peaceful look, given the destruction around us.

We found Glenna Green upstairs in her bedroom. She lay on the floor beside her bed, clad in her nightgown. She, too, had been shot. Glenna was the oldest victim, the mother of Lana and grandmother of the children. She lost her life and her family in one very violent night.

In the corner of this same room sat a blood-soaked couch. Tia's son Dayron Talbott, eleven, had been removed from here. Shot and beaten, Dayron nonetheless survived. Unknown to us at the time, he would be instrumental in solving this case.

Two more of Glenna's grandchildren had been assaulted but were still alive. Glenna Talbott, two, had been beaten so badly that hospital officials were unsure whether she'd been shot as well. Tia Green, five, had been shot through her right eye. Amid all the chaos, they, along with Dayron, had been whisked away by medics to an area hospital. Somehow, they survived.

This was the worst scene any of us had ever experienced. I was the new guy on the team, and I was hoping it didn't show. I talked to one of the veteran detectives.

"How does something like this happen?" I asked.

He told me not to focus on that, because however it happened, the circumstances would still baffle me, even if we uncovered every single fact possible. I knew he was right. People kill for lots of reasons, sometimes for no visible reason at all, or for bizarre reasons that exist only in their troubled minds. I'd already seen people killed over loud music, a parking space, a two-dollar debt, and more.

In a way, it doesn't matter. In a domestic violence homicide, which this would turn out to be, the immediate reason isn't what the killing is all about. That's just the trigger. Domestic violence is about control. The trigger is often something that no reasonable person would be violently angry about: a spilled glass of milk, or a baby who won't stop crying. It could be someone exerting the slightest bit of independence, in thought or action—which then threatens the psyche of the abuser. By its nature, domestic violence isn't rational or reasonable.

Still, I had to wonder: What is the trigger that leads to a massacre?

We soon learned that there was someone else who lived at the house but was not among our tally of victims: Glenna's boyfriend, thirty-one-year-old Samuel Moreland. As we worked the wretched crime scene and interviewed friends and neighbors of the deceased, Moreland was curiously absent. We would later learn that, during this time, he was having a few drinks at a friend's house, as if nothing had happened.

Through interviews, we discovered Moreland had been at the house earlier that evening, arguing with Glenna. The argument wasn't complex. Moreland wanted money for alcohol and Glenna wouldn't give it to him.

That's all it was. A fight over wine money led to five dead and three critically injured, many of them children. My veteran colleague was right. The immediate reason, the trigger, was absolutely underwhelming.

We put out a broadcast for Moreland. A broadcast was not an arrest warrant—we didn't have enough evidence for that yet. But we needed to find him, and quickly. We didn't know if the night's bloodshed was over.

Strangely, it wasn't hard to find him. He wandered home, appearing oblivious to the chaos he found. When officers quickly moved in and arrested him, Moreland told them, "You're too late."

There wasn't much notable about Moreland. He was of average size and somewhat unkempt, scruffy. The kind of guy who'd been on the street, but nothing about him suggested danger. He was not at all physically imposing. Of course, now he was dealing with a group of armed adults on their turf, not a houseful of children.

Moreland did not even attempt to feign surprise or shock over the slaughter. He was defiant, cocky, and obviously streetsmart. As we questioned him, Moreland was gauging our questions, trying to determine what we really knew, and making sure his answers matched what he thought we knew. Moreland was smart enough not to volunteer information but would respond to what we would say or ask, changing his story quickly to suit new information or questions.

For example, we asked him to submit to a gunshot residue test. The test, called a "GSR," looks for components used in ammunition that aren't normally found on one's hands.

Moreland told officers the test would do them no good, because he had been shooting at a range earlier in the day. But when asked questions about the range, he changed his story. Now he had been shooting down by the river. I quickly prepared a court order and got a municipal judge to approve it. Moreland submitted to the test, and the results were positive.

Moreland's story, or stories, continued to change. You can only bluff for so long. Ultimately, he invoked his right to remain silent.

"The Fifth Amendment is made for guys like me," Moreland said defiantly. "You got nothin' on me and I'll be damned if I'll help you."

Of course, Moreland was no lawyer. He didn't mean the Fifth Amendment. He meant his Miranda rights—the ones you hear read to suspects on televisions shows all the time. Either way, he didn't sound innocent. Despite his error, Moreland knew his way around the system—as we'd expected. We quickly tracked a history of violence and domestic abuse. He was unemployed and, in recent years, had gone from house to house, leeching off others until they tired of him.

Moreland had lived at the Talbott residence for more than a year, yet he showed no concern for his girlfriend or her family, who had been slaughtered. But even if he was done talking to us, he'd talked to someone else.

Moreland made a veiled remark to the friend he had been drinking with that the police were probably at his house looking for him. He also said he had fired a gun and "the bullet went in little but came out big." Our weapon was a .22-caliber long-rifle cartridge, a little bullet.

But we didn't have that rifle. Moreland was definitely our man, but for a successful prosecution, we would need more.

That came from Dayron Talbott the following day, after he'd recovered enough from his injuries to talk with us briefly.

Dayron told us that he watched "Sam" shoot his grandmother, and then Sam shot him. After that, Sam smashed a rifle butt into Dayron's face, causing him to pass out.

The contrast between Moreland and Dayron was unmistakable. Moreland had been almost nonchalant about the slaughter of several people in his home. Dayron showed all the expected signs of psychological trauma. Even after he left the hospital, the little boy was very quiet and withdrawn. He didn't make a lot of eye contact, and when he answered our questions, he usually just offered one-word replies. He wasn't trying to be difficult. Dayron was clearly, and understandably, in shock.

As we booked Moreland into the county jail, he remained defiant. Moreland wanted his phone call and he wanted it now. A deputy sheriff working at the jail glared at Moreland and responded, "Hell, Sammy, who you gonna call? You killed everybody you know."

We all went to the viewing of the deceased. Shiloh Baptist Church was prominent in Dayton's Black community and they had offered their services. Shiloh was a large church and it was packed. The people of Dayton were horrified by these crimes, with some standing in the street outside the church, just to be close to what was happening. The news reporters estimated seven thousand people attended, though it felt like even more.

I will never forget those five caskets stretched end to end across the front of the church. To this day, I have nothing to compare it to. Reverend Henry Parker told of how the community had opened up their hearts and pocketbooks for the family. One man donated $5,000. Another gave all that he had: twenty-one cents. During the service, the choir sang the hymn "He Knows Just How Much You Can Bear." I hoped that was true.

It would be a year before Moreland was tried in front of a three-judge panel. Facing the possibility of a death sentence, Moreland waived his right to a trial before a jury of his peers.

We knew we had a witness: little Dayron, who could identify Moreland as the killer. We hoped it would be enough. We had a tremendous amount of circumstantial evidence but Dayron's testimony would probably be our strongest piece of direct evidence. We were haunted by what we didn't find and couldn't present, particularly the rifle.

But life is strange, and when you work homicide, it's often stranger.

News media descended on the trial, starting from the first day. It seemed everyone was watching. One person in particular was watching because he knew something we didn't. After viewing a news broadcast, he realized how important his information was, and he called the police. Dispatch then called us.

"Got a guy you definitely want to talk to," the dispatcher said, giving us the man's name and number.

The caller, an employee of a local tree-trimming company, had been part of a crew working the Ardmore Avenue area the week of the homicides. The day after the slayings, a coworker found a discarded .22-caliber rifle. The coworker took the rifle home and boasted that he had the weapon used in the killings. The caller, who could not keep this secret any longer, gave us the name of the coworker.

Three of us left the trial, driving quickly to the offices of the tree-trimming company, leaving two other colleagues behind to continue assisting prosecutors at the trial.

At the office, we found a supervisor who told us the employee we were seeking was taking a day off. The employee lived near Ludlow Falls, about thirty minutes from Dayton. It probably took us only ten minutes to get there as fast as we were driving, but it seemed like an eternity.

We approached the residence with caution and enthusiasm. After we pounded on the door for a short while, the tree trimmer opened the door. His look told me he knew why we were there. After a brief discussion, he surrendered the gun.

It was a well-worn, cheap .22-caliber rifle. The man had crudely refinished it, but otherwise, it appeared unaltered.

We raced back to the crime laboratory. The toolmark examiner looked the weapon over. The checkered pattern of the butt plate matched perfectly the impressions left on the crushed skulls of Moreland's victims. When the examiner removed the plate, he found blood had seeped into the gun's wooden stock.

Guns often leave markings on bullets they have fired, markings usually as distinct as a fingerprint. But this rifle was in horrible condition. Making a match to the bullets recovered from our victims could be difficult.

Difficult, but apparently not impossible. The technicians at the crime lab quickly matched that rifle to the bullets that killed or injured nine people in the hell house on Ardmore, then led us to yet another victim.

The gun also matched a bullet taken from the body of Ulysses Russell, an elderly man who lived in Glenna Green's neighborhood. Russell had been shot to death just days before the Moreland massacre, though until now, no one knew the two scenes were linked.

It made sense. Moreland had probably taken the rifle from Russell, shot and killed him, and then used the same rifle on his victims on Ardmore. We had our murder weapon: there was no doubt this was what was used to kill Glenna and her family. We couldn't forensically put that rifle in Moreland's hands—the tests only showed the gun was used, not who used it. But Dayron could, and he did.

The little boy appeared so tiny in that witness seat. He was our star witness, and he delivered. You never know how well small children will testify, but Dayron's testimony was particularly strong. He told the jury exactly who had assaulted him and killed his family members: Samuel Moreland.

We hoped it would all be enough. We had a living witness, tremendous circumstantial evidence, and at last, the murder weapon.

Not that you necessarily needed to have a murder weapon to successfully try a case. In many cases, the weapon is never found. But when you have it, it becomes an important symbol. Judges or jurors can look at it, touch it, and hold it. It brings them closer to the crime, making the slaying less of an abstraction. Prosecutors love to hold up the murder weapon during their closing arguments.

"This defendant took this rifle and cold-bloodedly killed five innocent people, and tried to kill three more," the prosecutor told the judges.

It was more than a prop. It was the edge we needed.

Samuel Moreland was convicted and sentenced to death for the Ardmore murders. Through a series of appeals, Moreland has remained alive, but the convictions still stand. Though he has been on death row for almost three decades, time will eventually run out for Samuel Moreland.

Even still, Moreland has lived in prison far longer than most of his victims, and he has apparently gotten away with at least one other homicide: Moreland was never charged in connection with Ulysses Russell's death. There were no eyewitnesses and little evidence to work with. There is little doubt that Moreland killed Russell, but we could never prove it.

The homicide squad kept in touch with Dayron and his mother, Tia Talbott, for a few years. By then, Dayron knew us and was more outgoing. Always friendly and always polite, he no longer showed outward signs of trauma, and we didn't probe deeply. Once the trial was over, we never again discussed what happened on November 1, 1985. Instead we talked about his life: school, and as he got older, the kind of jobs teenagers take. You had to admire his poise, given all he'd been through.

We were grateful to that brave little boy and his important testimony. As the years went by, the contacts became more and more infrequent, until they stopped altogether. I would not see Dayron again until the summer of 1997. It would be a heartbreaking reunion.

2.
A TALE OF TWO CITIES

THERE ARE TWO types of cities in America: those that capture the imagination of people who have never been there, and those that don't.

Those that do usually offer some form of mental shorthand. If you ask someone what they think of when they hear the words "Las Vegas," they'll probably say something like "gambling" or "casino." For Nashville, it's "country music." For Los Angeles, it might be "movie stars." This shorthand is often reductionist, oversimplifying those communities, but people can picture something.

Dayton is in the second category. If you haven't been there, you might know nothing about it. It tends to get jumbled with the other midsized Ohio cities—Akron, Toledo, and Canton—if outsiders think about it at all. But Dayton is an average American city, and it has all of the problems that other cities have.

Dayton sits in southwest Ohio, less than an hour from the Kentucky bluegrass and the cornfields of Indiana. Many places call themselves the "crossroads of America," but Dayton has a legitimate claim. It's a Rust Belt city, solidly in the industrial

Midwest, while it's forty-five miles north of Cincinnati, often described as America's most northern Southern city.

Interstate 75, which runs from northern Michigan to southern Florida, cuts right though Dayton. Just eight miles north of the city, I-75 crosses Interstate 70, which runs from Utah to Maryland. That crossroads, bringing two of the nation's largest freeways together, makes Dayton a major transportation station for all types of products.

That includes illegal narcotics, as the Ohio State Highway Patrol can tell you. The I-75–I-70 corridor is known for drug busts.

We've had our fair share of famous people come out of Dayton. Mike Schmidt, perhaps the best third baseman in major league history, was born and raised here. Phil Donahue started his television show here in 1967, which became nationally syndicated three years later—though it moved to Chicago four years after that. His neighbor in suburban Centerville, Erma Bombeck, started as a local newspaper columnist before becoming a nationally known author and *Good Morning America* correspondent. More recently, three leads on TV's *The West Wing*—Martin Sheen, Rob Lowe, and Allison Janney—have Dayton roots, as local media never hesitated to remind us during the show's run.

This was as distant from my childhood as yours. The Dayton I experienced was more common: an industrial metropolis that lured people from other regions in search of work. Particularly mountain people. Dayton has a large Appalachian population—so large, in fact, that city ordinance prohibits discrimination against those of Appalachian descent.

Mention Appalachia and people often think of West Virginia. But Appalachia extends into Kentucky and southeastern Ohio. Dayton was one of the stops on the "Hillbilly Highway," the migration route during the first half of the

twentieth century that brought poor folks from Appalachia to
northern industrial cities. They were in search of better employment, and Dayton had plenty to offer—like auto plants. At
one point, Dayton had the largest concentration of General
Motors factories outside of Michigan.

There was NCR—originally known as the National Cash
Register Company—founded here by John H. Patterson in
1884. There was Mead, the paper company—you probably
had a Mead notebook when you were in school, right?—which
was headquartered in Dayton for more than a hundred years.
Frigidaire, at one point a division of GM, was based in Dayton.
McCall's magazine was printed here in a giant factory on the
city's near-west side.

Today, that *McCall's* plant is an empty, rotting shell. Most
of the auto plants are gone. NCR moved its headquarters to
Georgia in 2009. Mead's successor, MMV, moved its headquarters to Richmond, Virginia, in 2006, though some of the
paper mills in the suburbs are still running—albeit under different corporate ownership.

Today, much of Dayton's economy is based on health
care and universities—there are many across the Dayton area,
including the University of Dayton, Wright State University,
and many smaller colleges. The one part of the region's
original employment infrastructure that still stands tall is
Wright-Patterson Air Force Base, named for the aforementioned John H. Patterson and the Wright Brothers, who were
not from North Carolina. Though they did fly at Kitty Hawk,
they designed those airplanes at their bicycle shop in Dayton.

But much of the newer employment is white collar and
suburban. The loss of those factory jobs has devastated large
parts of the city, with poverty creeping into the inner-ring suburbs in recent years. Like many communities in the Midwest,
despair has led to the "hillbilly heroin crisis," as people abuse

and illegally trade prescription narcotics. For those who prefer the classics—cocaine, heroin, marijuana—the dealers keep shipping them in, making good use of the national interstate system, with its major crossroads lying in our northern suburbs.

Back during the migration, my parents were among those who were lured to Dayton, my mother from Paintsville, Kentucky, my father from Big Stone Gap in Virginia. Both had been farmers from poor families, and both came seeking a middle-class life. They arrived to find a good-sized city whose population crossed two hundred thousand back around 1930. In 1960, four years after I was born there, it was at two hundred and sixty-two thousand. Now it's just over one hundred and forty thousand.

My upbringing was pretty average. So was Dayton. And so, apparently, were my parents, if you believe *The Real Majority*, a 1970 book by two political analysts that attempts to identify the true "middle voter." You want to know who that is? The authors, Richard Scammon and Ben Wattenberg, say that it would be someone who is "middle-aged, middle-income, middle-educated, Protestant, in a family whose working members work more likely with hands than abstractly with head." Then they got even more specific: "Middle Voter is a 47-year-old housewife from the outskirts of Dayton, Ohio, whose husband is a machinist."

Though the authors didn't identify a specific person, the Dayton *Journal Herald* went out and found a woman who fit that profile, and *Life* magazine profiled her. But my parents were pretty close to those middle-voter descriptions as well.

My parents were east-siders for a simple reason: they were white. Despite being north of the Mason-Dixon line, Dayton has long been a segregated city. The Great Miami River cuts through the city. Though immigration from Mexico and other countries has blurred the distinctions a bit in recent years, for decades, everyone knew that the east side was white, and the west side was Black. Both sides were working class, but most people lived, worked, and played on their side of the river, with few exceptions.

My dad was one of those exceptions. We lived on the east side's Pleasant Avenue and my father worked at Smitty's Texaco on West Third Street, which is now also known as Martin Luther King Jr. Way.

Class is hard to describe in America. I'd say we were somewhere between upper-class poor and lower middle class. We didn't live in the projects, but there were no McMansions or yachts in our immediate future. I didn't know any other way of life, so I never felt "poor," though we probably were.

When school was out, I would help my father at the gas station for a little extra cash. This gave me a view of the "other" side of the city that my peers rarely saw in the late 1960s and early 1970s. Dayton was undergoing the same changes that other cities were, particularly by urban Blacks, who were tired of discrimination and wanted better schools, like we had on the east side.

Sadly, Dayton was ahead of much of the country, though not Watts, when we had a riot on the city's near-west side, not far from downtown. It was September 1, 1966, ten months before Detroit went up in flames and nineteen months before riots swept more than a hundred cities following the murder of the Rev. Dr. Martin Luther King Jr. In Dayton, the catalyst was the shotgun murder of a Black man who was sweeping his sidewalk. The perpetrators, a group of white men in a pickup truck, were never identified. The result was twenty-four hours of pandemonium, violence, and destruction. Half a century later, the scars are still there, but I saw them when I was ten and they were fresh wounds.

In the aftermath, my father and I would pull onto the bridge that leads to West Third and hand our work passes to the guards. Typically, we'd see two soldiers and a Dayton police officer in a jeep that had a machine gun mounted to the hood. If you didn't have a work pass, you didn't cross the bridge.

The destruction amazed me. Broken glass littered the street and buildings still smoldered. This is, as I recall, the first time I'd ever thought about racial discrimination and the divide represented by that bridge over the Great Miami River.

Overall, my childhood was uneventful. Dayton was home, and I didn't feel threatened, though that all changed one fall evening, when I was in elementary school.

Wilbur Wright High School was a block from my house, where our street dead-ended. On cool fall nights, I would walk to the grounds, sit on the hill that overlooked the football field, and watch the team practice. One night as I watched, I saw a young man—not a player—arguing with one of the coaches. That young man was disrupting practice and I heard the coach order him to leave the field.

The agitated young man refused, so the coach picked him up and put him on his shoulder so he could carry him off the field. I saw what happened next: the young man pulled a knife from a pocket and shoved it into the coach's back. This is, obviously, not the kind of thing you ever forget.

As I watched, horrified, some of the team helped the coach. Others restrained the assailant until police arrived. Most just stood there, stunned. Decades later, I still think about how traumatic this must have been for them.

I was still there when police arrived. Some were in uniform, others in plainclothes. I saw them cover the coach's body with a sheet and realized I'd just seen a man die. *Did this really happen?* I asked myself. As I sat there, stunned, and watched the police work, it never occurred to me that one day that would be me.

But looking back, I think that early experience helped me better understand victims and witnesses—how they felt, and the impact on their lives. Because if you are a witness or survivor of a violent crime, you are changed forever.

What I'd witnessed was more common than I'd ever realized. Dayton has long been a violent city, and at the time it was getting even more so. By the early 1970s, not long after this coach's slaying, the city's annual number of murder investigations would top one hundred. That's quite high, given the population. But when you adjust for that factor, Dayton has often been the most violent major city in Ohio—above much larger cities like Cleveland, Cincinnati, and Columbus. In fact, Dayton competes quite nicely in murders per capita against far bigger cities across the country.

Dayton is Everytown and Anytown. It's so representative of America that political scientists go there to find the middle voter. (They still do. In November 2016, NPR identified Montgomery County, Ohio, where Dayton is the seat, as one of thirteen bellwether counties that could decide the presidential election.)

It turns out that Anytown, USA, has its share of violence. Just like any other city out there. The number of homicides has declined considerably, but so has our population. When I was a kid, the city could see more than 100 homicides annually; during my career we've seen highs in the 60s and lows in the 30s. Most of our people are good people—solid, friendly Midwesterners. But there is a violent undercurrent, a small amount that causes a disproportionate amount of chaos, grief, and pain.

Ask any cop in any city in any part of America, and they'll probably tell you that's true. It's certainly true here.

3.

IT'S ABOUT TO GET REAL

AS FAR AS badges go, Dayton's was kind of plain. But to me it was beautiful. It was big and shiny and said everything it needed to: Dayton police, 623. That was my badge number, and it would follow me through my entire career. I would never forget that number, nor the date I first cradled that badge in my hands. That was on December 14, 1978, the day I graduated from the Dayton Police Academy.

Obviously, a lot had happened to me since I'd witnessed the coach's slaying. But it was hardly a direct line from child witness to rookie cop.

After I graduated from Wilbur Wright High School in 1974, I began taking engineering classes at Wright State University. I also worked full-time at a Kroger grocery store, stocking shelves during the night shift. I had little free time. While at Kroger, I met a police officer who moonlighted there as a stock clerk. I enjoyed listening to his war stories but had no desire to become a police officer.

One night, he asked me if I wanted to do a ride-along with him. That's when a civilian rides in the cruiser with the cop, observing everything the officer does. *Why not?* I thought. It was something different to do.

All I can say is I was hooked immediately. It's hard to explain why. I didn't see anything nearly as dramatic as that homicide I'd witnessed as a boy. Just routine patrol work. But something in it resonated with me.

Engineering is very abstract. I found it interesting, but not exciting. Police work is not abstract, and it is immediate. Even as a passenger, I caught the contact high of the adrenaline that an officer feels responding to a scene. We were in the fresh air, and we were engaging with people. I could see my friend had a lot of discretion in what he did on the job. Obviously, he was responding to calls over the radio, but when he wasn't, he patrolled where he thought he should. I remember us cruising the business districts to make sure there were no break-ins, and even visiting some bars where there had been trouble in the past, just to check in with the owners. He was watching out for the bad guys, but also helping regular people. I witnessed his mix of freedom and responsibility, and I was drawn to both.

I may have stumbled upon it, but I'd found my calling. From that night on, I wanted to be a police officer. I dropped out of college and began studying for the police entrance exams. To gain experience, I also volunteered as a neighborhood-assistance officer for the Dayton Police Department.

NAOs wore uniforms but didn't carry weapons, make arrests, or wear badges. We checked on people's homes when they were on vacation and directed traffic at accident scenes. Our role was to free up the sworn officers so they could focus on real police work. My NAO stint was volunteer work with no pay, but I would have paid to do it. It got me closer to police work and police officers, who were quick to caution me to stay safe and leave the big jobs to them. They would jokingly remind us that NAO also stood for "not an officer."

Three police departments were hiring. One was Kettering, a large suburb on Dayton's southern border. Another was the Ohio State Highway Patrol. The third was Dayton. I applied to all three and passed all three of the entrance exams. I chose Dayton in part because it was the first to call. I have to think this would be a much different book had I been hired by Kettering or the OSP.

Next, I underwent background checks, physical and psychological evaluations, a polygraph examination, interviews, and more. One day, the call came. I was told to report to the Dayton Police Academy at 8 a.m. the following Monday. Now the hard work would begin. Months of physical training, firearms training, exams. If you failed two exams, you were out. People dropped out, too, often after realizing they could never shoot someone, even if they had to. That happens in every academy class.

I arrived in a changing department. It was the late 1970s, and we were being taught by people who'd arrived in the 1950s or 1960s. Some had served in the Korean War. A lot had changed since then. Police departments were being pressured to diversify, and of the nearly two dozen people in my class, four were women. That was almost unheard of just a decade earlier. There was also a Latino man, but no African Americans. Forty years later, the department is still trying to diversify, with very mixed results.

Some of my classmates dreamed of becoming a field lieutenant or even a chief. I had no goals beyond passing the tests and becoming a police officer. I just wanted my own badge, and when I held it in my hands that December night, I felt elated.

The academy prepared me for the basics: what the laws were, what the department's policies and procedures were. What it didn't prepare me for, and couldn't, was how to wisely use that discretion I witnessed on that first ride-along when I was still working at Kroger. That would only come with experience. So the hard work wasn't over. It was about to get harder. It was about to get real.

Upon graduation, I was assigned a training officer in District One who would evaluate me and decide if I was a keeper. We would take calls together and he would watch my every move. Our shift was 6 p.m. to 2 a.m., which quickly exposed me to the nastier side of the city's nightlife. After a few weeks, my training officer deemed me suitable to fly solo, so I would need to choose a permanent shift. I was called to the district commander's office.

"Son," the commander said. "We have one opening on midnights, and two openings on three to eleven. Which would you like?"

"I would like midnights, sir," I blurted out.

I'd given this a lot of thought, long before that day. Midnights were known as the toughest shift. When you were growing up, your mother may have told you that nothing good happens after midnight. That is often true.

The midnight-shift officers were legendary. Most were long-time veterans. They were tough, smart, and well respected. Even hardened criminals had grudging respect for them. They were the real deal, and I knew I could learn plenty from them.

The commander grinned and said, "Those guys will eat you alive if you can't keep up."

I knew what he meant. These veteran officers would mentor me, but they would expect me to work hard, to take the toughest calls, to learn as quickly as possible. They didn't have time to babysit me. To earn their respect, I would need to show that I could think for myself.

"I'll do my best, sir."

"Let's hope that's good enough. Show up on midnights tomorrow."

By this time, his slight smirk had broadened into a smile. The commander knew that the night shift was challenging, and I think he respected my willingness to try it.

My first night on my new shift, my sergeant paired me up with one of the toughest officers on the shift. He was cordial enough but made it clear to me that my name was Rook until either I proved myself or I was gone. He knew police work, but even more importantly, he knew people.

"Rook," he said. "We work nights, in one of the roughest districts, in one of the most violent cities in the country."

During the day shift, you will encounter many law-abiding people, he explained. At night, many of those people are asleep. Who is left? After midnight, you've got people who've been drinking, so street fights and bar fights are more common. Those drawn to criminal activities, such as burglars, usually prefer the cover of darkness. You will encounter some law-abiding citizens on the night shift, but the ratio skews more toward meeting troublemakers, just as they're ready to make trouble, he said.

During my time on midnights, I watched these officers carefully. They dealt with many dangerous situations with dangerous people. But I also watched them stop by and check on elderly residents. These were people who'd worked hard, only to watch their neighborhoods deteriorate around them, leaving them nearly prisoners during what should have been their golden years. The officers were deeply protective of them.

On midnights, we generally worked in single-officer crews. About a month after I'd started midnights, on February 28, 1979, I found myself alone in a cruiser on a very cold winter night. There wasn't much radio traffic and not many people were out. I anticipated a long, slow night.

The radio's emergency tone, long and loud, jolted me back to reality. A dispatcher had issued a signal 99, which meant "officer in trouble."

"Shots fired, officer down," the dispatcher yelled.

I flipped on my lights and siren and sped toward the intersection of Wayne Avenue and Medford Street on the city's near-east side. By happenstance, I was one of the first to arrive.

We saw the cruiser, but we didn't see the officer. We were slightly puzzled until one officer looked under the cruiser. There he was. The officer, David Koenig, had been my academy classmate. I was horrified.

All he'd done was initiate a traffic stop after he spotted a car without license plates. The vehicle's driver gave the name "Harvey Lee Jones," but he was really Harold Ray Redfeairn, a convicted felon. The previous day, Redfeairn had held up a Howard Johnson's, then visited a car dealership. While taking a car out for a spin, Redfeairn had pulled a gun on the salesman.

"Well, pal, this is the end for you," Redfeairn said, according to the salesman's later testimony.

The salesman begged for his life and Redfeairn allowed him to exit the vehicle unhurt. He showed no such consideration for Officer Koenig.

Dave was checking the stolen car's vehicle identification number when Redfeairn left his vehicle, then jerked open the cruiser's door. He started firing a handgun, striking Dave three times. According to an interview Dave gave to Southern Poverty Law Center's *Intelligence Report* in 2003, Dave was wearing a bulletproof vest, but because Dave was seated in the cruiser, his side was exposed. Redfeairn entered the cruiser and fought with Dave, taunting him and calling him a "fucking pig."

Dave told the SPLC that when Redfeairn left the cruiser, Dave got out and was ready to return fire but instead he passed out.

Bullets had penetrated Dave's neck, liver, and shoulder. Briefly regaining consciousness, he told us the shooter had wrecked the car just up the street then fled on foot into nearby Woodland Cemetery.

I joined the search for Redfeairn, which was intense. Woodland Cemetery is huge, more than two hundred acres, and has plenty of hills and trees. The final resting place of the Wright Brothers and poet Paul Laurence Dunbar, it's an older cemetery, dating back to 1842, so there are plenty of old mausoleums and larger gravestones. I knew I didn't want to be buried there, not yet anyway. I held on to my Remington 870 pump shotgun like it was my prom date. This guy had shot a cop. He had nothing to lose by shooting another.

Walking through that huge cemetery at night, in that eerie silence, looking for the man who'd just shot my friend, remains the scariest moment of my life. The search took hours, although it seemed like days. The search area expanded as we cleared one cemetery section and moved on to another.

We were still searching when the radio came alive with activity. Crews had found the shooter in another car, driven by his stepfather. We were able to arrest him without further shots fired.

Thankfully, Dave recovered. A few years later, he moved to a smaller department outside Cincinnati.

As for Redfeairn, he was tried and convicted, then paroled in 1991. In case you're wondering why the SPLC, which tracks hate groups, was so interested in Redfeairn, he later became the leader of the Aryan Nation in Ohio. He died in 2003, not long after Dave gave his interview to the SPLC. We do not miss Harold Ray Redfeairn.

But that experience was key to my development as a cop. After that, those tough, hard-nosed midnight officers stopped calling me Rook and started calling me Burke.

That experience also underscored the danger of the job. What Dave had done, instigating a traffic stop, is something that cops do every day. Most of the time, nothing terrible happens. But there is always that possibility.

It might strike law-abiding people—those who automatically defer to the authority of an officer, those would never dream of assaulting a peace officer—as bizarre, but there are plenty of people out there who have no such hesitation. Experienced criminals don't want to get locked up. Their other choices are fight or flight. If they flee, it's our job to chase them and catch them. If they fight, it's our job to fight back and subdue them using the *minimum* amount of force necessary to obtain control, or to eliminate a threat to human life. Survival and personal safety are often secondary concerns.

* * *

It would be several months into the job before I took a homicide call. My first was at a "boot joint," Dayton slang for a bootleg-liquor joint, usually a private residence functioning as an unlicensed bar. Kind of like a 1920s speakeasy, but dumpier. Typically, the owner would renovate the first floor or the basement into a bar area.

They sold booze whenever people wanted it, but the boot joints really came to life in the early morning hours, after the real bars had closed for the night.

Quality varied. Some joints were as posh as a Las Vegas casino; others were just a trashy place to drink. The one on Diamond was just a trashy place to drink.

I was one of several officers dispatched to the scene. We charged inside with weapons drawn. Surprisingly, several people were still there.

"Too drunk to run," one officer said.

We lined up the living and frisked them for weapons. The victim lay on floor, in the corner. At that point, I was no expert, but it was clear he was DRT, cop slang for "dead right there." No need to call an ambulance.

Like most of the patrons, the victim was an older Black male. His head was tilted back and his eyes and mouth were open, as if he were pleading for help. The cause of death appeared obvious—the gunshot wound in his chest. Blood surrounded him.

"Must have got the mud vein," one officer said. (More slang. The "mud vein" was any major organ or artery that held or carried a lot of blood.) The amount amazed me. For the first time, I noticed that blood has a unique odor that is hard to describe, but you never forget. This smell would follow me through my career.

As we secured the scene, we found a revolver that smelled like it had been recently fired, along with one spent round, behind the bar.

As noted, it was my first homicide scene, and it was a lot to take in. One of the other officers noticed me looking around and approached me.

"Burke," he said. "It's about to get real."

I was confused. "What do you mean?"

"They're calling out the homicide dicks," he said, grinning. "You ain't seen nothing yet."

This filled me with anxiety and curiosity. These midnight officers were my heroes. To me, they were larger than life. I couldn't wait to see who *they* looked up to.

Soon, three well-dressed detectives entered the room. One of them stopped.

"Mornin', Gerry. Rex. Ron," he said, acknowledging the other officers. Then he looked at me. "New guy?"

"That's Burke," Gerry said. "He's okay."

That was apparently good enough, because the detective said, "Good morning, Burke."

I stood there starstruck. It's hard to explain why, but they had a commanding presence. I don't mean that they were rude or intimidating. If anything, they were quiet, professional, and methodical, so much so that everyone deferred to them: the other cops, the witnesses. Except for one.

The boot joint's owner, a man they called Buff, was getting mouthy.

"Burke," one of the detectives yelled out. "Put this asshole in a can."

I knew what that meant. Put him in the back of a cruiser. Buff stayed mouthy all the way to my car. His demeanor changed instantly once he was in the back seat and I was in the front.

"How you doin' tonight, suh?" he asked with a drawl.

"Good. You?"

"Oh, can't complain."

This led to several minutes of chitchat with my new friend Buff. Suddenly, one of the detectives hopped in the back seat and asked, "Okay, Buff, what happened?"

Without hesitation, Buff described how two men argued about a woman. One pulled a gun and ended the argument. Buff described the suspect, including what he was wearing, and noted that he was still inside the bar. Buff said he'd picked up the gun and placed it behind the bar. I was dumbfounded, and the detective noticed.

"Burke, Buff here is a good guy," he said. "Makes a little money on the side at his joint. But Buff doesn't want any trouble and he always cooperates."

Now I got it. Buff wanted to talk. He just couldn't do it in there in front of everyone else. His mouthing off was a signal for the detectives to pull him away from the crowd, but in a way that didn't reveal he was cooperating. For the first time, I realized there was more to being a detective, especially a homicide detective, than reading reports and lab sheets. You had to be able to read people.

We loaded the rest of the patrons, the suspect included, in several cruisers, and took them to headquarters so they could be interviewed. I took my new friend Buff, who was pleasant during the whole ride. As soon as we arrived and I pulled him from the car, Buff put on a show.

"Motherfucker, I can walk," he said as he tried to jerk away from me.

"Call me 'motherfucker' one more time and you won't be able to walk," I barked back, falling into my supporting role with ease.

I learned a lot that night. One thing that resonated with me was that these detectives were going to work that case until it was done. As a rookie patrol officer, I would take a call, then go to the next one, and the next one. Follow-up was done by other people. I wanted to be one of them.

Most importantly, I knew where my career path was headed. I didn't want to be a sergeant, a lieutenant, or even a chief. I wanted to be a homicide detective. From that point on, I read every book I could find on death investigation. Whenever I was at headquarters, I'd stop and talk with the homicide detectives. Once again, I was all in.

After four short years on the street, I applied for an open position in the detective section. It was for burglary squad.

No one starts on homicide. You work your way through property-crime squads, then to violent crimes, and then maybe, just maybe, to homicide. But this new position would put me in the same building as homicide, and that's what I wanted. It was a start.

Three years later, I would achieve my goal. In 1985, I was "temporarily" assigned to homicide. I stayed on the squad for twenty-two years.

4.
DEAD FOLKS

THE BANK LEADING to the river was steep and covered with snow. At the bottom, near the frozen river, lay the nearly nude body of a sixteen-year-old boy. Identified a few days later as Anthony Dyer, he was wearing only his socks. Children sledding down the bank had discovered his body.

I thought back to the hill at Wilbur Wright High School, where I had witnessed my first homicide. These children were much younger than I had been. I hoped they hadn't seen too much.

It was January 10, 1997, in the midst of one of the coldest winters Dayton had seen in years. Late that night, we were called to the Wolf Creek Bridge. For an outdoor scene, it wasn't particularly large, but given the weather, it wasn't easy to get to. Firefighters set up a system of ropes to help us up and down the bank.

This was misery. It was so cold, the ink in our pens actually froze. We would climb down the bank and make notes of our observations. When our hands and pens became so cold we could no longer write, we would then climb back up the hill to the warmth of a cruiser. After we thawed out, we would repeat the process until we completed our scene work.

Our victim had clearly been beaten. We found a small pile of clothing nearby that had been set on fire but not consumed. Part of a burnt coat was adorned with symbols I had not seen before. The only things missing were shoes and a motive.

The Algonquin Street housing projects, a place that kept street cops busy with complaints about addicts and gangs, sat just across the street from the river. I doubted that was mere coincidence. But Anthony and his mother didn't live there. Once we identified the boy, we needed to speak with her.

One of our first tasks, as always, was interviewing the victim's relatives. With a younger victim, that usually meant a parent or other adult with custody. It was often a mother, sometimes a father or a grandparent.

I spoke to hundreds of parents during my homicide career. The conversations could be stunning. Some could not have cared less about their children's deaths. Some were even incensed that we had the audacity to waste their time.

"That's why I hate the living," I would often say. Until those times that I didn't. Anthony Dyer left behind a loving, grieving mother who was devastated at the loss of her son. Through tears, she told us about her son and all she had done for him. She worried about him. He was staying out late, sometimes not coming home at all.

She had just purchased an expensive pair of gym shoes for him. She showed me the box, which had a picture of the shoes on the side. I snapped a photo of the box. It might come in handy later.

I felt sorry for this woman. Her son deserved justice, and maybe even more so, she deserved justice. Perhaps we could bring her some. Not enough, but some.

As I left the Dyer residence, my mind wandered from the dead boy on the riverbank to my home, where I had a teen-age son and a young daughter. Though my son was near the same age as Anthony, he rarely gave me any trouble. But I won-dered. . . . Sometimes my son came home late for one reason or another. What if he had gotten involved with the wrong crowd? How much can any parent do to keep their children safe, no matter how hard they try?

I went home that night and hugged and kissed my son and daughter until they thought I was crazy.

"What's wrong?" they grumbled.

"Nothing," I replied. "Nothing at all."

* * *

In the days after Anthony's body was found, we did what we usually did: neighborhood canvasses, talking to anyone we could find. One name kept coming up: the Folks Gang. Also known as the "GD" or the "Gangster Disciples," the Folks had set up shop at an apartment on Algonquin Street, right in the very housing project I'd noticed that first night.

A little research showed the Folks originated in Chicago but had several factions in Ohio. Their sign, a crude six-pointed star, matched one of the symbols on the burnt jacket found at the scene.

The people we interviewed gave us plenty of names, none of them proper names. Every one of the Folks seemed to be known solely by a nickname: TT, Natti, Spank, Spade, Wolf, Nose, and Psycho.

This was not uncommon. Lots of people went by nick-names, and we'd have to figure out who belonged to each one. Sometimes you had what you thought were nicknames, but were really what was on their birth certificates. And while there was nothing wrong with creative names, you did have to wonder what some parents were thinking. Particularly people in the lowest socioeconomic margins, whose kids would need every advantage possible. Did the parents of twins Orangelo and Lemongelo—named after two favorite flavors of Jell-O—ever think that they might be setting up their children for ridicule and failure? I knew a young man whose first name was spelled "Shithead," though he was always quick to remind us, "It's pronounced 'Shu-THEED.'" How is naming your kid that not cruel?

Sometimes we laughed about these names. That's not nice, but it's true. A favorite was one D'Alcapone Alpacino Morris, named for a famous gangster and a famous actor who played iconic gangsters in the movies. We did chuckle ruefully about self-fulfilling prophesies as he moved through the juvenile system. But no one laughed when Morris went to prison at age twenty for murder.

But the Folks' nicknames were new to us. It would take some time to match proper names with them.

Five days after the discovery of Anthony's body, we identified seventeen-year-old Chris Campbell as "Spank." When we found him, Campbell was wearing Anthony Dyer's new gym shoes.

Campbell and his sixteen-year-old girlfriend quickly admitted their involvement and described what happened, but not before laying out the oldest gang story in the world: "It's not a gang; it's a club." Because we'd never heard that before.

The Folks Gang, they said, was a "youth group." GD stood for "growth and development," not "Gangster Disciples." It didn't matter what they called it. Like any organized gang, the Folks had a structure.

There was a leader, known as TT, plus enforcers and officers. Apparently, Anthony had disrespected TT's girlfriend by flirting with her. The punishment TT handed down was a six-minute beating. Campbell and several others volunteered to participate. So, in the confines of that tiny kitchen, Anthony received his punishment.

When the beating was done, they looked at Anthony's lifeless body and realized they'd gone too far. TT ordered them to dispose of his body. They stripped Anthony of his clothing, then placed him in a wheeled garbage can. Next, they rolled him over to the river, dumping him like trash. But, to their surprise, Anthony wasn't dead. He shocked them as he started trying to crawl away. So, TT ordered Campbell to "six-nine" him, meaning to kill him. Campbell then stomped the already critically wounded boy to death.

After they set his clothes on fire, they rolled the trash can back to Algonquin. Campbell's girlfriend then mopped up the blood in the apartment, though we soon found she didn't do a particularly good job.

Luckily, we'd broken Campbell early in the investigation. We obtained a search warrant, then hit the Algonquin apartment. No one was there. The Folks had fled, but they had left behind damning evidence. Blood was still visible where Anthony had been beaten. A bloody mop stood in the corner. A book of regulations for the Folks Gang lay on a table. So much for "growth and development."

We had our victim, we had our crime scene, and we had our motive. We even had two suspects in custody—Campbell and his girlfriend. But there were more out there, so we kept working, interviews leading to arrests, and arrests giving us more information on those still out there. Spank knew who Spade was, and Spade knew who Nose was and Nose knew who Natti was, and etc. In nearly every occasion, a proper name led us to past arrests and juvenile records for petty crime. Every time we placed a real name with a nickname, a new search started. Until I found someone I didn't expect to find.

One gang member described Psycho to me, adding that he didn't know his last name. But "Psycho's" first name was Dayron, he said.

I sat silently, stunned. Was it possible? There had to be more than one Dayron in the city. Surely it wasn't our Dayron. Nevertheless, I decided to check it out. I really had no choice.

I visited Tia Talbott, who came home to 35 South Ardmore Avenue to discover Samuel Moreland's massacre ten years earlier. She'd lost her mother, sister, niece, and two of her sons that night. Another son, Dayron Talbott, had been our pint-sized star witness, the brave little boy who had seen the slaughter and nearly died himself. *It was enough to make you "psycho,"* I thought.

Tia said she didn't know Dayron to use the name "Psycho." She also said she didn't know him to be in a gang. Instinct told me she wasn't lying. But that didn't mean she was right. As I thought when I met Anthony Dyer's mother: parents don't always know what their kids are really doing.

It would be summer before I located Dayron, with the help of his mother. Dayron was avoiding all contact with his family, friends, and certainly me. It was a bittersweet reunion. I was still a detective but Dayron was no longer a victim. Dayron was now a suspect—a murder suspect.

I hadn't seen him in years, but Dayron looked the same, just older. He still looked clean-cut, and he was still polite.

"How are you, Mr. Burke?" he said to me with a shy smile. He seemed almost a little embarrassed. Dayron wasn't sarcastic and he wasn't defiant—but he wasn't talking, either. Instead, he just politely explained that he didn't think it was in his best interest to say anything. I felt a tinge of sadness when I booked him into the jail.

Tia called me the next morning. Dayron had changed his mind, she said. He now wanted to speak with me.

I brought Dayron from the jail back over to our office and placed him in an interview room, very similar to the room he had sat in years before, identifying Samuel Moreland as his family's murderer.

I took his statement and placed him back in jail. He admitted how he and the other Folks had all participated in Anthony's beating. Dayron said he was the one who put Anthony in the trash can, but that everyone except for Campbell's girlfriend went to the river to dump the body. He remembered TT giving Campbell the six-nine order, and Campbell stomping Anthony to death.

Months later, Dayron pleaded guilty to involuntary manslaughter. As always, I stood at one table with the prosecutor. Dayron stood at the other table with his defense attorney. The judge sentenced Dayron to four to seven years in prison.

I took no pleasure in watching his sentencing. The boy who had survived Samuel Moreland's horrors, then bravely testified against him, had helped take a life and was going to prison. This was nothing to celebrate. Dayron's life should have had a different outcome. Did we, as a community, fail him? Or was this inevitable, given the trauma he'd endured? None of the potential answers were comforting.

It took a year to round up the Folks Gang, identifying them, arresting them, and charging them. One by one, they pleaded guilty to felony charges. Each new conviction led to new information about another suspect. That trail stopped with the leader, "TT," whose real name was Terry Brown. Now twenty-two, Brown refused to plead guilty, electing to take his chances before a jury.

When we arrested Brown, he had admitted to his involvement in the "group." Like Campbell, he preferred not to call
it a gang.

Brown gave us a short, lie-ridden videotaped statement.
Everything that happened concerning Anthony Dyer, according to Brown, happened around him. Not because of him. Not
under his direction. He downplayed his role considerably, even
ridiculously. But TT was a gangster, and it showed on the tape.
He could lie about what happened, but he couldn't change who
he was.

During his trial, Brown sat at the defense table, wearing
a perfectly pressed suit. He looked very much like the bewil-
dered, innocent young man, wrongfully accused and stunned
to be there.

I took the witness stand for the prosecution.

"Is there a videotaped interview of the defendant?" the
prosecutor enquired.

"Yes, there is," I said.

"Do you have that tape with you?" the prosecutor asked.

"Yes, I do," I replied. So, we played the tape, and I had the
honor of introducing our jurors to the real TT.

For the first time, the jury saw not Terry Brown, defendant,
but TT, murderous gangster. I watched the jurors carefully.
They would watch the tape and then quickly steal a glance at
the defendant. You could see it on their faces. They couldn't
believe it was the same person, but it was. Once they had seen
the real Terry Brown, it didn't take them long to convict him.
He was sentenced to ten years in prison.

When it was all over, seven gang members had been
convicted and sentenced to prison terms while two mothers
grieved. Anthony Dyer's mother had lost her son to street violence. In a different way, so had Tia Talbott, at least for a while.

Eleven years earlier, she'd almost lost him to Samuel Moreland's madness.

The question lingers: What if Dayron Talbott hadn't been at home that night in 1985? Would he have ended up beating another boy to death, then helping dump the boy's body by a snowy river? There's no way to know, and I'm not making excuses for Dayron, though our entire squad had hoped he would have a better life.

I never saw Dayron again. In January 2018, the *Dayton Daily News* reported that he had completed his sentence and was now living in Louisville, Kentucky. He was married, had stepchildren, and "operates a business that sells custom T-shirts and dental jewelry," according to the paper.

Dayron and Tia still hope that Samuel Moreland will be executed for his crimes. Now in his forties, Dayron told the *Daily News* that he still has suicidal thoughts, three decades after his family was slaughtered.

"I don't need triggers," Dayron said. "Everything around me is a trigger. Every day, I have to stay busy and find things to keep from taking myself out. It has affected me that much."

He also told reporters that he had survivor's guilt, adding, "I'd rather them be here than me. Plain and simple."

I sincerely hope for better things for Dayron. But when I think back to the poise and the promise he showed as he entered his teens, it seems obvious there was so much going on inside him that I just couldn't see. Even today, he hasn't escaped Samuel Moreland's madness.

There's no doubt: one violent death changes many other lives, in many other ways. When you work homicide, you see it over and over again.

5.
THE TEAM

WE REFER TO the homicide squad as a team, but it's also like a second family for most of us. You actually spend about as much time with the squad as you do with your real family. This second family offers much of what blood relations do, with all of the kindness, love, humor, and occasional dysfunction you might imagine.

It was another long, hot day. We were exhausted and the building's air-conditioning was out. The five of us were housed in an office meant for three people, and everyone was cranky. I was looking over some lab sheets when two of my squad mates started to have a heated argument. I never did figure out what it was about, but one grabbed the other and you could see punches were going to be thrown. The rest of us just jumped in and separated them. As we were trying to sort out what the fight was about, a call came in.

"Homicide on Rockwood," the dispatcher said. So much for the argument. We headed that way.

We arrived to find a woman who had been beaten to death inside a flophouse. Her boyfriend/pimp was on scene and was not cooperative. Our sergeant hadn't arrived yet, so I was in charge.

"You two guys take him downtown and let me know what you get," I said. "I'll stay here and do the scene."

The whole squad looked at me in disbelief. The two detectives I'd ordered to transport the suspect had, minutes earlier, been ready to go to blows. They dutifully took the suspect to a car and went back to headquarters.

"You think that's a good idea?" another detective asked.

"They'll work it out, and I bet they'll get a confession," I said, laughing.

They did both, and the argument was forgotten. I knew that their dedication to the job would overcome a momentary personal dispute.

If we were all brothers and sisters on homicide squad, then we also had a lot of cousins. We certainly didn't work these cases alone. People from other parts of the police department, other agencies, other lines of work, helped us.

First up on the team were the detectives themselves.

You don't just fill out an application to become a homicide detective. You start off as a street officer, then usually work your way into a detective squad, probably handling property crimes—burglaries, stolen cars. You learn a lot, but when you make it to homicide, you have to learn even more.

The department sends you to numerous courses and seminars to learn the art of death investigation. Usually you take something from them, even when the course is somewhat bland. You also learn to read people and to talk to them to get what you want. Most importantly, you hone your instincts and what you've learned as a police officer. That learning process never ends.

Probably the most intense but rewarding course of study was blood-spatter interpretation. This was extremely important because while some people will lie to you, blood never does. Look at it closely and it will tell you exactly what happened—or that what the suspect told you cannot be true. The ability to "read" the blood at a death scene is priceless.

In one case, our victim was an older man who had been stabbed to death in a friend's kitchen. There were cards on a table and two overturned chairs. The friend was talkative from the time we arrived.

"He came at me with a butcher knife," he said. "I grabbed his arm and he ended up stabbing himself."

Interesting, I thought. We were in a kitchen, so the butcher knife fit. But nothing else did. We could see that the victim had been stabbed at least twice. But we suspected he had been punched, as his nose appeared broken. The knife didn't do that.

Looking at the blood on the wall adjacent to the victim, we could see that all of the blood came from the ground up. That meant the victim was flat on his back when he was stabbed. There was no doubt. Confronted with this evidence, the suspect finally admitted the truth: There was an argument over cards; the two men had come to blows; after the victim was down, the suspect grabbed a knife from the sink and stabbed him. Blood never lies.

But none of that blood evidence would ever see the inside of a courtroom were it not for some other members of the team, the evidence technicians, or "E-crews," as we called them. These were highly skilled officers trained in the art of evidence collection. It was a thankless job with long hours. These were the officers who would prove what we thought happened or prove us wrong and send us down another path. They were armed with high-tech equipment that could fluoresce blood by use of alternate lighting techniques, map out a scene in 3D, lift a fingerprint or shoe print we couldn't even see, and much more. But they were also armed with a keen sense of observation. They knew what would be important and they did their best to find it for us.

The E-crews would gather up their bounty of potential evidence, then deliver it to the next members of the team, the crime-lab technicians. There, our forensic teammates would analyze blood, hair, fibers, DNA, and anything else we had found that might identify or rule out a suspect.

We were quite comfortable with the medical members of our team, the forensic pathologists at the coroner's office. Usually, we sat in on the autopsies ourselves.

The autopsy would reveal how many times a person was shot or stabbed, the angle of the wounds, and much more. We would then compare the medical findings to the other evidence. Once, we had a female victim who had been shot in the head. Her husband said he had struggled with her for control of the handgun when it fired accidently. The autopsy, however, showed that the fatal shot was fired from over four feet away. Gotcha.

When crediting teammates, I could never overlook the street officers. If we needed help looking for a suspect, they were there. If we were having trouble controlling onlookers or family members at a homicide scene, they took care of it so we could focus on the investigation. At times, they shared info they received on the street, directing us to new leads. At times, the Dayton Fire Department assisted us. Having the heavy equipment and ropes we lacked, they got us in and out of places we couldn't dream of going without them.

Although it may sound odd, the news media was also—at times—a member of the team. Reporters and videographers monitored us daily. They listened for our crew numbers on their scanners and some even camped out at the rear of the headquarters, especially if a hot case was unfolding. Sometimes, we would grab our shotguns—a sure attention-getter—then run to our cars and drive off. The reporters would follow us. After a short drive, we would split up in two or three different directions. Depending how many news stations were following, they would split up themselves or just stick with the lead car. While they followed our decoys, other detectives were sneaking a frightened witness into headquarters. Sometimes it was better not to garner attention.

Most of the time, however, I wanted to be on the news. The media used us and we used them, and all of us were okay with that. Most times, it worked to everyone's benefit. Reporters loved video of us walking around, sleeves rolled up, guns and badges exposed.

Videographers would shoot footage of nearly any civilian we walked in with. Many times, a cameraman would quietly ask, "Anything worth keeping?" I would tell them the truth, because credibility was precious. You couldn't afford to lose it. So, if we were working on something that wasn't newsworthy, I would let them know. Other times, I would tell them, "Guard this one with your life, it's going to be big." They were always happy to hear that.

I didn't give them anything that could hurt us or the case. Often, they just had video of us walking around trying to look official. But what I was really doing was using the media as my marketing firm. I was using them as salesmen, but I wasn't selling used cars. I was cultivating witnesses. The more heinous the murder, the more often that video of us would be aired. I wanted people to see it and be appalled about what had occurred, and to know that we were working hard. I wanted to put pressure on the suspect, sometimes before we even knew who the suspect was. Many times, we would receive a call with information because someone had seen us on the news.

Those were the team members from the early parts of the investigation. Then, if all went well and you identified a suspect, you visited the county prosecutor's office. To obtain an arrest warrant, we'd meet with several attorneys there to determine what, if any, charges should be filed—based on the evidence we had obtained. These meetings could become very heated and animated. While the attorneys would sit and read our case reports and look through the scene photos, we would become antsy. We pushed hard, trying to get the highest level of charges for the evidence. The attorneys pushed back, questioning us and demanding more. They wanted the safest, most airtight case possible. We wanted justice, right now. The tension between the two sides was inevitable—and usually healthy, because however hard we challenged one another behind closed doors, the defense attorneys would challenge us even harder in open court.

You don't get to choose your victims or your witnesses, and there aren't many nuns hanging around in dope houses. Many times, our witnesses were addicts, prostitutes, or other violent felons. The prosecutors focused on the weaknesses—after all, they knew the defense attorneys would do the same. We focused on justice, arguing hard for charges. Sometimes, it all worked out well. Not always. Sometimes we left with an arrest warrant and sometimes we left with nothing.

The members of the prosecutor's victim-witness division were always helpful. They sat in the courthouse hallways with our witnesses, often for hours, as those witnesses waited to testify. They comforted and protected our witnesses and informed us of any problems. Overall, they saved us a lot of time and energy, allowing us to focus on assisting the prosecution.

If everything worked out, and you were able to identify and charge a suspect, you could place a name on the final member of the team: the annual homicide board, an iconic presence in our office for decades. It was simple but powerful. On the left were the victims' names. In the center were the names of the detectives assigned to that particular case. To the right was a column that always started as a blank space. That blank space was what you worked all those hours to fill. That blank space was where the name of the suspect went. One thing was clear: you never wanted your name on that board, on the left-side column or the right.

As for the middle column, you didn't want your name beside too many blank spaces. You wanted to fill every blank space on the suspect side, but that never happened.

6.
THE LOOK

WE WORKED ROUND the clock on homicide, all year long. I can't stress that enough. Killers don't work nine-to-five and we didn't either. Sunny and dry or cold or rainy, we worked, often outside. But no matter the weather, no matter the hour, you were expected to have "the look."

Appearance is important in police work. Arrive at an incident, and you will be the center of attention. As they say in the police academy, there are no shy effective cops. If you are shy, you'd better get over it.

A police uniform is a powerful statement, as it should be. From the DAYTON POLICE patch on each shoulder to the badge on the chest, the uniform is a symbol of authority. Add to that the wide leather belt loaded with gear, like Batman's utility belt, though the officer's belt carries guns, ammunition, radios, pepper spray, Tasers, and handcuffs. Put it all together and people recognize the uniformed officer from a mile away.

We wore a different uniform. We never responded to a scene without wearing a suit and tie, even before police cars had air-conditioning. The suit was always a dark, professional color, black, blue, brown, or gray. We didn't wear bright, happy colors because it wasn't appropriate for the job.

And no, we didn't do casual Fridays.

Detectives learn to purchase suit coats one size too large, to help conceal their guns and handcuffs. Your badge, however, would be clipped on your belt, in a place of honor: right up front, where it was always visible.

In the colder months, we all wore long black leather coats. Again, this was a kind of uniform, identifying us as the squad, showing we were working together as one, and hopefully creating an air of professionalism. Even our notepads were black leather. No bright-colored sports logos here. We meant business. The look was as important to us as Samson's hair or Superman's cape.

The look did make a difference. It still does today. If you don't believe me, try this. Put on a suit and visit a jewelry store or new-car lot. Watch how fast salespeople flock to you. Formal dress sends the message: you mean business. Now put on a T-shirt and old jeans. Go to similar establishments. See how long it takes to attract the attention of a salesperson. The look makes a difference. We were already good at our jobs. But looking good made us better.

The look doesn't stop there. Most of the male detectives had mustaches. Dayton police policy would not allow for a beard, so a big, thick mustache was the best alternative. It was just another statement, another part of the look. It was our persona, our reputation, our identity. It was even a form of marketing, kind of like the special business cards we had made.

The city provided business cards for us. They were nice, white with black lettering, with a little badge in the corner. The standard information: names, phone numbers, fax numbers, and eventually, as technology evolved, email addresses. These were great for handing out to officers from other agencies or attorneys or doctors. But attorneys and doctors rarely solved our cases.

We needed something bold and simple. When we were looking for you, whether you were a witness or a suspect, we needed a card that would grab your attention. We had our own made. The card was simple. It was solid black with gold lettering. The outline of a huge Dayton Police badge sat squarely in the center. HOMICIDE SQUAD was printed from one side of the card to the other, across the outline of the badge. But the only personal information listed was your name and phone number. These were designed for the kinds of people who never faxed anyone anything. This card was simple but it got results. People called when they found this card on their door. It was part of the look.

The look boosted you, made you feel confident. And that was the most important message: We are confident. We are confident in our abilities. We are confident in our team. We are confident in ourselves. And we are confident we will solve this murder. Many times, we would approach a scene and quickly realize it would be a tough one, maybe impossible to solve. But you can't let people see that. A lack of confidence emboldens all of the wrong people, particularly the suspect. The look cloaked any doubts we had in a particular case.

Next, add the stereotypical trademark of the homicide detective, the cigar. Almost all of us had a cigar or two in our jacket pocket or desk drawer. You were never allowed to smoke in public, and most of us didn't smoke anyway, but there is a practical need for the cigar. When you were dispatched to check on the poor soul who hadn't been seen or heard from in a month, you grabbed a cigar from your desk drawer and headed to the scene.

It's informally known as a "decomp call." I remember one in particular on the city's east side, and yes, I grabbed a cigar before heading to the scene.

Decomposed bodies were always the worst call you could get, particularly in the hot summer months. You would be met at the door, always outside the door, by uniformed officers, with Vicks VapoRub dripping from their noses.

"I've told you a million times," I would say with a laugh. "Vicks is designed to open up your nostrils."

It was true. Most officers believed you could rub some Vicks on your nose, and it would take the smell away. In reality, all it did was give you a minty fresh smell of death. We would stick with our cigars.

We'd been called out after a mailman noticed a large number of flies in the windows. Flies in the windows were never a good sign.

"Whatcha got?" I asked the officer at the door.

I expected one of a few sad scenarios. A friendless man whom no one checked on and no one missed when he died alone. Perhaps an elderly woman who had outlived all of her friends. Or a homicide that hadn't been detected earlier, for whatever reason. This one matched none of my expectations.

"I'm not sure of anything, other than it smells like hell in there," the officer said, gagging. "We've got an elderly white male who is blind and deaf and barely speaks. Apparently, he's been sleeping with his wife, who is even older than he is."

"Sleeping like sawing logs, or sleeping like sex?" I asked.

The officer laughed.

"Shit, Doyle, he's eighty-five years old," he said. "He's sleeping."

The officer explained that the couple had been somewhat estranged from other family, though those family members told police that the man could not do anything without his wife's help.

"So, who's our victim?" I asked.

It was the wife, he said, whose corpse had apparently been lying in the bed for about a week. The old man had been lying with her the whole time.

"He doesn't even know she's dead," he said.

"Well, that's different," I said, turning to head into the house.

"You want a moon suit or something?" the officer asked.

He was referring to the bright white suits we carried with us for the really bad ones. We called them "moon suits" because they made you look like an astronaut. These disposable plastic suits covered you from head to toe. The problem was, for them to be effective, you also needed to wear a gas mask so that no skin was exposed. And the stench would still reach your nostrils. It just wouldn't be as strong. On a hot summer day like this one it would be like wearing a sauna suit. I decided to skip the moon suit and just deal with the odor.

The stench from a decomposing body is like nothing else. You will never forget it and will certainly recognize it when you smell it again. Many an officer has asked how I can work a scene with that horrible smell.

"It's an acquired taste," I would joke. But it really wasn't. It was just part of the job. I never got used to the smell. I just learned to tolerate it.

The elderly female lay in her bed. She was on her back. It was hot outside and even hotter in the house. She had probably been dead for four or five days, though the heat had accelerated her decomposition.

There is a time-tested rule of death investigation: heat accelerates decomposition and cold slows it down. Why do we refrigerate the dead? To slow down the decomposition process.

The scene was horrible. The woman had already popped, police slang for when the body bursts. Leave a body to decompose naturally, and it will fill with gases and expand until it ruptures, releasing the gases and bodily fluids. This is one of the reasons it is so hard to keep a body underwater, even if you weigh it down.

The bed was soaked with her bodily fluids and liquefying organs. Maggots were everywhere, swimming in and feeding on her juices. Maggots always go for the dark, moist areas first, eye sockets, nostrils, mouth, or in this case, bodily fluids. It was a huge mess with a horrible stench. The maggots looked like someone had dumped several bowls of rice on her body, rice that was moving, slimy, and stinky. When we brought bodies like this in for autopsy, we would first put them in the morgue freezer to kill the maggots. If we didn't, the maggots would be everywhere.

This poor lady was on all kinds of medications. We counted the pills in her prescription bottles she kept by the bed. It appeared she had taken her last dose six days earlier. It seemed to be a natural death, and the autopsy would confirm that the next day.

Her husband was unaware she had died and lay helplessly beside her until rescued by the officers and the mailman. He was dehydrated and suffered from malnutrition, but he would live. Sadly, as often happens, he died a few months after losing his lifelong companion.

The smell is also quite persistent. It attaches itself to your clothing, your hair, and even your eyebrows. On this call, like so many others, I would call my wife on the way home.

"Leave me a clean set of clothes and two paper bags in the garage," I would say. She didn't have to ask. She knew why.

I would pull in the garage and shut the door. Next, I would take off everything I had on. Watch, gun, belt, shoes, and like items would go in one bag to air out. Clothing would go in another. I would then put on the clean clothes my wife had provided and run to the bathroom. There, I would strip down again and take a long, cold shower with lots of soap. You only had to take a post-decomp hot shower one time to realize that hot water makes the odor stronger, while cold water washes it away.

I would then redress myself and take my bag of stinky clothing to the coin-operated Laundromat. No way was I washing those clothes in my washer at home.

The next day, it would be back to work, and back to the look.

* * *

If I've made it seem like we all dressed exactly the same, like a bunch of drones, that's not true. There were several ways to personalize the look, to express your individuality while projecting that confidence. One of my partners always wore a kerchief in his suit coat pocket that matched his tie. Others sported expensive watches. Quite by chance, I took my look one step further.

Ohio Loan is a pawnshop on the city's west side, and I became familiar with it long before joining the force. My father and I would drop in and see what deals were available. Along the way, I became friends with the people who worked there. Even after I became a detective, I still dropped in to say hello and see if there was anything that, as the guys would say, I "couldn't live without." One particular time, there was.

"Have I got something for you," my friend said. He went to the back room and reappeared with a small box in the palm of his hand. I opened the box. It was a solid-gold ring—a gold skull ring with ruby eyes.

"Wow, that's badass," I exclaimed.

The employee explained that it had been custom made for a man who had since died. His wife then sold it to the pawnshop. I snatched it up.

I wore that ring every day—still do. To me, it was a constant reminder of the victims I dealt with. A constant reminder of the career I had chosen. Nothing more, nothing less. But it meant other things to other people and soon became my trademark. Little did I know that one day it would attract the attention of a serial killer.

7.
OH SHIT

WE'VE ALL WATCHED the cop shows on television. From *Adam-12* to *CSI*, one thing remains constant. There is usually some officer or detective reading the bad guy their constitutional rights, or "Miranda rights," as we call them.

Miranda v. Arizona was a 1966 U.S. Supreme Court ruling designed to protect the rights of the accused. In a sense, to level the playing field between the police and criminal suspects, who are often, but not always, the bad guys. Sometimes, a person initially becomes a valid suspect, only to be eliminated by further investigation. But consider this: Ernesto Miranda, the plaintiff in the case, was a career criminal with a record that started in his teenage years and ended with his stabbing death at age thirty-four. Though the nation's highest court overturned his conviction for rape and kidnapping, finding that his confession was not valid because he had not been informed of his rights, prosecutors in Arizona retried him without the confession and convicted him again. This time he stayed in prison, at least for a while.

So, if you want to use any information given by suspects while in custody, you'd better make sure they have been read their rights. In fact, most police departments go further—we get their waivers in writing. Every department has a rights waiver form and a rights card that each officer carries with them every day.

For those of you who have watched television, ever, this will probably be familiar. But Miranda requires us to let the suspect know the following:

- You have the right to remain silent.
- Anything you say can and will be used against you in court.
- You have the right to an attorney.
- If you can't afford an attorney, one will be provided to you free of charge.
- You have the right to stop anytime you wish.

Miranda warnings have existed for five decades. But police work changes constantly. New laws are passed, and courts hand down new rulings on evidence collection, searches, and statements. Miranda remains, and so does its importance, because despite changes in forensics that would have seemed like science fiction in Ernesto Miranda's day, a confession is still the most damning piece of evidence you can get. It's always easier to convict someone who admits they did it. In fact, confessions are so powerful that courts have ruled that we cannot convict someone on a confession alone—this is to keep criminal justice's hacks from prosecuting the deranged, who first come forward to confess their involvement whenever there is a high-profile case, then will go on to tell you that they also kidnapped the Lindbergh baby and helped John Wilkes Booth shoot President Lincoln.

Most people, police included, are dumbfounded as to why a guilty person would talk to us after being given these warnings. My opinion is there are many reasons. Some murder suspects think they can outwit us. Some are proud of what they did. Others just can't help but talk. Still others become so nervous that they confess to relieve themselves of the tension, only to quickly realize that they've put themselves into deeper jeopardy. Whatever the reason, the successful homicide detective is always ready to listen.

We never fooled ourselves. I was fortunate to get most of my suspects to talk, but I know I obtained very few "true" confessions. I obtained hundreds of "lie-fessions" though. A true confession, I believe, is when the suspect tells why and how they committed the murder, with no excuses, justifications, or spin. It did happen occasionally, but rarely. A lie-fession is when you get the suspect to admit they pulled the trigger, but . . . insert justification. Such as, "I shot that piece of shit, but he had threatened me, so I was scared." If the other evidence shows this was an ambush, not a self-defense situation, that's a lie-fession.

A lie-fession is usually more than enough. First off, it cuts off any alibi defense—the suspect has admitted they were there. Typically, you have at least one witness. Hopefully, you have forensic evidence that supports your theory, and a little circumstantial evidence as well. Now add in the "I did it" lie-fession and your case is in pretty good shape. A lie-fession may not be the whole truth, but usually it is still an admission of guilt, particularly when you throw in the other evidence. But even lie-fessions take a lot of work to obtain, and it starts long before you ever speak to a suspect.

When I was at a scene, I would take note of what I saw. That's probably not surprising. But I would look at every piece of evidence and give it some weight. It was like loading bullets in your gun. I would fire these information bullets at the suspect during the interview. An important item has a lot of weight, while other items may have little or no weight. Sometimes, the same type of item would take on a different weight during the interview. Confused yet? Let me explain.

We were dispatched to a nice housing development in the north end of Dayton. The call was a possible suicide. As usual, the first responders would brief me.

"Wife is in the bedroom with a hole in her head," one officer said.

"Been there awhile, blood is starting to dry a little," added another.

"How about a gun?" I asked.

"Revolver, probably a .38, lying beside her," the second officer added. "The husband found her; he's outside."

"Not real broken up either," the first officer added.

Ah, police intuition. I believe in police intuition. We dealt with more varied personalities in a day than many psychologists would in a week. Police intuition was a combination of experience and observation. If something felt wrong, it usually was. Consider the person who was too polite, too cooperative. Usually, these people had outstanding warrants for their arrest, or some other secret they were hoping to smile and joke away with a pleasant, cooperative demeanor. The husband fell into this category. He was way too helpful.

I introduced myself to the husband, who by now had been joined by his next-door neighbor, a single woman, attractive and friendly—way too friendly, especially to the husband. The husband had now piqued my intuition.

"'Never have your girlfriend with you right after you kill your wife,' I always say," I said to the officers before walking over to the husband.

"I'm Detective Burke from homicide," I told him. "Homicide" was a powerful word, which is why I often used it with suspects. It definitely got their attention.

"Hi," the husband replied. "I came home from work, where I've been all day, and found my wife."

It's always a bad sign when you give your alibi in your introduction, I thought. I planned to interview him thoroughly once I had a few more facts. For now, I would just hit the basics. He was not in police custody so, under law, I didn't need to read him his rights.

"So, how did you happen to find her?" I asked.

"I had just gotten home, you can check my time card," he said. "I went down the hall by the bedroom and saw her. I never went in the room, you can check my clothing for blood, no blood on me."

Nothing weird here, I thought. "You never went in the room?" I asked.

"No, I watch a lot of *CSI* shows," he said. "I knew it was best to leave the scene unaltered."

Idiot, I thought. Might as well put a neon sign on your head that said, "I killed her!" A man who cared about his wife would have rushed to her aid. His first and only concern would be her well-being, not preserving a crime scene. And even if he didn't care, wouldn't he have at least approached her to see if she were really dead?

That was enough for now. I reviewed the scene with my partners and an E-crew. The gun was a .38-caliber revolver. Investigation would quickly reveal that it had been purchased days earlier—by the husband.

The revolver held six cartridges. Five were unfired. The fired round had passed through the wife's head and the gun lay on the bed in her right palm. We would learn from family and friends that the victim was right-handed. Friends would also tell us of marital problems. The victim was unhappy and thought her husband was fooling around on her. *She was correct*, I thought. But marital problems can lead to suicide. The deciding factor for me was my intuition that the husband's actions were all wrong. But intuition is not evidence.

The wife lay in her bed in her nightgown. She was on her back with her arms at her sides. There was a moderate amount of blood on the headboard and wall. Her eyes were black and puffy. To the untrained person, she would appear to have been beaten. We knew otherwise. The eyes rest on orbital plates that are wafer thin. When the head of a victim sustains a strong blow, such as a bullet passing through, the plates shatter. This allows blood to fill the eyelids, making them darker. We called them "raccoon eyes."

We found the first piece of damning evidence quite quickly: The hole in the wife's head was going in the wrong direction. The bullet had entered the left side and exited the right.

When a bullet is fired into a human head, it encounters a number of obstacles. First, there is the skin, then the skull, then the brain. As it exits, it encounters the other side of the skull and skin. All of these obstacles alter the bullet. This is why, in most cases, the entrance wound is much smaller than the exit wound.

You could also feel the beveling around the holes to determine the directionality of the bullet. There was no doubt she had been shot left to right. The gun, however, had been carefully placed in her right hand. This shot would have been awkward, if not impossible to do with her right hand. Next, we looked at the entrance wound.

An entrance wound is an evidentiary treasure trove. When a gun is fired, the bullet is not the only thing that leaves the barrel. Unburned gunpowder leaves the barrel, but only travels a short distance. So do hot gases and flame from the burning gunpowder. All of these components are observed around an entrance wound if the gun was fired from close range.

We observed nothing like that around this wound. This was not a close-range shot. This does not mean that the woman had been shot from a hundred yards away. A distance of four to five feet would usually be enough to eliminate these close-range signs. It could have been a shot from the hallway, or even from a few feet away in the bedroom as she slept. But she did not hold that gun to her temple and fire. This was no suicide.

At my request, the coroner's investigator performed a "liver stick." He made a small incision near the abdomen, then stuck a meat thermometer into the liver. This provided a body core temperature so we could determine a time of death. It was really pretty simple but very effective.

"She's been dead approximately eight to ten hours," the coroner's investigator estimated.

Perfect, I thought. *He kills her in the morning and clocks in at work, creating his alibi.*

I talked to my partners and our evidence technician. There was no doubt: the husband was our suspect. We just had to prove it. So, we went to a local judge and obtained a search warrant for the house.

Most people don't understand why we always got a search warrant for a victim's house when the victim had been killed there. But we were also in the suspect's house, and that required a warrant. Within a few minutes, our E-crew tech motioned us to the basement.

In a laundry basin there was diluted blood where the killer had probably washed his hands. That was good, I thought. Of course, any competent defense attorney would argue that the wife had cut herself earlier and washed her hands. Or even if it had been the killer washing his hands, the blood didn't identify the husband as the culprit.

"Oh, but wait, there's more," the tech said. He was beaming when he pointed to a brand-new bar of soap sitting on the sink.

"So?" I asked.

"Look in the trash can."

There it was, the piece of evidence that had more weight than even the revolver. It was beautiful. There in the trash can lay the wrapper for the new bar of soap. On the wrapper was a perfect thumbprint, in blood. The killer had used a blood-covered hand to hold the bar of soap while the other hand peeled the wrapper off.

The tech was justifiably proud of this find.

"Even a blind squirrel finds an acorn every now and then," I said. I couldn't resist.

"I love you too," he said. "Now, go do what you do."

What I do is get confessions. It would be at least a day before the bloody print was matched to the husband's hand. It would be days, maybe weeks, before the blood was matched to the wife. But the husband didn't know that.

I listen to everything a potential suspect says. I had listened to the husband when he said he'd watched a lot of *CSI* shows. *I'll bet you do*, I had thought. And in those shows, lab results come back in an instant. I was sure he believed that. I would use his *CSI* fascination to my advantage.

It was the husband's print, I was sure of that, even before the results came back. Remember how I said the same type of item could have different weight? This was his print in his house. His print on the door meant nothing. Even his prints on the revolver meant nothing, since he had handled it in the past. No weight could be given to those prints. But his print in her blood, on a package that had probably been opened the day of her death, carried tremendous weight. I was ready to attack.

I never interview suspects at their homes or in a car. There are too many ways to escape. I don't mean a physical escape. I mean a mental escape. No daydreaming, no looking out a window. You don't want a suspect to get comfortable in his surroundings. And I wanted all attention focused on me. I had an officer take the husband to headquarters and place him in an interview room.

Those rooms are Spartan by design. Drab blue walls, no windows, no pictures on the wall. There was a small table with no drawers, and two chairs. Other than those barest of furnishings, there would be nothing but you and me.

The husband sat in one chair. I entered the room with my interview face on. I was no longer the friendly detective he'd met at the scene, politely addressing a victim's spouse. Now the message was clear: this was business, he was the suspect, and I intended to get the truth.

I asked the husband to move to the other chair. He complied. They always do. In reality I didn't care which side of the table he sat at. I just wanted to establish who was in charge.

I went over the rights form, which he willingly signed, adding, "Let's get this cleared up."

We will, I thought.

"I've been at the scene for a little while and I have a whole CSI team still there," I told him. In actuality, my partner and the E-crew were just finishing up, but I wanted his mind to race. "Your wife didn't kill herself," I said, now looking directly into his eyes.

Suspects hate that. Even guilty children turn away during a scolding. The concept doesn't change as we age. That's why the interview rooms were designed the way they were. There was nothing in this room to turn away to.

"I can't believe you have no blood on you," I said.

"Sir, you can take my clothing," he said. "You can check my skin. I have no blood on me."

"So, you really never went in the bedroom?"

"No, sir."

"So, there is no way you should have even a drop of your wife's blood on you?"

"Absolutely not a single drop," he said.

I reached in my pocket for a photo of the bloody thumbprint.

"The killer washed your wife's blood from his hands in the basement sink," I began.

"No way!" he said. "What balls."

Indeed, I thought. I lay the photo on the table between us and said, "We also found this."

He stared at the picture for several seconds, then very slowly said, "Oh shit." He knew we had him. The confession was just a formality now.

The husband admitted that he'd been seeing the pretty neighbor. His wife became suspicious and wanted a divorce, which he feared would leave him penniless. A staged suicide was, in his mind, the only way out. "How is that fair?" he asked.

Ask the woman you murdered because she objected to your infidelity, I thought.

Whether we gained a confession or a lie-fession was usually determined by the suspect and how much information we had at the time of the interview. We would yell with some suspects and pray with others. We would talk and we would listen. As long as a suspect was talking to us, we never stopped the discussion. Some interviews lasted for five, six, or seven hours.

I've known many competent detectives, but the interview room is what separated the great from the good. The power of that room intimidated even us. Winning sometimes meant the difference between getting a statement and getting nothing. We didn't always win. No one does. But we worked hard for that "oh shit" moment.

8.

COD MOD TOD

SCIENCE HAS CHANGED how we do our jobs. The ability
to use blood to identify a single suspect—to the exclusion of
everyone else on earth—would have sounded like science fiction when I first went into homicide. Back then, we could only
use blood type to exclude potential suspects. That's obviously
a big difference.

You see that in the true-crime shows on television, as well
as fictionalized versions, such as the *CSI* series. But we still fall
back on the basics, concepts we've used for decades to solve
crimes. Allow me to introduce you to COD, MOD, and TOD.

COD, MOD, and TOD are needed in every death investigation. No, these are not names of detectives or pathologists.
Quite simply, "COD" is "cause of death." "MOD" is "manner
of death." And "TOD" is "time of death." They are separate
but always linked together, and they are critically important to
all death investigations.

Let's start with cause of death. In most cases I can tell you
at the scene what the cause of death is. Say we were dispatched
on the report of man who had been shot in the head. We would
arrive, find a body with an obvious bullet hole in the cranium.

"Bullet to the brain. Bet that's what killed him," we would sometimes joke. Often it really was that simple—but maybe not. It should be noted that sometimes people are shot post-mortem, meaning after death. For the purposes of the trial, we would still need a full autopsy to tell us exactly what happened.

The autopsy would trace the path of the bullet through the brain. All other organs would be examined for defects and/or disease. The pathologist would weigh each organ to see if it matched normal anatomical weights. Then each organ would be sectioned and preserved, forever, if needed.

Fingernails would be scraped in the hopes of finding the suspect's DNA. Tubes of blood, samples of tissue and hair would all be examined and preserved. The entire autopsy would be photographed. The pathologist would measure the wound and remove the bullet from the brain. That bullet would be sent to the firearms section of the crime lab. There, if a weapon had been recovered, it could be matched to that weapon.

The end result? It was a bullet to the brain that killed him.

* * *

Time of death is critical. Those who lead a high-risk lifestyle, such as a prostitute or a narcotics user or seller, come into contact with strangers on a regular basis. Stranger-on-stranger murders are the hardest to solve because nothing ties the victim and suspect together except for the crime itself. If you have a high-risk victim, it is imperative that you shorten the killer's window of opportunity through an accurate time of death. The less time you have to retrace the victim's last moments, the better.

There are several ways to make an educated guess as to time of death. I am often asked at the scene what time I thought someone was killed.

"When was he found?" I would ask.

"Early this morning, about 7 a.m.," the officer might reply.

"When was he last known to be alive?"

"Left his girlfriend's house at about 3 a.m."

"It's sometime between those two points," I would say with a grin. To determine time of death, you needed both a beginning and an end. Then you would try to narrow it down further.

The body goes through a number of changes immediately upon death. First, I check for what is known as "rigor mortis." "Rigor" is a stiffening of the muscles. Everyone has heard the term "stiff as a board," or corpses referred to as "stiffs." Rigor is why: in ten to twelve hours, depending on conditions, the entire body becomes rigid, or stiff as a board.

This doesn't happen all at once. Rigor is a gradual process that starts with the smaller muscles. Early on, fingers and wrists will be stiff while elbows are not. In looking at the progression of rigor, you can get an idea of the time of death. If just fingers and wrists are stiff, it may only be a few hours. If larger muscles are stiff, it could be eight hours or more.

The next thing I check is "lividity," which is the settling of the blood in the body due to gravity.

Once the heart stops pumping, the blood naturally settles in the lowest point of the victim's body. For victims lying faceup, their backs should appear purple because of the settled blood.

As a test, I will press on the area of lividity. If the blood is still fluid, it will blanche out for a moment—kind of like pressing on your tanned arm in the summer. If the blood is not fluid, lividity is deemed to be fixed, and it will not blanche out no matter how hard you press on it.

For this reason, lividity is also useful in determining if a body has been moved. The blood remains fluid and can shift if the body is moved during the first ten hours after death. If we find a body floating facedown in the river with lividity fixed on his back, we're likely dealing with something more complicated than a drowning.

The final thing we look at is body temperature. The liver, the body's largest internal organ, retains body heat more accurately than other organs. To take a body core temperature accurately, you need to perform a liver stick.

A living person maintains a normal temperature of just under ninety-nine degrees Fahrenheit. After death, the body usually loses one degree of heat each hour. So, if the liver stick shows the body has cooled to ninety-four degrees, then the time of death should be about five hours earlier.

Once we have obtained findings on rigor, lividity, and body core temperature, we compare them with when the victim was last known to be alive and determine an approximate time of death. It can be surprisingly accurate, particularly with a fresh body. Most importantly, it gives us a segment of time to focus on.

If a body has not been found for days, all of these observations are meaningless. Rigor has come and gone. Lividity is most certainly fixed and body core temperature has fallen to room temperature—or worse, outdoor temperature. Thankfully, there is another method for those cases, one that uses stomach contents found at the time of autopsy. It takes the human digestive system four to five hours to digest a meal. If you know what your victim last ate and when, you've got a shot.

Let's say a body is found on May 5, but we know that person has been missing since May 1, and that they ate at 11 p.m. before they left home that day. If the meal has been digested, we're stuck with a four-day window. But the presence of stomach contents would indicate that he was killed within hours of leaving home. In the modern world of DNA analysis, this technique probably sounds a bit antiquated, even crude—but, as you'll see later, it would be critical in helping us solve a local case that drew nationwide attention, involving the disappearance of a four-year-old girl.

Many times, bodies are not found for weeks, or even months. This requires extra work to determine time of death, and some real expertise. One typical scenario is when hunters find a body in the woods. Another is when city workers mowing vacant lots find a body in an abandoned field. In those situations, we still treat the crime scene as if the crime had just occurred, but with one exception—the addition of forensic entomology. This is when the maggot, ordinarily among the most repulsive of the earth's creatures, becomes a friend.

Forensic entomologists help us pinpoint a time of death based on the life cycle of the blowfly. At a scene like this, we would pull out one of our prestocked entomology collection kits. We would carefully place live maggots in one marked bottle and dead ones in another. We also had a third bottle for dead flies, of which there were usually hundreds. The fourth bottle gave us the most trouble. It was marked Flies Live. Each collection kit contained small butterfly nets. We must have looked pretty silly trying to catch flies in our tiny nets, but we did it.

After our collections were complete, we would send them to a forensic entomologist. We would also send weather reports for the appropriate time period, even if it was weeks or months. The weather reports were important because blowflies are not active at night or when it's raining or snowing. Without this information, even the best entomologists could be weeks off in their time-of-death estimation.

Within a few days, we would receive a report back estimating a time of death. In those cases that we solved, I was often astounded as to how accurate the time-of-death estimate was.

Many murderers are in prison today due to the "testimony" of the flies and maggots.

* * *

People outside of law enforcement often confuse "cause of death" and "manner of death." They are not the same thing.

Cause of death lies predominately with the medical or forensic-pathology realm of the death investigation. Meaning we watch the forensic pathologist do the autopsy and wait on the test results. But manner of death is a team effort, and the captain of that team is the coroner's office death investigator.

Cause of death is virtually limitless. You can be shot, wreck your car, overdose, have a heart attack, fall off a ladder, or any other way you can think of to die. Manner of death is much more limited.

Most states, like Ohio, have a limited but comprehensive selection of manners of death that are acceptable on a death certificate. The big four are "homicide," "suicide," "accident," or "natural." A homicide occurs when the victim is killed by another person. Please note that this is not synonymous with "murder," which is a legal charge. In rare occasions, a homicide can be justifiable, such as in a self-defense situation.

"Suicide" is obvious: the victim purposely killed themself. "Accident" also speaks for itself. "Natural" means you died of natural causes. And for the very few cases (fewer than 2 percent) where you cannot determine an accurate manner of death, the final selection is "undetermined." This can happen when a badly decomposed body is found and there is no obvious wound, like a bullet hole in the skull.

In some cases, the pathologist cannot determine manner of death without input from the investigators. Let's go back to the man shot in the head. The cause of death is the gunshot wound. Now it's time to determine manner of death with information provided from the scene investigation. It may be a homicide: the scene investigation may have disclosed that the victim had been shot by someone else in a bar fight. It could be a suicide: investigators may have found a weapon and a suicide note at the scene. It may be accidental: the deceased may have been cleaning his "unloaded" gun when it discharged. Certainly, with a gunshot wound to the head we can rule out death by natural causes. But without input from the scene investigator, manner of death could never be determined.

Manner of death is often hardest to determine in autoerotic asphyxiations. Autoerotic asphyxiation has nothing to do with a car. It is, in fact, a highly disturbing practice. Somehow, someway, someone discovered a method to heighten arousal during masturbation: by cutting off the blood and oxygen supply to the brain. This is nothing new. Autoerotic asphyxiation activity has been documented back to the ancient Mayans. Unfortunately, like with other types of artificial highs, things can go very dangerously wrong.

Typically, the autoerotic asphyxiation practitioner does the act in a private or secluded place. Some are found nude, while others are discovered in elaborate attire. Others are dressed normally. Most are white males in their mid-twenties, though the youngest one I've dealt with was fifteen and the oldest was sixty-eight. Most are married.

The mechanisms used to facilitate the act are varied as well. They range from intricate setups involving props and sex toys, to a simple trash bag over the head. Now, cutting off oxygen to the brain is not a good idea—that goes without saying. So, why would anyone do this? Some like the idea of taking a risk. Others want something their spouse won't or can't provide sexually. Others still just enjoy the sensation.

Almost always, it is a friend or family member who discovers the deceased autoerotic asphyxiation practitioner, and when that occurs, the scene is usually altered. Often, those unlucky loved ones don't know exactly what they've found, but they know it isn't good. So, those scenes will be altered to make the death appear natural or as a suicide or sometimes even as a homicide. This manipulation, however well-intended, makes determining manner of death much harder.

One fall day, we were dispatched to a nice home in a quiet neighborhood on the south side of town. A woman had returned home from work to find her husband hanging in the garage. Uniformed crews had determined the scene was suspicious, so we were called out.

"What you got?" I asked the first officer at the scene.

"Got one swinging in the garage, but it is a weird one," he replied. "He's got towels around his neck to protect him from the rope and he had the door locked from the inside."

As if he didn't want to be disturbed, I thought.

The scene appeared simple and typical, though the victim was wearing a dress, but even beyond that, it didn't feel right. I grabbed a nearby ladder and examined the ceiling beam that the rope was tied around.

"Lot of wear marks up here," I said. "Either this guy is horrible at suicide or he's done this before, a lot."

I figured it was probably autoerotic. The wear marks on the wooden beam were evidence of prior activity. He had done this so many times before that he had worn grooves in the wood. He would just kneel while masturbating, to tighten the rope around his neck and create just enough pressure to cut off the flow of blood to the brain temporarily. Had he survived, after he was done masturbating, he would've simply stood up. This time he had waited too long.

"Why the towel around the neck?" one officer asked.

"Can't show up for work tomorrow with rope burns on your neck," I said. "Someone might start asking questions."

Now for the hard part: talking to the wife. I walked into the house, introduced myself, told her I was sorry for her loss, and added that I had a few questions. She nodded. I started with the usual questions: When did you last see him? Was he depressed? Has he ever talked about suicide? Then I moved directly to the tough one.

"Did you change or remove anything from the garage before calling for help?" I asked.

This woman was no criminal. She looked at me with surprise and fear. I felt sorry for her.

"I don't understand," she said.

"Ma'am, your husband didn't commit suicide," I said. "He died from what's called 'autoerotic asphyxiation.'"

She understood. That was a huge clue. Many police officers couldn't tell you what an autoerotic asphyxiation death is, so for a civilian to know is very telling.

"He wants me to do weird things in bed and I won't do them," she said. "I've caught him playing with himself before with a bag over his head. When I came home and found him, I knew what he had been doing."

She explained that he had his laptop computer with him when she found him and that she'd stashed it in the coat closet before calling police. She was almost trembling as she handed it to me.

"I'm so ashamed," she said. "Will I go to prison?"

This was so sad. She'd lost her husband, in a manner that she probably wouldn't want to explain to anyone. And now she was terrified. She'd altered a death scene, but there was no criminal intent here.

"No, ma'am," I said. "It will all be okay."

I turned on the laptop. It was full of photos of individuals in various stages of bondage and torture. I could see why she didn't want to participate. The manner of death was ruled accidental. This man wasn't committing suicide. He was just engaging in a very dangerous activity and went too far.

I teach a weeklong death investigation course at the Ohio Peace Officer Training Academy. I always include a lecture about autoerotic asphyxiation deaths. Though they are rare, they are unique and they can be misleading. It is very important that they be recognized for what they are and not labeled as suicides, or worse, homicides.

One of the examples I use in class is a video I obtained long ago of a man performing an autoerotic asphyxiation act. It is common for practitioners to take photos or videos of themselves during the act. In this video, the man places a pair of panties over his head, then places a rope around his neck. He then leans into the rope to apply pressure but goes too far. For the next ninety seconds he struggles to breathe, clawing at the rope to free his airway. Then, slowly, his arms drop to his sides as he dies. I must have watched this video one hundred times in my lectures. You almost find yourself rooting for the guy to make it. He never does.

9.

YOU NEVER KNOW
HOW SOMEONE LIVED
UNTIL THEY DIE

IT WAS AN uneventful day in August 2004. Hot but—oddly for Dayton's Midwestern climate—not humid. The police radio was busy but not crazy busy. The kind of day when we would follow up on our open cases, which is what we had been doing before we pulled into the back lot at headquarters.

"Crew 613: give dispatch a 400 right away," the radio blared. That got my attention. I was "crew 613," a "400" was a phone call, and "right away" meant it was not a social call. I called dispatch.

"Dayton police dispatch. Do you have an emergency?" the dispatcher answered.

"Yes, I do," I said. "I can't decide which gun to wear to the Policeman's Ball this year. Can you help me?"

"Wear a big one to compensate for your lack of police balls," he chuckled back. "All kidding aside, I've got a weird one they didn't want put out over the air. Grab a couple uniforms and go to 88 Pioneer Street. I'll fill you in on the way."

There were several uniformed crews milling around the rear entrance to headquarters. "Who wants to go with me on a mystery call?" I asked.

"You buying?" one asked.

"Depends on what they're selling," I replied.

On the way, I learned dispatch had received an anonymous call about a dead body on Pioneer. Of course, the call was only somewhat anonymous. Caller ID showed the call originated from the office of a prominent local defense attorney. The caller was a receptionist who did not give her name but would not be hard to identify.

This attorney, a fixture on the local news broadcasts, is instantly recognizable to many Dayton residents. His practice attracts a lot of potential clients—so many that they have "teller lines" set up in the waiting room like a bank. An attorney then screens the potential clients to see if there is a case worth taking. On this particular day, the room was very busy. A man who lived at 88 Pioneer approached the receptionist.

"My name is Matt Caddy and I need to see an attorney," the man said. When the receptionist tried to assign him a number, Caddy responded, "I have a dead man in my basement."

That was enough to move him to the front of the line. The receptionist immediately took him out of the reception room and in with one of the firm's attorneys.

The receptionist was intrigued. She overheard Caddy telling the attorney that he ran a bondage house in his basement. It seems Caddy had gone a bit too far and killed one of his bondage customers. The body was still in the house. Some more routine questions followed: value of the home, finances, etc. After a short while, Caddy exited the room and walked away.

Imagine the receptionist's surprise. Caddy had admitted to killing a man and was now casually walking away. She confronted the screening attorney as to why.

"Can't afford us," the attorney said.

Not that we could use this admission. Caddy had been talking with a man who was, however briefly, acting as his attorney. That meant the conversation was covered by attorney–client privilege. Even though the receptionist overheard the conversation, that information would never be admissible in court. Her call to dispatch may have just as well been anonymous, because this information was never coming in at trial.

That didn't mean we were helpless. We sent out Caddy's description over the KDT units in the officers' patrol cars. KDTs are closed-system laptops that we use. You can receive calls, run names and licenses and registrations, and even communicate with other crews, all without putting anything out over the air. It was important to keep this one off the scanners until we figured out what we had. We also had a responsibility as police officers to check on the "dead" body on Pioneer Street. Perhaps he was just unconscious and needed assistance. We would soon find out.

The uniformed crews and I pulled up to 88 Pioneer Street, parking a safe distance away and approaching on foot. There was always a chance this was a setup. That's uncommon, but it does happen. Someone will make a call that they know will merit a police response. When the police pull up, they then ambush the officers. Considering how weird this call was, we had to be extra careful. The state of Caddy's property added to the apprehension.

"Geez, do the fucking Munsters live here?" one officer asked as we approached the house.

"The Munsters' house was cleaner," I said.

We were looking at a two-story structure in serious disrepair. The weeds that surrounded it were several feet tall. *Another spooky old house*, I thought.

"Cover it and I'll try to make contact," I said. The four uniformed officers surrounded the house, while I stood to the side of the door, glock in hand, and began to knock.

"Dayton police," I yelled several times, then turned back to the officers and asked, "Anything?"

"No movement," the uniforms replied. They hadn't seen any sign of life from any of the windows or doors.

I tried the front door, but it was locked. An officer alerted me to a large window on the side of the house that was unlocked and partially open. I decided to do the sniff test. Believe me, once you've smelled a dead body, you will recognize that smell for the rest of your life. I took a big whiff of the air through the open window.

"Shit," I said.

"Got one inside?" one officer asked.

"I don't know," I said as I reached into my coat pocket for a cigar. "The place smells so bad I can't tell. Going to have to go in. Exigent circumstances."

Usually, we can't just enter a home, due to the Fourth Amendment of the US Constitution, which requires that we get a search warrant. Exigent circumstances are the exception, usually in emergency cases, particularly those involving personal safety. Bottom line: we had reason to believe there was someone inside who might need help urgently and we didn't have time to get a warrant. We crawled through the window.

Conditions inside mirrored those on the outside. We saw dog hair and even dog feces that looked to be several years old.

"I didn't know dog turds could mold," one officer said.

"Learn something new every day," I said.

We carefully made our way through the filth and clutter. Finally, I worked my way to the basement.

The basement was really just a damp, moldy old root cellar that now housed the furnace and offered a bit of storage. A blue sheet lay in the middle of the floor. Underneath the sheet was our victim. He was obviously dead. Lividity was fixed. His skin was blistering from the gases in his body expanding. Skin was slipping off in other areas. He was, as we say, DRT. The exigent circumstances were now gone. There was no one here we could save. Time to back out and get a search warrant.

Once outside, we saw three men. Two we recognized as public defenders. The third matched the description we had broadcast earlier.

"Is this Mr. Caddy?" I asked.

"Yes, and he does not wish to give a statement," one of the attorneys replied.

"That's fine," I said. "We'll just arrest him for murder."

We handcuffed Caddy and placed him in the back of a cruiser. As I looked at him, I could see he looked familiar, but I didn't know why. The attorneys left, having made it clear that Caddy did not wish to be interviewed.

Fair enough, but we still had the right to ask standard booking questions. The arresting officer was going through Caddy's wallet, logging its contents, which is common practice. Inside, the officer found a Minnesota driver's license in the name of Daniel Everson.

"This you?" the officer asked.

"No," Caddy replied.

Caddy wasn't lying. Everson, we would quickly learn, was our deceased victim. *Probably kept the license as some sort of trophy*, I thought. These weird ones usually want something to help them relive the event.

"How the hell does a guy from Minnesota end up in a basement in Dayton?" one officer asked.

"We'll soon find out," I said. "You know, you never know how someone lived until they die."

Every homicide detective knows this is true. Once you die, all your secrets go on display. We were going to learn a lot about Daniel Everson—more, probably, than he'd ever wanted anyone else to know.

As Caddy was being booked into the county jail, we worked on the search warrant. Our guess was that these two had met through the Internet. How else could you explain a guy from Minnesota ending up in Caddy's haunted house? We added computers and digital storage devices as items to be taken on the search warrant.

After we obtained a judge's signature, the search began. The house was not huge, but it was crammed full of everything and anything imaginable. Boxes and boxes of videotapes. Computers, zip drives, books, magazines. Many boxes just contained trash, which Caddy apparently kept around. There wasn't an area of the house you could walk through without having to squeeze by boxes of junk. A few years after this, the term "hoarder" became common due to a reality television show of the same name. Caddy could have been on the Halloween episode.

We decided to split up and each take a floor. Though it would probably be impossible, I told the crews to look at everything.

"Our reputation depends on not overlooking a severed head or something," I said.

That was kind of a joke, but not entirely. It was completely possible that Everson was not Caddy's first victim. I did not want to be remembered as the guy who missed a head.

I couldn't get past my familiarity with Caddy. It wasn't from his police record, which was nearly nonexistent. Many times, our suspects had arrest records, known as "rap sheets," that would rival a small library. Not here. But that didn't mean

Caddy hadn't been doing strange stuff for a long time. How strange, we were about to find out.

I took the basement, which was as cluttered as the rest of the house. There were a lot of political signs, for both Republican candidates and Democrats. That, too, was strange. Usually, you only helped out your own party. Then I knew where I'd seen our suspect before.

Caddy was one of several protesters who stood outside the courthouse every Friday. We called them the "cause-of-the-day men," because whatever was trending at that moment is what they would be promoting or protesting.

I grabbed my cell phone and called a criminal personality profiler I had worked with in the past. Caddy wasn't your average gang enforcer or wife beater, and I wanted the profiler's insight. Despite the limited information I could provide, she quickly delivered.

The suspect, she said, would be living alone, probably in his dead mother's house. He would be either unmarried or divorced. A desire to be part of something bigger would lead him to volunteer for causes or political campaigns. His Internet presence would be larger than life, to compensate for his pathetic real-world existence. She was spot-on.

Since I was the squad's senior investigator, the newer detectives looked to me for answers. I had none. This was uncharted territory for all of us.

"You ever had one like this before?" one detective asked.

"Oh, hell yeah," I said. "Back in the eighties, we had two or three like this a week."

I made my way through the basement toward our victim's body. We had a name from the driver's license, and the corpse matched the license's description. Though the body was starting to decompose, there was no odor. The damp, cool basement had slowed down the decomposition process.

Everson was totally nude, and I didn't see any obvious injuries. His head and pubic region had been shaved. Both his nipples were pierced. A cheap pair of handcuffs was locked around his wrists, and the cuffs were tied at the center with a nylon rope that was a little thicker than a clothesline. The other end of the rope was tied to a four-by-four piece of wood that lay just below a ceiling joist.

It was easy to visualize. The rope and four-by-four had been wrapped around a ceiling joist, keeping Everson in an upright position, hands over his head, with little mobility. But why didn't Everson yell for help when his fantasy life went out of control? Maybe he had.

I asked an officer to stand outside the house, then I returned to the basement, adjacent to where the officer was standing. I began screaming as loud as I could.

"Hear anything?" I asked when I returned outside.

"Not a thing," the officer replied.

The cinder-block walls were so thick they'd muffled my voice, and probably the victim's as well. But how did he die? Hanging in Caddy's homemade contraption would be uncomfortable, but I doubted it would be fatal.

I continued searching. In the far corner of the basement was an old coal cellar, about the size of a modern walk-in closet. Inside I found a large, freshly dug hole. Caddy's first instinct was probably to bury his victim. He probably abandoned the idea when he realized it was too much work. Caddy, like others, had found out it takes an awfully big hole to bury a body.

We also found an open bag of lime, a shovel, and a garden tiller. Even a garden tiller couldn't help out here. I went back upstairs.

"Look at this shit," one detective exclaimed. They had found our victim's wallet—minus his license—plus chains, studded leather straps and tie-downs, and more. There was a stun gun and two large dildos. Every time you thought Caddy's house of horrors couldn't get worse, it did.

"What were the odds on finding this stuff here?" I said.

Our E-crews boxed up the sex toys, the computers, the videotapes, and just about anything else I was afraid to leave behind. There was so much crap here that I didn't know what would be important.

The coroner's office removed the body while the news crews set up shop outside the residence. Everyone wanted to get a live shot in front of the torture house.

Unsurprisingly, this was a particularly strange autopsy for the pathologist. Caddy hadn't been in a rush to get legal advice—the victim had been dead for seven to ten days. Everson was dehydrated and suffered from malnutrition.

"So, basically, Caddy neglected to feed and water him?" I asked.

"In a nutshell, yes," the doctor replied. "With his arms suspended over his head, it tightens up the chest muscles and makes it harder to breathe. But the coup de grâce is blunt-force trauma to the abdominal area."

"With what?" I asked.

"Probably a lightweight linear object," the doctor said.

"Like a dildo?" I asked sheepishly.

"Yes, that would do it," he said.

There it was. Caddy had cuffed and roped our victim, rendering him defenseless. He then deprived him of food and water to soften him up. Finally, he repeatedly smacked Everson in the abdomen with one of the dildos we had found. Yep, this was a weird one.

I had noticed Everson had been bleeding from his rectum. The doctor explained why.

"He's in renal failure," he said. "His internal organs have shut down and he's just bleeding out the anal orifice."

Geez, you can't make this stuff up, I thought. But there was no doubt: this was a homicide.

Our computer-forensics people quickly found Caddy's website, slave4master.com. It offered cock-and-ball torture, mummification, piercings, shaving, gags, cuffs, bondage, and a whole host of other options. The webpage described how "it" would be chained to the floor by the master's bed. "It" would live only to serve the master. I don't know about you, but I am immediately turned off once I'm referred to as "it."

None of us understood this. Who would travel to Dayton to be treated this way? We were about to find out.

My partner talked to Everson's brother, who knew little about his brother's unusual proclivities. He did know that Everson had a history of meeting people on the Internet and had even traveled by bus to do so. That made sense, since his car had been found parked near a bus terminal in Minnesota. The brother also said that the piercings and shaving must have occurred after Everson arrived in Dayton.

Talking to a victim's loved ones is never easy, but this one was particularly difficult. How much should we say? How much did they know? It's hard enough to comprehend a "normal" homicide, such as a drug-related shooting or a bar fight gone bad. This case was beyond comprehension.

Everson was not the first person to visit Caddy's dungeon, nor was he the first to regret it. Our computer techs found email exchanges between Caddy and a wide assortment of people from across the country and beyond. One by one we made contact with them, and each new contact left us even more amazed and dumbfounded.

We found one man from Australia who had traveled thousands of miles to visit Caddy's filthy basement. That man had contacted police but decided not to press charges after realizing he would have to return to Dayton to testify. Another man told us his wife sent him to Caddy to "train and discipline" him. Dude, you need a good divorce attorney.

Most of the rest had similar stories.

"I have to know: What did you think when you saw how low-rent filthy this place was?" I asked one.

He patiently explained to me that it was part of the whole experience. He described the anticipation of what he envisioned happening as he traveled to Dayton. The excitement, he said, increased with every mile. Once he arrived, the house's condition was irrelevant.

"He could have come to the door with horns on his head wearing goat leggings," he said. "It wouldn't have mattered to me."

I can't say I understood, but at least I had an answer.

Our next task was getting the prosecutors to approve charges. Given the circumstances, this would not be easy. Our cause of death was difficult to understand, but our larger problem was that our victim had willingly participated in the activities that led to his death. The usual debates between the detectives and the attorneys went longer, but eventually charges were approved.

A year later, Matthew Caddy went to trial. The jury was selected and seated, then they were taken to view Caddy's house. The attorneys gave opening statements, then the forensic pathologist testified about the autopsy. It was a busy first day, but it was all the dungeon master could take.

The next day, Caddy pleaded no contest to reckless homicide, gross abuse of a corpse, and possession of criminal tools. "Criminal tools" meant he had used the dildos, cuffs, and other sex toys to cause Everson's death. "Gross abuse of a corpse" stemmed from how Caddy treated the body after Everson died. "Reckless homicide" meant Caddy's reckless actions had caused the death.

I don't believe Caddy intentionally killed our victim, but he was still responsible for his death. The charges were adequate even though they didn't carry much prison time. The maximum sentence would be only seven years. I don't how much time is sufficient, or if any time is ever enough, but that was the way it was. Thankfully, we don't have to deal with that sort of case regularly.

A few years later, while Caddy was still in prison, the house on 88 Pioneer burned to the ground. The fire was ruled an arson. The case was never solved. Caddy himself died in December 2017, undoubtedly taking many gruesome secrets with him.

10.
NOTHING EVER HAPPENS
UNTIL IT DOES

THE REAL WORLD of death investigation and police work is a far cry from the run-and-gun police shows on television. Police work was once described as hours of boredom punctuated by moments of stark terror and pure adrenaline. That is an accurate statement, even for homicide detectives. We spent a lot of time tracking down leads and witnesses, reviewing lab sheets, and talking to people. All very routine, but it could change in an instant.

We had been searching for a shooting suspect for several days. This suspect was the real deal. Many suspects would turn themselves in after they'd had enough time to assemble their stories. Others vowed to never be taken alive, but most of them were bluffing. Not this one though. This one was a stone-cold gangster who fancied himself as the Jesus of the Bass Boys gang. By "Jesus" he meant "leader."

The Bass Boys plagued the region they named themselves after. DeSoto Bass was a huge housing project on Dayton's west side. The city had many housing projects, and we'd had callouts to all of them. But the Bass stood out. It was like its own little world. The narrow project streets made it difficult for police to get anywhere quickly. You could effectively block any of these streets with one or two of the wheeled trash containers the city provided. This made the Bass a nightmare for us. We always had to be careful in the Bass.

Detectives from suburban departments would sometimes work with us for training.

We had a suburban detective with us that day as we cruised the Bass, searching for our shooter. Sure enough, as we drove those narrow, winding streets, we came across a trash can barricade.

"I'll get it," our guest said.

"Hold up," my partner said. "Those are there for a reason."

We explained this could be just an inconvenience, but it could also be a trap. It was not unheard of for officers to exit their cars to move the cans, only to be pelted with rocks, or worse yet, shot at.

"You got to be shitting me," our guest said.

"Nope," I said. "That's life in the Bass."

Seeing nothing unusual, we moved the cans and continued our search. We didn't find our shooter in the Bass but our sources there told us that the suspect was also known to hang around the Blueberry Apartments, which were further west. It had been a long, unfruitful day, so we decided to wait until morning.

The next day we drove out west toward the edge of the city limits. The Blueberry Apartments were well known to us. They had rows of buildings. Some were two stories, some were three, others were ground level only. But all were potentially dangerous. Before we left our car, we advised dispatch of our location. This is always a good idea, and it would be especially helpful that day.

"You need more crews?" dispatch asked.

"Not now," I said. "Just looking at this point."

My partner and I went to the second floor of the first building we found. There were supposed to be some vacant rooms upstairs. Our source told us our suspect sometimes hid there when he was "hot"—or wanted by police. We drew our glocks and carefully started down the hallway.

There were a lot of vacant rooms. Some had wide-open doors. Some had no doors. Some doors were left slightly ajar. We looked in each room carefully, slowly. There were homeless people lying on urine-stained floors. There was an addict or two, looking to score, but no shooter—yet. The scene was about what we expected.

Then, through a partially open door, something caught my eye. It was a gun lying on the floor. My partner and I kicked back the door and entered the room, yelling, "Dayton police."

There was our shooter, lying on the floor, just waking up. My partner grabbed the gun before the still-sleepy suspect could, then I handcuffed him.

That's when we realized we were not alone. Our cries of "Dayton police" had aroused the other "residents," and they were not fond of the police.

"Where you think you're taking him?" one asked.

"He's under arrest," my partner said.

"Don't mean shit here," another said.

Now, on television, the cops would just draw down on everyone, shoot two or three and be on their way. This wasn't television though. In real life, to use deadly force, you need to be able to articulate a legitimate and immediate threat to someone's personal safety. We didn't have that—yet. What we did have was a mob of about a dozen angry, threatening people who were enjoying themselves.

They knew we couldn't shoot them, at least not yet. If we threatened them with our glocks now, they would laugh. They would probably dare us to shoot them, knowing we couldn't. As you can probably imagine, this was not good, because by the time deadly force would be justified, one of us could be very, very hurt. If you lose control in a situation like this, you're done.

"Let us through," my partner said. "We've got no beef with you."

"Fuck you, Five-O," someone said.

I was holding my glock in one hand and the suspect with the other. I had a radio, but I couldn't let go of the suspect or my gun to get to it, and my partner had left his radio in the car. We didn't have any good options.

"Take these motherfuckers down," the suspect ordered the crowd.

Time to do something, I thought. I shoved my glock right into the suspect's ear.

"Do it, but he's the first to die and he won't be the last," I yelled to the crowd. Then I turned to the suspect. "That's right, you motherfucking waste of flesh," I screamed. "Back them off or I put one in your head."

I really was screaming. Half of this was an act to make them believe me. The other half was my being utterly terrified. I had no intention of executing this man. But to get out of here alive, I had to make them believe I would do it.

"You ain't gonna do shit," the suspect said.

"You willing to bet your life on it?" I asked.

By now, I looked like a madman, probably because I was. But I got my point across. We began to back out of the room.

The next thing I heard shocked me: sirens. Apparently, this hellhole had at least one good denizen, and that person had called the police. Waves of uniformed crews arrived. I was never so happy to see that many cops in all my life.

Now we had the numbers, and I took advantage of it. The boldness of our angry mob evaporated quickly. In fact, some of them even gave us statements about how the suspect had bragged about the shooting.

As they converted themselves from potential defendants into helpful witnesses, we had to forgive and move on. We realized that putting the shooter in prison was more important than a few misdemeanor menacing arrests. Just another day at the office.

"Well, this went to shit quickly," my partner said.

"Nothing ever happens until it does," I replied.

"That doesn't make any sense."

"Does to me," I laughed. Truthfully, we were just happy to be alive.

Times like these would restore my faith in humankind. Make no mistake about it: A good Samaritan had probably saved our lives simply by making that call to dispatch. We just didn't know who. When you drive through a "bad" neighborhood, it's easy to assume from the safety of your car that everyone in it is bad too. Not true. There are good people, and they put up with more mayhem and unpleasantness than most of us can imagine. They are usually poor, work hard at multiple jobs, then come home, afraid to sit on their front porches for fear of being struck by an errant bullet. This is a basic and daily injustice. I would have liked to have thanked whoever made that call, but frankly, that would only put that person at risk of retaliation.

* * *

But because nothing happens until it does—meaning that the worst could happen anytime, with little warning—we trained with our weapons constantly. We were issued handguns, shotguns, OC spray (tear gas), Tasers, and Asps (a collapsible steel baton). After every officer-involved shooting, the police academy's range staff would incorporate that scenario into our training. We were well armed and, more importantly, well trained. But we were not gunfighters. Many officers never fired their weapons during their entire careers. You were taught to use your weapons, but you were also taught restraint. We would wait, maybe less than a moment, for a threat to emerge and react.

This happened quite rapidly during a high-risk stop one evening.

A man on his way to work in a purple truck was shot and nearly killed. We quickly identified a suspect, as the man told his girlfriend he was responsible for the shooting. This was a case of mistaken identity: His intended target drove a purple truck, and so did our victim. It was all over a botched narcotics deal.

We identified a suspect but needed to find him. He had several residences throughout the county. Some were dope houses, some were stash houses, and some he actually lived in. A dope house is where drugs are sold and/or used. A stash house is where the drugs and money are kept. The stash-house location was usually closely guarded. We knew he could be at any of them, but more than likely, he was at none of them. With help from the Montgomery County Sheriff's Office and other Dayton crews, we had enough manpower to put two investigators on every location.

My partner and I were exhausted, having worked double shifts for days. Looking at the list of properties we were staking out, we chose one that seemed unlikely, largely because the suspect had rarely been seen there. But sure enough, two hours into the stakeout, we spotted the suspect driving a car.

"What are the odds?" my partner asked.

"Never fails," I said.

I put the car in drive, then followed the suspect from a distance, trying to keep him in sight, while my partner worked the radio, calling for other units to get there.

"We're going to have to make a move soon," I said. "Any idiot knows this is a cruiser."

We were in my unmarked car, but it was still a fleet vehicle. The drug unit had undercover cars; we had unmarked cars. There was a big difference. An undercover car could be anything from a hot Mustang to an old pickup truck, whatever fit the officer's cover. Unmarked cars were plain, with basic colors, such as white or silver. They were fleet cars, midsize four-door family cars. Basically, our cars were cruisers without markings or overhead lights, but we usually weren't fooling anyone.

As we approached a red light, the suspect's car was behind another vehicle, which was first in line. I pulled in behind the suspect's car.

"This is our best shot," I said as I exited the car.

My partner approached on the passenger side with his shotgun, which must have drawn our suspect's attention. The suspect was looking over to his right, at my partner as he approached. The suspect's right hand reached for a potentially loaded gun lying on the seat beside him.

"Do it and you're a dead man," I told the suspect.

My glock was pointed right at his head. He had been so fixated on my partner that he never saw me. He slowly raised his hands and turned to see my gun now pointed squarely at his face. Other crews were arriving, and the arrest from that point on was quiet and uneventful. We were lucky—again.

But I could have shot him. He was a dangerous criminal, wanted for a shooting, who was reaching for what could have been a loaded gun. He was clearly going to shoot my partner had I not acted. And I did act. I acted the way we were trained. Had the suspect not complied, or had he lunged for his gun, I would have shot him. And I would have been totally justified. But he did comply. I reacted to his action. It happens that quickly and you are forced to make a split-second decision. Remember, nothing ever happens until it does.

* * *

Back in the spring of 1987, we were sent on what would be one of the strangest cases of my career. It didn't start out that way: A young man washing a car had been shot to death. Tragic, but hardly unusual. This was in a high-crime area known for narcotics. Shootings were frequent here.

"Car pulls up, shotgun blast, and here we are," the uniformed officer said.

We had a vehicle description and a few witnesses. Overall, the scene was pretty simple, and quite small. There were shotgun pellets, which, unlike bullets, cannot be matched to a particular gun. There were no spent shell casings. The mystery wasn't what had happened. The mystery was why, and who was responsible.

The answers came the following day, and from an unusual source: local newspapers the *Dayton Daily News* and the *Journal Herald*. Usually, we told reporters who the suspects were. But the news said that one "Buffalo Soldier" had declared a "Holy War" on drug dealers.

His real name was Christopher Malone, and his girlfriend had called the newspapers to read a letter she said Malone had written.

What's not clear, even today, is why he assigned himself that moniker. The Buffalo Soldiers were a proud group of Black cavalry troopers active from the late 1860s to the early 1950s. Obviously, Malone had been born too late.

In his letter, Malone specified the target of his holy war: crack dealers. Unheard of in Dayton a few years earlier, crack had saturated the city's west side. Malone also wrote that he had killed the man who had been washing the car. The reason, Malone wrote, was that the victim was working at the house of a crack dealer.

"The number one crack king must die," Malone wrote. "I will not shoot at police officers, but only crack dealers."

The letter included a promise: "I leave fire and death in my path."

Malone was well known to the Dayton Police Department. He was one of those guys who drifted into trouble, not the kind that made the news reports, but enough that we noticed him. He rarely did any substantial jail time, but we knew he was not to be taken lightly.

At least we now knew our suspect's name. But we had to find him, and soon, or there were going to be other shootings. Malone had a minor criminal history, so at least we had some records, giving us addresses to visit and stake out. Not that it mattered. We searched every one of Malone's known hangouts, with no luck.

Uniformed officers were already looking for the large, dark four-door GM car. We had a plate number to a vehicle registered to Malone, but it didn't match the vehicle description given by witnesses. It wasn't unusual for wanted suspects to switch tags on cars.

I didn't like stakeouts. It seemed like it was always either blazing hot or numbing cold during one. You couldn't run the AC or heater because, by sitting in a running car for hours, you would attract too much attention. Plus, the stakeouts were usually boring.

Ultimately, our supervisor decided we would work in teams of three, staking out areas known for open-air drug sales, in the hopes that the Buffalo Soldier would arrive. I offered to use my unmarked car, a newer Ford Taurus with air conditioning that we probably couldn't use and cloth seats that reclined. My two partners agreed.

Under Dayton Police Department pursuit policy, officers must terminate a pursuit if that chase is more dangerous than allowing the suspect to escape and be caught at a different time. This was not an issue in our case. Malone had publicly declared war and vowed to kill again. Common sense demanded we capture the Buffalo Soldier. And so, we sat, in West Dayton's Hilltop area.

We waited and waited. When it was my turn to rest, I reclined my seat and daydreamed about being anywhere but there. I didn't rest long.

"There he is," my partner yelled, nudging me from the passenger seat.

"Leave me alone, I'm tired," I grumbled.

"He's not bullshitting," my other partner said from the back seat. "There he is."

I raised my seat up quickly, almost chest-bumping the steering wheel. "Holy shit" was all I could think to say. There was the suspect car, slowly cruising the alley, stopping occasionally. My two partners decided to approach the suspect on foot while I manned the car. It was a good plan, but it didn't work. As soon as they got close, the Buffalo Soldier took off, sideswiping an elderly pedestrian as he fled.

My two partners scrambled back into the car, and I drove off while the detective next to me manned the radio. The one in the back yelled at the pedestrian, asking if he was okay. The man nodded, and one of my partners shouted that we would call a medic for him.

"It's on now," I said, and accelerated rapidly.

Malone's car was much faster than mine, but it was also much bigger. In a drag race, I would lose, but we were racing through alleys, onto residential streets, onto main roads, and back to the alleys. I could corner much better than Malone, so with every turn he made, I picked up any lost ground.

"Don't let him get away," one of my partners said.

"I'm not losing him," I said.

I was like a machine now, focused completely on driving. My two partners could handle everything else. We went sixty, seventy miles per hour and more, in alleys not designed for those speeds. The chase seemed endless. My partner would broadcast our location to the other crews, but by the time they arrived, we were gone. Had we stayed on one road long enough, we could have intercepted him with another cruiser, but Malone changed direction constantly.

I will admit this: as dangerous as these pursuits are, they are every bit as exhilarating. My front-seat partner was calling out streets like a subway conductor, only a lot faster. My partner in the back seat was not as excited. There is no worse place to be in a pursuit than the back seat of the pursuing vehicle. In the back seat, you are no more than an observer. Sometimes a frightened and helpless observer.

"Be careful," he would say over and over. At one point, he shouted, "Look out!" so loudly that dispatch thought we were on Lookout Street. Later, we would all laugh about that one.

We flew up Young Avenue, approaching West Third Street. West Third Street is a major roadway with many lanes. I could see traffic passing through the intersection. To run the stop sign would be suicide. I slammed on the brakes. The Buffalo Soldier ignored the stop sign.

The sound was unbelievable. One witness called dispatch and said someone had detonated a bomb at West Third and Young. The Buffalo Soldier had rammed into the side of another car, almost splitting it in half. He then continued for a short distance before crashing into the concrete steps of a nearby house. I stopped my car right behind his.

The caller was right. Between the smoke, the concrete dust, and the devastation, it looked like a bomb had exploded. Amazingly, Malone was uninjured. We dragged him from the car and placed him under arrest.

A young couple had been in the car that Malone hit. They suffered minor injuries, though in the surrounding chaos, their empty car seat startled a uniformed officer.

"Where's the baby?" the officer screamed.

"He's not in the car," the mother replied.

"I know that. Where is he?"

"At home," she said.

"Oh, thank God."

The final tally of this pursuit included three injured people—thankfully none seriously—one damaged house, and two destroyed vehicles. Oh, and one very rattled back-seat passenger in my car. But we got our man.

The major who supervised the investigations division approached me. At the time, I didn't know him well. He had just moved to Dayton and had been in charge for only a few weeks.

"Not a scratch on my city car, Major," I said.

"This looks like a war zone," the major answered.

"It was a tough pursuit, but necessary," I said. "My partners are getting a confession from our suspect right now. I figured you would want me to stay here."

"Oh yeah, you got that right," he said. He surveyed the devastation with his chin in his hand. "Burke, Burke, Burke. I don't know whether to suspend you or give you a medal."

"I don't have time to be suspended and I don't need any more awards," I said. "How about we call it even?"

The major smiled and said, "I can do that." I drove back to headquarters in my undamaged city car.

The Buffalo Soldier may have appointed himself judge, jury, and executioner, but the state gave him a four-day trial. His girlfriend testified about the letter he had dictated to her that ran in the *Dayton Daily News*. Our eyewitness identified him as the shooter. My partner testified to his confession. It was about as strong a case as you could have.

Malone made it a little stronger though. In one hearing prior to the actual trial, Malone said, "There is no codefendant. I did it." And of course, this was admissible at trial.

The jury took only a few hours before convicting Malone of murder, and he was sentenced to eighteen years to life. While serving that sentence, our public avenger severely beat a fellow inmate, almost killing him. Malone was convicted in that case as well, which added eight more years to his sentence. The Buffalo Soldier spent the rest of his life in prison. He died on April 16, 2020, from COVID-19, the virus that killed so many people that year.

* * *

As you can see, it's not uncommon for police officers to find themselves in unexpected company. Occasionally, the results can be humorous.

You may recall the Y2K scare in late 1999. The whole country was afraid that when the clock struck midnight on January 1, all of the world's computers would shut down and we'd be thrust back into the Stone Age. As you know, it never happened. Nevertheless, some people embraced the impending doom the old-fashioned way: a crime spree. The crime rate sky-rocketed as January 1 approached.

Dayton put out three-officer crews on twelve-hour shifts, and that included homicide, which worked roving patrols city-wide. We still wore our suits and long black leather coats in case we had to respond to a scene. But we mostly monitored the radio and backed up the uniformed crews when we could.

At one point, we heard a crew chasing a burglary suspect, and realized they were nearby. Burglars look for uniforms when they run, not long black leather coats. The suspect ran right into us and we quickly apprehended him.

"Looking for this?" I asked the uniformed officers when they caught up.

"Thanks, guys," one of them said. "I kind of like the extra patrol."

"Don't get used to it," I said. "If the world doesn't end, I'm going back to my day job."

As we were pulling away, I noticed some blood on my coat. It was coming from my partner's finger. We headed to the local twenty-four-hour grocery store, then went in the restroom to examine the injury.

"It stings," the injured partner said. "Must have cut it when I hopped the fence to get around the uniformed cops."

"Well, we can't go to a hospital," my other partner chimed in.

"Got that right," I agreed. "We would be doing reports for hours."

I grabbed a paper towel and handed it to him. "You've got some blood on your gun," I said.

It was then that we heard a muffled sound come from the restroom stall. I peered inside. It was a man and his young son. The boy looked to be about four or five years old. The man, who looked terrified, had his hand firmly across the boy's mouth to keep him quiet. We must have been pretty intimidating standing there in our long black leather coats talking about blood, guns, and cops. I smiled and pulled back my coat to reveal my badge.

"It's okay," I said with a grin. "We're the good guys." A look of relief came over the man's face. I still laugh when I think about it.

11.
I WANT MY BABY BACK

MY FAMILY AND I were enjoying a much-needed vacation in Myrtle Beach, South Carolina. It was late July 1995 and the weather was perfect. Extended time off was rare. The job followed me, even while on vacation in another state. I'd brought my case notes with me so that I could study them for an upcoming trial.

While my family slept in, I turned on the local news. The top story was about the trial of Susan Smith, a South Carolina woman who had killed her two children the prior October. Though she initially told police that she had been carjacked and her two small children kidnapped, she later admitted to drowning them. I switched to a national news station.

To my surprise, the national news was also focused on Susan Smith. The national interest on this case surprised me, but not as much as when I saw the next story. It was about a missing four-year-old Dayton girl named Samantha Ritchie. The similarities to the Susan Smith case were astounding. Prior to her confession, Smith had pleaded on television for the safe return of her children, even though she knew they were dead.

Now we had Samantha's mother, Therressa Jolynn Ritchie, making a similar plea.

Ritchie stared into the news cameras. She was only twenty-four but looked much older. Ritchie had a cast on one of her arms, which she nervously massaged with her other hand as she spoke. Her eyes were lifeless and seemed to look not at, but beyond, the viewer. She sobbed but there were no tears.

"I want my baby back," she said repeatedly. It may sound callous, but my first thought was: here is someone who is clearly enjoying those fifteen minutes of fame that Andy Warhol spoke of. I knew that neighborhood where she lived. Poverty was rampant and living conditions were often dreadful. Some people didn't even have functioning toilets. Many who lived there were good, hardworking people, but my instincts told me Ritchie wasn't one of them.

Samantha's parents were divorced, and her father, Denton, was the absolute opposite of Jolynn. While Jolynn scheduled news interviews, Denton avoided them. Instead, he spent days looking for his daughter. When he spoke to the news crews, clearly exhausted, he seemed concerned, a parent whose sole objective was finding his daughter.

Samantha had been missing for three days. *That's not good*, I thought. I had investigated many missing-child cases. If you didn't find the child within the first day, you had a problem. Occasionally, a missing child would turn up in the care of a relative, but I doubted that would happen here. Juvenile/missing-persons squad had the case for now. I trusted them and had worked with them many times. They usually sensed if a missing-child investigation would morph into a homicide case.

My phone rang. It was one of my partners.

"You see the news?" he asked.

"Yeah," I said. "Are they turning it over to us yet?"

"I think soon," he said. "Want to come home a little early? It's going to get busy, fast."

"I'll drive back Friday and be ready to work Saturday, okay? That'll give you a few days to find her." It was only Wednesday. Perhaps the case would be solved by Friday.

"You know she's dead," he said.

"Yeah, I know," I said. "See you soon."

Was she dead? This was tricky. Even when we strongly suspected a missing person was dead, we still had to search for them with the assumption that they could be alive. It was possible, after all, but highly unlikely. After that initial twenty-four hours was up, these cases almost never ended happily. Samantha was surely dead, but where was she?

Sure enough, before I returned from South Carolina, the case was sent to homicide. The ostensible reason was to get a different perspective on the scant evidence, but on a deeper level, no one working had any real expectation of finding this little girl alive.

Samantha and her mother lived in a depressed area of north Dayton, just across the Great Miami River from downtown. The difference was astounding. A freeway overpass paralleled their neighborhood, with homeless people camped out underneath. A large, abandoned factory sat nearby. Dope addicts wandered the streets. There were vacant houses, and occupied houses that should have been condemned. A registered sex offender lived down the street. An ex-convict lived nearby. There was no shortage of possible suspects.

News reporters descended into the neighborhood, shocked by the depravity of some of its residents. Cathy Mong, a veteran reporter at the *Dayton Daily News*, wrote that "talk on Jolynn's street ranged from a six-year-old child describing a neighbor trying to 'get it off Grandma' to incest and its offspring, bestiality, and the rampant abuse of drugs and alcohol."

Mong noted that neighbors spoke of four-year-old Samantha as "the sweet innocent type" and said she had a "cute butt." It was unreal.

This neighborhood had plenty of crime, but nothing like this. Child abductions are actually quite rare. And child abductions by strangers are ridiculously rare. If a child goes missing, the person responsible is usually someone who knows them.

News trucks covered two city blocks. They came from all over—local Dayton, Cincinnati, Columbus, and beyond. Even national news organizations sent crews. I'd almost never seen so many raised antennas. It looked like something from NASA.

Dozens of locals gathered around the trucks. Some wanted to be on television. Some wanted to help search for Samantha. Others just wanted to take it all in. Clearly, the circus had come to town and it was drawing quite a crowd. People gave interviews to news crews about the neighborhood, their suspicions, and their thoughts. Everyone had a theory, but no one had any answers.

People went door-to-door, handing out flyers with Samantha's picture. That photograph of an innocent, smiling little girl in pigtails stuck with me. I can still see it today.

As I watched the news in the hotel room, my mind wandered. In truth, my vacation was over. On Thursday, one day after I saw the news, we started the six-hundred-mile drive back to Dayton.

GHR Foundry had been in Dayton for decades, employing hundreds through the years. One of my friends used to work there. "GHR stands for 'go home and rest,'" he would say. It was hard work, for sure.

Now vacant and somewhat dilapidated, the GHR campus covered a large area with several buildings. It sat a few hundred yards from the Ritchie house, just across the freeway, but within walking distance. Some of the buildings had been razed, but those still standing had broken windows and doorways without doors. Graffiti covered the walls. Inside were remnants of homeless camps, including urine and feces. Believe it or not, that was the better part of the campus.

Even worse was what was left behind after the other buildings had been razed. All had basements, generally ten to twelve feet deep. Most of the heavy machinery and equipment was outdated, so it was left behind in those deep holes. Over time, rainwater mixed with oil and sludge from the machinery. Then the local people started using these pits as a dump for refuse, chemicals, and old tires. The murky, discolored water had a foul stench. It was impossible to see more than a few inches into it.

The GHR area had been searched multiple times. The basement pits had been looked at but not searched. By day five of the search for Samantha, GHR remained a logical place to find her remains, regardless of whether someone had abducted her or she had wandered away from home on her own. It was time to search the pits.

We couldn't use divers. No one knew exactly what was in the pits, and with zero visibility, it was too risky. Cameras wouldn't work either. But a nearby sheriff's office had a legendary cadaver dog and offered to help.

Cadaver dogs are trained to be alert to the smell of human flesh and human remains. A true cadaver dog should do nothing else. No drug sniffing, no tracking, no patrol activities. An all-purpose police dog was good in most situations, but for this, we needed a true cadaver dog.

The deputy arrived with her dog. Fittingly, the day was rainy and overcast.

"Won't matter to this one," the deputy said, motioning to her dog. "Best one I've ever seen."

I was still traveling home from my family vacation when our new four-legged partner began sniffing around the sprawling GHR campus. A short while later, the dog began barking by one of the sludge-filled pits. Next, a Dayton firefighter probed the water with a pike, a long sturdy pole with a hook on the end.

I was pulling into my driveway about the same time that the firefighter was pulling the pike from the water. Slowly and solemnly, the lifeless body of Samantha Ritchie floated to the surface of the sludge. My partner phoned me and said, "We've got her."

I just said, "Okay." It was clear he didn't want to talk about it. Though we'd known better, we'd all quietly hoped Samantha would be found alive. Sometimes, you hate being right.

There was only one thing left to do: find Samantha's murderer. I threw on a suit and drove over to the scene. When I arrived, I worked my way through a large crowd of onlookers and news reporters, to the scene tape.

"Welcome to hell," a uniformed officer said as he lifted the tape for me.

"Good to be back," I said.

I could see my partners just up ahead. Despite their umbrellas, they were soaking wet. Their faces were grim but determined. They looked emotionally exhausted.

I didn't sleep much that night. Images in my head kept me awake. Changes occur when a cadaver is submerged in water. The term is "adipocere." The skin takes on a waxy appearance, similar to a partially melted mannequin. In my mind, I compared two faces: One was the girl who had been pulled from that filthy pit, where she'd been dumped with the garbage. The other was the smiling little girl in pigtails on the posters. I prayed that Samantha died before she'd been thrown into the sludge. I didn't want the last thing she saw to be that filthy black hellhole.

The following morning, the autopsy revealed how Samantha died: her skull had been crushed.

"Could she have fallen or something?" my partner asked.

"Not with this type of wound," the pathologist said. "She's definitely been beaten to death with something. Multiple blows too."

So, we knew: it wasn't an accident, and she had been murdered prior to being dumped. Interestingly, she had not been molested. We were not looking for some pedophile from the sexual-offender lists. We were, in all probability, looking for someone quite close to home.

As with all autopsies, the organs were weighed, examined, and sectioned. When the pathologist opened the stomach, he called us over. Inside was an undigested meal. Though the food had been chewed and swallowed, it had not yet left the stomach when Samantha was killed. The pathologist identified onions, potatoes, and a white meat—judging by the texture, possibly pork.

This is not as amazing as it may sound. Onions have a very vein-heavy texture. Meat retains its color and texture as well. Potatoes, whether whole, sliced, diced, or chewed, still look like potatoes. If you've ever had a child throw up on you, then you know how easy it is to identify undigested food. But this was a very important clue for us.

We needed a good estimate for time of death. Given that Samantha had been missing for five days and had been submerged in the sludge, all of the traditional observations and tests we used to determine time of death would be useless. Stomach contents could help us though. It takes a human, regardless of age, about five hours to digest a meal. If we could determine when Samantha last ate, we could narrow the period of time we needed to concentrate on.

"I think we have that," one of my partners said as he thumbed through the already massive case notes. "I'm sure it's in here."

He switched to the file the juvenile squad had given us of the initial interviews with family and neighbors. Moments later, he held up a witness sheet and said, "Got it."

There it was. Samantha's older brother told of how he had boiled pork chops, onions, and potatoes for dinner. The meal matched the stomach contents. All the children, including Samantha, had eaten some. The time of the meal, Samantha's last meal, was around 10 p.m. the night she disappeared.

The viewing and funeral were a week after she was reported missing. With the autopsy now complete, her body was turned over to a local funeral home for burial. We decided to stake out the viewing. We would not interfere with the proceedings or even approach anyone. Our purpose was to see who came and how they acted.

Samantha's father was there. He worked for the city as a garbage collector and we knew him as a good, hardworking man, always friendly and upbeat. He was not the same man today. Denton Ritchie had fought for Samantha's custody since the divorce. He was still fighting when she was reported missing. Today, he looked tired and broken.

"We've got to solve this," one of my partners said. "Not for justice, not even for Samantha, but for him."

"Samantha and her father deserve better than this," I said.

Then Jolynn and her media entourage entered the room. Jolynn was enjoying her newly found fame, trying to stretch her fifteen minutes into thirty or more. She played to the cameras.

"She has never felt right to me," my partner said.

"Me neither," I replied.

Therressa Jolynn Ritchie, twenty-four, had her first kids when she was ages fourteen and fifteen, and her boyfriend, known as Junebug, had been her mother's boyfriend in the past, as reported by the *Dayton Daily News*'s Cathy Mong, who visited Jolynn's house while the search unfolded.

"The television with its frequent updates of the search provided constant interference," she wrote. "Men carted case after case of beer into the house. As the alcohol level rose, so did the frustration and agitation. Old wounds were opened and kin accused other kin of one thing or another (everyone seemed to be related, a cousin or an aunt or an uncle). Jolynn, whose temper flared at those around her, downed prescribed relaxants with beer and never left her porch or living room to search for her child."

I had not interviewed Jolynn yet. She had been interviewed though, multiple times, by several detectives. Everyone felt she was hiding something. But she hadn't been interviewed as a suspect yet. I wanted a shot at her.

Nothing about Jolynn's behavior indicated innocence. My partners had noticed how strongly Jolynn followed the media circus that surrounded the search for her daughter. The news coverage was constant. Jolynn would watch the television monitors about the latest search site. We watched her. No matter where we searched, she was unconcerned. Until we searched the pit at GHR—that got her attention. Jolynn knew Samantha was in that pit long before we did. I was sure of it.

We watched Jolynn as much as we could, but we also kept track of who came to the viewing and who didn't. A large jar had been placed in the reception area so visitors could make donations to the family. It was a nice gesture for many reasons. The family could certainly use the financial help. But it helped the public also. People wanted to do something—anything—to help Samantha. Everyone gave generously, including us.

After a short while, I noticed Jolynn was gone. We looked all over the funeral home. She had been seen leaving a few minutes ago, we were told. It was strange: the woman who craved media attention had quietly slipped out.

"You've got to be shitting me," my partner exclaimed.

"What?" I asked.

He pointed toward the donation jar, which was now empty.

"She stole money from her daughter's funeral," I said.

"That is about as low as you can get," my partner replied. None of us were surprised.

* * *

We were still working the case two weeks after Samantha's body had been found. We had interviewed almost everyone we could think of. Some came to us. Others we had to seek out. One man asked my partner how we found him. "We are detectives, you know," my partner replied.

The squad sat down and studied the witness sheets to make sure we hadn't overlooked anything. My mind wandered. I ran the case through my head, trying to strip away the extraneous and focus on the most important points: Jolynn said she put Samantha to bed with her at 2:30 a.m. The window in the room was open because the house had no air-conditioning. Jolynn awakened in the morning and Samantha was gone. Jolynn guessed that Samantha had crawled through the open window, while others feared the girl had been abducted through that same window. Rumors swirled around, about how a neighborhood dealer had kidnapped Samantha because of her mother's drug debt. Some focused on Jolynn's friendship with a local ex-convict. None of this felt right.

There are times in an investigation where a piece of information that once seemed benign and unimportant becomes, after further investigation, important or even critical. Context changes with new information, and in this case, that new information was the stomach contents.

As we reviewed witness sheets, I found the initial interview of the next-door neighbor. It wasn't exciting and upon first reading, didn't contain much information. The neighbor said that on the night she disappeared, Samantha had wandered to her house. The neighbor said she could see a light in the basement of the Ritchie house. "I told her to go on home and I watched her go in the house," the neighbor had said. This was at 1:30 a.m.

That statement had been taken just after Samantha was reported missing, but long before her body was found. It was merely information at that point. There was no body—at that point, police were looking for a living girl—and more importantly, no autopsy.

As I pointed this out, one of my partners yelled, "Stomach contents!"

"Absolutely," I said.

If Samantha had eaten at 10 p.m., the meal would have been fully digested by 3 a.m. But it was not digested, and so Samantha must have died after she returned to her house at 1:30 a.m., but before 3 a.m. There was little doubt: Samantha had been killed in her own house. There wasn't time for anything else to have occurred anywhere else. And no, Jolynn most certainly did not put that child to bed at 2:30 a.m.

Though we'd already interviewed him, we decided it was time to talk to Jolynn's friend, the ex-con, one more time. Ernest Vernell "Vern" Brooks was a forty-three-year-old career criminal, in and out of correctional facilities for most of his life. He would drift from house to house, staying with anyone who would have him. He now lived by Jolynn and they talked frequently.

We found Vern at a relative's house. A thin, gaunt man, Vern looked like a living corpse. He was courteous but nervous. This was a very pronounced nervousness. Prior to this, our discussions with him were cordial. The upcoming interview would not be as pleasant, and I think he realized it. Vern fidgeted the whole ride to headquarters.

"What's your problem, man?" I asked sternly.

"Just don't know what you all want," he said. He was now visibly shaking.

"The truth," my partner said. "No more bullshit. We want the truth."

"And we will get the truth, Vern," I added. "With or without your help."

It was all a mind game. I doubted we could make Vern any more nervous than he already was, but I was sure going to try. We placed Vern in an interview room.

Our next stop was Jolynn's mother's house, where Jolynn was now staying. The news coverage had shifted, with reporters speculating about whether Jolynn had been involved in her daughter's death. The media circus was no longer fun for her, and she was avoiding the old neighborhood.

We told Jolynn we needed her to come to headquarters and "clear up a few things." She agreed, grabbed a ball cap, then slid into the back seat of our car.

But first, we needed to do something about the reporters. The feeding frenzy kept growing, particularly now that the focus had changed from grieving mother to possible suspect. If we walked Jolynn into headquarters, where news crews were usually staked out, we would have utter chaos. My partner let me and Jolynn out at the nearby courts building, then I walked her to headquarters through the enclosed, secure prisoner walkway that connected the two buildings. As a diversion, my partner drove up to where the news crews were lined up, then got out and walked into the building alone. It worked.

I placed Jolynn in an interview room in a separate part of headquarters, far from where Vern sat. We would have no chance meetings between those two.

I closed the door behind us as my partner and I entered Vern's interview room.

"We know a lot more now than we did two weeks ago," my partner said, staring directly at Vern.

"A lot more," I added.

"Like what?" Vern asked.

At least he was interested, I thought.

Without giving up any secrets, we told Vern how we knew Samantha had been killed in her own house—a house where Vern spent lots of time. He was there when she died, we were sure of it. Vern became visibly more anxious. He started to speak but caught himself.

"You'll feel better when you tell me the truth," my partner said in his most soothing voice.

Vern could take no more. We didn't make him confess; he made himself confess. Vern was a small-time criminal. This was way out of his comfort zone.

"I was there, but I didn't kill her," Vern blurted out.

We had it. We were finally getting somewhere. And then Vern told us his story, about how he and Jolynn were having sex in her house, at the foot of the basement steps. It was well after midnight, and Samantha had come down the steps and interrupted them. This enraged Jolynn, who struck Samantha in the head with the cast on her arm. Next, she picked up a pipe wrench and finished off her four-year-old daughter.

"She looked at me and told me to get rid of the body or she would blame it on me," Vern said. "She knows I'm an ex-con. Who's going to believe me?"

The two wrapped up the girl's lifeless body and walked over to GHR. *What could that have felt like?* I wondered. Carrying a dead four-year-old under your arm at two in the morning to toss her into a dark, filthy, smelly, watery grave.

Vern clearly wanted our sympathy, but we had none to offer. He wasn't our killer, but there wasn't much commendable about him. Even now, he was helping us for one reason: because after a lifetime of petty criminal activity, he found himself in far more trouble than he could handle. Vern may not have been a killer, but he was a parasite, a pathetic man living a pointless life.

We left Vern in the interview room and went to Jolynn's room. Some of our squad had been interviewing her. We told them about Vern's confession.

"We haven't fared as well," one said.

"No knock on you," I said. "She's evil. Vern at least has a conscience."

We took turns talking with Jolynn, trying to figure her out. She talked about her past. She talked about her future plans. She avoided talking about Samantha unless specifically asked. To get her to confess, we would need to prove to her she was guilty, just as we would later have to prove her guilt to a jury.

I stared out of the windows into the parking lot behind headquarters. It was packed with news crews and members of the general public. They knew something was up. But we knew there was no way we could make a case against Jolynn based solely on stomach contents and Vern's statement.

"We make this case, or we all get transferred to midnight shift in uniform," I said.

"I'll take that," one said.

It was make-or-break time. We decided on our next move: We would hit her hard with the truth. We would divulge what Vern had said. She would either realize we had her and confess, or she would continue her denial—and she'd know what we had. We could only try this once. No matter what the outcome, we had to try.

One detective went in first and began to speak with Jolynn. I stormed in, acting as if Vern's confession had just occurred, and confronted Jolynn with Vern's story. It clearly affected her. She trembled a moment and then she spoke. Her story was similar to Vern's: the two of them had been having sex in the basement, Samantha interrupted them, and Jolynn struck her in the head with the cast. Next, she used the pipe wrench, then Vern disposed of the body.

When she was done, Jolynn began hitting her head on the table and trying to hurt herself. We calmed her down, but there was no way we were going to get a taped confession from her. Instead, prosecutors would have to rely on our testimony.

We were done here. It was time to give the people what they wanted: the perp walk.

Videographers loved the perp walk. You've seen it before on your evening news. The police walk the handcuffed suspect over to jail as the media follows. We took Vern over first and were immediately mobbed by news crews. From the rear of headquarters to the jail sally port was about half a city block. We took our time. When we finally entered the jail to book Vern in, the news crews were in a frenzy. Little did they know that Vern was the undercard. The main event was about to begin.

When we stepped out of headquarters with Jolynn, the frenzy gave way to pandemonium. We worked our way to the jail with our prize. Cameras rolled and microphones were thrust into our faces. The camera lights were blinding. Jolynn realized she had been exposed for what she was: a child murderer. As a final classless gesture, Jolynn stared through the booking-room glass and gave everyone the finger.

We had a body. We had a cause of death. We had a manner of death. We had a suspect. We had a confession. And now we had a crime scene. Up until Jolynn and Vern confessed, we didn't know exactly where the murder had occurred, though the stomach contents had narrowed it down to the house. Police had searched that house earlier, including the basement, but that was when we were looking for a missing child, not a homicide scene. We obtained a search warrant and drove to Samantha's house.

The first stop: the basement steps. The wall had been freshly painted.

"Look for the only clean spot," our E-crew tech said.

"Never fails," I agreed. "Who paints a piece of a wall at the base of the steps?"

"A murderer trying to cover the blood," my partner said. "That's who."

A few years ago, it might have worked. Not now though. The E-crew tech offered to "Luminol it."

Luminol was a group of chemicals you mixed just prior to application. Once mixed, you sprayed it anywhere you suspected there may have been blood. If blood was detected, the Luminol would glow a bright blue for just a moment. Even if the killer had mopped up the blood, there would still be microscopic remnants invisible to the naked eye, and Luminol would reveal them.

We had used Luminol on carpets, in cars, and even on grass. This would be my first attempt on paint. We suspected that, as the wet paint had been applied to the blood, it had also mixed with the blood.

The E-crew tech sprayed the Luminol, and we stood there staring at the freshly painted wall as if it were a Rembrandt. It was better. The paint glowed a bright blue. There was blood there, Samantha's blood. We had our crime scene. More importantly, we now had physical evidence that backed up our two suspects' confessions. The E-crew tech would scrape the wall and get as much of the bloodstained paint as he could.

"Time for the hard work," I said. "I'm out of here."

"Don't forget to take all the credit," the E-crew tech said.

We drove back to headquarters to piece it all together. To our surprise, there were signs everywhere. Some were hand-written, some were painted on vacant buildings. Even busi-nesses had changed their signs. "Thank you, DPD," "Bless you, DPD," and "Good job, DPD," the signs said.

"They like us," my partner said.

"For now," I replied. It was a good feeling, though it wouldn't last.

Jolynn went to trial in January 1996. Vern, who would tes-tify against her, pleaded guilty to three felonies: gross abuse of a corpse, tampering with evidence, and obstructing justice. He was sentenced to five years in prison.

Vern would probably never be anything other than a small-time criminal, but as he testified, you could tell he spoke the truth. Jolynn sat at the defense table with her attorneys, taking it all in. She was the center of attention once again, and she was clearly enjoying it. One by one, each of us testified. The defense tried to discredit Jolynn's confession, pointing out that we did not have a taped admission.

The jury reached a verdict in five hours. The judge sum-moned everyone back into the courtroom. As is customary, the judge reviewed the verdict forms and handed them to the bailiff. The bailiff then read the verdicts. "We, the jury, find the defendant, Therressa Jolynn Ritchie, guilty of abuse of a corpse . . . guilty of tampering with evidence . . . guilty of inducing panic . . ."

Those charges didn't mean much to me. You could find her guilty of those and still believe Jolynn didn't kill the girl. Then the bailiff read "guilty of murder," and I knew we had won. Justice had prevailed. Samantha could rest now. We had done all we could for her.

At her sentencing, Jolynn maintained her innocence. They were hollow words. Samantha's father also spoke. Denton Ritchie said he suspected Jolynn from the start. Jolynn had betrayed not only him but the entire community, he said. He then turned to Jolynn. He looked at her for a moment, then spoke.

"May God have mercy on your soul because I have none for you," he said.

The judge sentenced Jolynn to fifteen years to life for the murder of Samantha Ritchie, plus an additional seven-and-a-half years for the additional charges. We should never see Jolynn Ritchie again.

I was, however, over-optimistic about Vern having a conscience. After the trial, he moved to the Columbus area. In 1999, he was convicted of raping an 11-year-old girl a year earlier. Released after four years in prison, he fondled a 9-year-old girl in August 2005. He pleaded guilty to one count of rape and two counts of gross sexual imposition. Vern died in prison of natural causes in October 2012.

Concerning justice for Samantha, it was a good win, but all victories in death investigation are temporary. We congratulated one another and headed for the streets. There were plenty of other cases that required our attention.

12.
I'M STUCK IN THE ELEVATOR

THEY WEREN'T ALL homicides. Sometimes we got called out on suspicious deaths that turned out to be accidents. There wouldn't be any criminal charges, but that didn't make them any less tragic.

Sometimes our mysterious accidents involved positional and compressive asphyxiations. That cause of death is unusual with adults. Positional asphyxiation was a contributing factor in the death of Daniel Everson, Matthew Caddy's victim. But that case is atypical.

Usually, compressive asphyxiations are seen in infant deaths. Different jurisdictions use different terms—"overlay," "layover," "rollover"—to describe the same circumstances. They generally occur when parents sleep with their babies, whether on a couch or in a bed. The adult goes to sleep, then rolls over onto the infant, cutting off its breathing. It really doesn't take much—the adult doesn't have to be totally on top of the child. If the child is wedged between a sleeping adult and part of the furniture, that position can be enough to kill the baby.

We often see parents who are so intoxicated—on alcohol or marijuana or whatever—that they never notice the infant underneath them. Other times, we find well-meaning parents who have lain down on the outside edge of a couch, forming a barrier to prevent the infant from rolling off. Instead, the parent falls asleep and rolls over onto the baby. This is why Children's Services officials always say: "Babies belong in baby beds."

These cases are usually ruled as accidental unless there are extreme circumstances. In most cases, no extreme circumstances exist, just a heartbroken and guilt-ridden parent. We had one in south Dayton on a cold winter evening in 2005.

The call was for a deceased two-month-old infant. Dayton Fire was already there. Their medic unit had removed the baby from the crib and administered CPR, but could not resuscitate her.

I couldn't recall ever responding to an infant who had died in their crib. We would always get to the scene and find that the infant had been on the floor, in the parent's bed, or on the couch. Never in a crib. A crib was always present at these scenes, though it might be full of clothing, toys, or other items. The one thing it never contained was a baby. This one was different.

"She was lying on her side in the crib," one young paramedic said. "I knew she was dead, but I had to try."

I glanced at the infant's body. Lividity was fixed. Rigor was in place. She was obviously dead, and he was clearly shaken. I reached out and put my hand on the medic's shoulder.

"It's all right," I said. "I would have done the same thing."

I knew why he felt bad. Not only had he been unable to help the child, but he'd also altered our death scene. This was a constant tension between the two departments. We wanted a virgin scene, one in which everything was intact and the deceased had not been moved. Paramedics had a different mission: to render aid and save anyone they could. Obviously, we understood. But when someone was blatantly dead, regardless of age, we wanted that victim to be left alone. This child was blatantly dead.

"She's just a baby," the paramedic said. I didn't know him, but he appeared to be in his twenties. There were hundreds of firefighters and paramedics in the department, so I didn't know all of them. Actually, I didn't even know everyone on the police force—we had more than five hundred sworn officers and more than one hundred civilians. It was impossible to know everyone.

"How long have you been on the job?" I asked.

"Almost a year," he said.

I continued to examine the infant. It was clear she had died hours earlier.

"Son, this baby was dead hours before you even got the call," I said. "There was nothing you could have done."

"I should have left her there, sir. I know that."

"Sometimes emotion gets the best of all of us," I said. "If you weren't passionate about your job, you wouldn't be any good at it." Then I grinned. "And don't call me 'sir.' I work for a living."

He finally cracked a smile. I made a new friend that day. Yes, the baby should have been left where she was found. But his intentions had been honorable, and we could still work with this scene. I was much more interested in how she died in a crib.

The baby's lividity was mostly frontal, indicating she had died facedown. But some of the lividity was blanched out, as if her face had been pushed down into something. The lividity also had a grainy-looking pattern to it.

I looked in the crib but saw nothing unusual. The house was clean and well kept. The crib was clean as well, with nothing in it but a tightly pulled sheet. There was nothing in this crib that could have caused that grainy pattern on her face.

While I was examining the scene, my partners were interviewing the young parents. They seemed solid. Both of them worked. There were no family troubles, and this was the couple's first child. The mother said that before she left for work that morning, the baby was cranky and restless, but that wasn't unusual.

The father told another detective that the parents worked different shifts so that they didn't need to hire a babysitter. That night, the father arrived home just before the mother left for work.

"Dad said the baby was a little fussy, so he laid her on the couch with him," my partner said. "A short time later, he woke up and the baby was sleeping, so he put her in the crib. Seems to be a good guy."

There was no one else in the household. Baby was alive when Mom left. Dad was the only one with the baby. But we didn't know what happened to her. Nothing in the crib could have caused the grainy pattern. Given that my partner believed the father was telling the truth, we had a genuine mystery.

We talked with dad again. This is never easy. It may sound heartless, but to have a successful investigation, you need to talk to the principals as soon as possible—even a grieving parent. Lock down the stories. Don't give a possible perpetrator time to develop an alibi. So, we had the baby's father walk us through that day.

He said he'd come home from work dead-tired. The baby was cranky and wouldn't sleep in her crib. So, he placed her on the couch and then fell asleep next to her. Hours later, he woke up and saw that the baby was "sleeping" quietly, so he picked her up and put her in the crib. He then went back to sleep for about an hour. When he woke up, he checked on the baby, noticed she wasn't breathing, and called 911.

We looked at the couch, which was leather and had a grainy texture. Obviously, that caught our attention. So, we decided to use ALS ("alternate light source"), a process that uses different wavelengths of light to detect various bodily fluids. The E-crew tech would use different-colored goggles for different types of fluids. So, he started, and moments later said, "Got it."

"That didn't take long," I said.

"I'm just that good," he said, handing me a set of orange goggles. "Take a look."

There it was: a stain on the dark leather. Probably blood, purging from the baby's mouth or nostrils. It was invisible to the naked eye but not to the ALS. We had our death site.

"You know what this means?" I asked.

We did: rollover death. The "sleeping" baby was dead when the father carried her to her crib.

"He never knew it," my partner said, shaking his head.

"He still doesn't," I said. "I'll tell him."

"No, I've been talking to him," my partner said. "I'll do it."

We had only been at the scene for a short time, but it is surprisingly easy to bond with people, even strangers, at a time of loss. My partner had clearly bonded with the dad. I watched from a distance as my partner told the young dad how his baby girl had died.

"Oh my God, I killed my baby!" the dad cried out. He fell to his knees, sobbing with his face in his hands.

My partner knelt beside him, reassuring him it would be all right. The young dad would not be arrested or charged. This was a tragic accident, nothing more, and this seemingly decent young man would have to live with this tragedy forever. His wife consoled him. Sometimes a tragedy like this tears a couple apart. Sometimes it brings them closer together. We all hoped they would stay together.

One of our most tragic, and oddest, compressive asphyxiation cases occurred in May 2000. We were in our office at headquarters when we got the call.

"Head for the homeless shelter downtown," the dispatcher said. "Female stuck in the elevator."

"Stuck in the elevator?" I asked.

"Beats me," my partner said.

"Maybe Dayton Fire is tied up and they're calling us in to save the day," another added.

"We could walk to this one," another said. The shelter was just a few blocks from our offices.

It was good that we joked around when we could. We would have nothing to joke about when we arrived at the scene.

Downtown Dayton's biggest homeless shelter was housed in what used to be a firehouse. It was an old multistory brick structure with a basement. The city had sold it to a charitable agency for a dollar many years earlier. It had been a homeless shelter for as long as I could remember.

We had been there frequently, generally to interview potential witnesses among the city's homeless population. The homeless may be nearly invisible to you as you hustle past them, but they certainly notice you. They constantly watch people—often, they have absolutely nothing else to do—and sometimes they were our only witnesses to a crime.

The homeless were allowed to stay in the shelter from 7 p.m. to 7 a.m. on a first-come, first-served basis. Then they went back to the street, and there was no one at the shelter except a priest and some nuns. We pulled up to the scene, and prior jokes aside, Dayton Fire was already there.

"It's not good," one firefighter said to me. "Not good at all."

Firefighters and paramedics are generally tough. They see as many horrifying scenes as we do, maybe more. But this time, they were visibly shaken. *What's the deal here?* I wondered. *Someone stuck in an elevator. How bad could it be?*

My guess was that some old nun got stuck in the elevator and had a heart attack. I wondered why we were even here. But my guess was wrong.

The large, older freight elevator looked like something out of an old black-and-white television show. The doors were open. I glanced inside and saw no one. Then a uniformed officer directed me to look down, and I saw her.

This was not a nun, or a priest, or a homeless adult. This was a girl, lodged between two floors. All I could see was the top of her head. Most of her long blonde hair was hidden by the concrete and steel of the elevator shaft. She was not moving.

"What the hell?" I asked.

"It's a long story," the uniformed officer said.

"I've got nothing but time," I said. "Let's hear it."

The officer filled me in on what they knew at this point. For the purposes of this book, let's call her Alice. The twelve-year-old girl had been suspended from her suburban middle school. Her parents had agreed with school officials that Alice should do some form of volunteer work during her suspension. In fact, it had been Alice's parents who chose the homeless shelter. Her main task there was to remove the bedding from the rooms on the upper floors and take them to the basement to launder them. She would then take the clean bedding back upstairs. This, of course, required the use of the elevator.

Alice had been volunteering for a few days. The nuns liked her and found that the girl enjoyed helping out and was a good little worker who required little supervision. I was impressed by how much information had been gathered before we arrived, but we still didn't know what had happened. So, I spoke with the nun who had called for help.

"I heard Alice screaming, so I ran to her voice," the nun said. "She was saying, 'I'm stuck, I'm stuck in the elevator.' I told her to hang on and I called 911."

"Did Alice ever say anything else?" I asked.

"No, I ran right back to the elevator after I called and didn't hear a sound," the nun replied.

Unbelievable. How did this child get stuck on the outside of the elevator? For answers, we needed outside help. I called one of the large elevator companies located downtown, and they sent two repairmen over. After I showed them Alice, they became visibly disturbed.

"Oh my God, is that a little girl?" one asked.

"Yes. I apologize, but I wanted you to see what we have here," I said. "We need your help. How does this thing work?"

This was a freight elevator and was not designed to transport people, they told us. They recommended that we contact the U.S. Occupational Safety and Health Administration, the government agency that responded to work-related and industrial accidents. OSHA could have some inspection records, they said.

As my partner called OSHA, the elevator experts explained the elevator's two major safety features. One was a gate that covered the interior side of the elevator's entrance from ceiling to floor. This inner gate slid back and forth horizontally on a track.

"You see this here?" one expert said, pointing to a metal contact. "The gate has to be shut and make contact here before the elevator will run."

Next, he turned to the outer door, which opened on hinges, not unlike a door in your average house. However, the door was steel, far heavier than what you buy at Home Depot. It had a pneumatic closer, similar to the spring-loaded closers on a screen door, only much stronger because of the door's weight. The expert again pointed to some metal contacts on the door and its frame.

"Just like the gate, this door must be closed and making contact here or the elevator won't run," he said.

At our request, he checked the gate and door safeties. To my surprise, all functioned as it should.

Meanwhile, OSHA officials had checked records and responded to my partner's inquiry. The elevator had been inspected regularly. It was out of compliance in some areas but nothing drastic. Classified as a freight elevator, it should have had a sign stating it was not to be used for passengers. However, by 1989, inspectors were referring to it as a passenger elevator anyway.

The item that drew the most attention from our elevator experts was the gap between the gate and the inner door. It was well out of compliance.

"Shouldn't be more than an inch or so," one said as he pulled out a tape measure. "This one is four inches. Not unusual on these older ones. No one is going to fit into a four-inch gap."

Maybe he was wrong about that. I certainly couldn't fit in that narrow space, but maybe Alice could. Firefighters were trying to remove the girl's body, but even with their heaviest rescue equipment, they were struggling to move the elevator's floor. The steel-and-concrete shaft was not going to budge either. I went downstairs to get a better look at Alice.

One level down, I could see what happened. Alice was trapped at chest level between the heavy floor of the elevator and the substantial wall of the elevator shaft. Her body hung there limp and lifeless. Alice was average size for her age, small but not petite, weighing just below one hundred pounds. Though I didn't know how she got there, I could already see how she had died. Her chest was trapped but did not appear to be crushed. With her chest, and more importantly her lungs, being unable to expand and contract, she had asphyxiated. That also explained why she'd been able to call out briefly for help. She hadn't been crushed. She was just unable to breathe.

"This elevator will not move unless both of these safeties are engaged?" I asked our experts.

"Will not move," one replied.

"And these safeties are working correctly?" I asked.

"Absolutely," he said.

"What happens if the elevator encounters a load where it strains to go up?" I asked.

"That's the final safety," he said. "It stops."

It was starting to make sense. At this point, the firefighters had freed Alice. I examined her with a coroner's office investigator. What we were looking at was a cute twelve-year-old girl with few observable injuries. She looked as if she were just taking a nap.

As I write this chapter, I think of my youngest daughter. I'm on my second marriage now and this daughter is our only child together. She is a cute little ninety-four-pound blonde. I never realized until now how much Alice and she looked alike. I couldn't imagine something like this happening to her.

"Not a broken bone that I can tell," the investigator said.

It was as we had suspected. I looked at the folds in her clothing. Her shirt had been forced downward slightly.

"She was definitely going up," I said. "If she were coming down, the shirt would have been pulled upward from the friction."

We also learned that her hands had still been gripping the gate. That gate was still closed. I had an idea of what had happened. Now I needed to speak to that nun again.

"Was the elevator running when you heard Alice yell for help?" I asked her.

"No, not at all," she said. "I pressed the button, but it wouldn't do anything. The outer door was shut, so I couldn't see anything. I just thought she was stuck inside the elevator."

Now we knew. Alice had been in the basement when she pressed the button to call the elevator. After it arrived, she opened the heavy outer door. As she grabbed the gate, the heavy door closed behind her, trapping her between the door and the gate. Alice was just small enough to fit into that four-inch space.

Next, one of the nuns, not knowing the girl was trapped several floors below, pressed the button to call for the elevator. Though Alice was stuck, the gate and outer door were both shut—so all safety mechanisms were engaged. The elevator went up, taking Alice with it. When she got stuck between the floors, the third safety device kicked in, shutting it down. All of the safety features had worked perfectly. Ironically, if any one of them had failed, Alice could have survived.

The autopsy would show our suspicions were correct. Alice had died as a result of a compressive asphyxiation. Not a bone was broken.

Cases like these take their toll on you. You never forget them, and you are never able to block the images from your memory. Years later, I can still remember how Alice looked—every piece of clothing, her hair, her face. These scenes change you. Change is not always a good thing.

13.
AND I DIDN'T HELP HIM

IT WAS JANUARY 7, 1993, and the worst, we thought, was behind us. Other industries, other vocations, slow down during the end of December. Not us. "Peace on earth" sounded nice on a Christmas card, but usually our caseloads rose as the year closed.

"Nothing like a holiday to bring out the worst in people," my partner said.

"Maybe we can catch up a little this winter," I said.

The cases kept coming all year, but winter was usually our "slow" time, except during the holidays. Summers were brutal. When it's hot, tempers flare and bodies drop. Spring and fall were comparatively better, but they weren't slow. Then the holidays came, and with them, a lot of crazy. For most of us, bringing the family together is a blessing. But for some, it's time for feuds and rivalries to resurface. Add some alcohol, a few weapons, and some good old family dysfunction to the mix, and we were a busy squad.

But now it was winter. The snow and cold slowed down people's lives and kept them inside. We still got callouts, but not as many. It was a good time to get caught up on older cases, and we needed a break. That winter, we would not get one.

We did monitor television news, and that day's broadcast brought a big story: two-year-old Erick Nobles had been abducted from the Salem Mall. This shopping center was in Trotwood, a suburb of Dayton. *Thank God it's not ours*, I thought.

My mind wandered as I watched the news. Trotwood was an inner-ring suburb that bordered Dayton, right next to some of our more dangerous neighborhoods, and some of the poverty and crime from our city had spread across the border. We jokingly referred to Trotwood as the "Sixth District," as Dayton was divided into five districts. We knew the Trotwood police as an experienced department with good detectives. They clearly could handle this case, but I could already tell it wouldn't be easy.

The broadcast included an interview with Erick's mother, Tanisha Nobles, a single mother in her early twenties. *She killed him*, I immediately thought.

Intuition isn't evidence, but it counts for something. Tanisha was way too calm. She sounded like she was reading cue cards. She avoided eye contact with the reporters and the cameras. Staring down at the ground while talking about your missing child was never a good sign. It was clear she had not anticipated the media attention.

Obviously, no one is the same. People react differently in stressful situations. But Tanisha was not acting right. She had something to hide. I was sure of it.

As I drove into work the next day, I kept passing people distributing posters with Erick's picture.

They tacked them to telephone poles. They placed them in storefront windows. The posters were everywhere. Though the Salem Mall was in Trotwood, the Nobles family lived in Dayton. Both cities were flooded with Erick Nobles's picture.

It always takes a case like this to bring a community together, I thought.

When I walked into our office, I could see one of my partners eyeing one of those posters.

"For once, it's not ours," I said.

"Yet," he said.

"It's a Trotwood case," I said. "We'll help if they ask."

"She lives in Dayton, in the Hoover Avenue projects."

"So?"

"You know he's dead, and you know she's the most logical suspect," he said.

"Yeah, but the Salem Mall is still in Trotwood," I said.

"She didn't kill him at the mall, you idiot," he said. "She had to kill him at home, and that, my friend, is in Dayton."

He had me there. But I had to poke at him a little. "How do we even know he's dead, much less that his mother killed him?" I asked.

My partner stared at me, peering over the poster and grinning from ear to ear.

"Please," he said. "This isn't your first rodeo."

We laughed and went to work on our own cases. Deep down, I knew he was right. The odds were, the boy was dead. In most of these cases, a family member is the most logical suspect. Particularly the family member who reports the child "missing." Nevertheless, I hoped Erick would be found alive. That hope faded quickly.

For several days, the news reported the exact same story about Erick—largely because there were no new details. That was typical in these types of cases: lots of hype, not much in the way of facts. In a genuine abduction, media attention can be very helpful. Think of Amber Alerts. However, in a case where we have doubts but can't say that yet, media attention does nothing but add stress to the situation. So, the reports were padded with interviews from citizens who gave their opinions—child abduction is bad!—sidebar stories about other missing children, and whatever small updates the Trotwood detectives could give them. Still, it was clear in the coverage that people were beginning to doubt Tanisha's story. That was not explicitly stated in the news, but you could feel the shift, both from the reporters and the interview subjects. Not that it helped. There was still a missing child somewhere.

Five days after Erick was reported missing, Trotwood detectives were ready to put some pressure on his mother. They brought her in for another interview. But by this time, they had developed a lot of information and discovered that her original story was full of holes. What she'd originally said was that the boy had gotten away from her when she'd been in a stall in a public restroom.

Since then, the detectives had done a lot of work, and they let her know what they had learned: that several neighbors said they hadn't seen Erick since Christmas—two weeks before Tanisha reported him missing. When those neighbors asked about the boy, Tanisha told them that Erick was staying with his grandmother. This was not something that Tanisha told detectives, and when they contacted the woman who was the boy's paternal grandmother, she said she had not seen the boy since Christmas.

The grandmother also said that she had planned to pick up the boy from Tanisha's home on New Year's Day, but Tanisha said she couldn't—because Erick was staying with neighbors. Instead, Tanisha told her that she could pick up the boy on the evening of January 7—the day that Erick just happened to disappear.

The detectives had more damning information. There was only one bus route from Hoover Avenue to the Salem Mall, and they had interviewed the driver. Tanisha and Erick were regulars on that route, and the driver recognized Tanisha when she boarded the bus on January 7. She was alone but carrying Erick's winter coat. When the driver asked where the "little man" was, Tanisha said that he was with friends.

Detectives also had interviewed one of Tanisha's friends who happened to be on that same bus that day. She had also asked where Erick was, and received the same response as the driver: with friends. The friend also told detectives that she found Tanisha's demeanor odd, in that she was clearly uncomfortable with the question and she stared at the ceiling when talking about her son.

Obviously, detectives also spoke with mall security officers. They had been the first to hear Tanisha's story on January 7, when she told them that, while she was using the restroom, two-year-old Erick had crawled out from under the stall and started washing his hands in a sink. When she exited the stall, the boy was gone. She gave them a photo of the boy and his winter coat.

Those security officers searched the mall with Tanisha. But every time they approached a store, Tanisha told them she had already checked there. She seemed genuinely uninterested in the search, and the officers found her to be unusually calm for the mother of a missing toddler.

Trotwood Police uniformed crews, who assisted in the search, echoed the mall security officers' observations. They also noticed that Tanisha wouldn't make eye contact with them.

When detectives met with Tanisha on January 8, after her son had been supposedly missing for nearly twenty-four hours, she remained incurious. She never asked about the status of the investigation. She never asked if Erick had been found. She didn't ask any questions at all. In fact, from the time she had reported her son missing, she had never shown any interest in the investigation.

When the detectives presented all of that information, including the overwhelming evidence that Erick was never at the mall, Tanisha changed her story. In this version, Erick had not been abducted, and wasn't even missing. She told detectives that she had given the boy away to a grieving young couple whose child had recently died. This bizarre act of maternal generosity supposedly happened at a local grocery store in Dayton. Tanisha gave the detectives the first name of the woman but said she didn't know the man's name. She also said she may have had a phone number for the couple, but she couldn't find it. Tanisha explained that she gave her son away because she had no freedom and he was getting on her nerves.

As bad as her mall story was, this one was even less plausible. Tanisha had no way to contact the people she gave her son to. She didn't know where they lived or worked and added that she thought they were moving out of Dayton. Caught in a number of lies surrounding the abduction story, Tanisha now expected police to believe she just gave her kid away to strangers at a grocery store. For Trotwood detectives, it was time to start treating this case as a probable homicide and to contact the department where Tanisha lived. So late on the afternoon of January 12, a dispatcher called and told us to give Trotwood PD a call.

Over the phone, Trotwood detectives gave us an overview of the case. Then we rode out to their headquarters, where they greeted us warmly. We all knew one another and frequently worked together.

"You don't know how happy we are to see you guys," one said.

"Wish I could say the same," I said.

"Come on, now," another Trotwood detective said. "We've done most of the work for you."

We all laughed. As expected, our Trotwood colleagues had done a solid job. We knew who our suspect was. But we didn't know where the boy was. The hard part was to come—we needed a true confession, or even a lie-fession. Something closer to the truth than the obvious fictions Tanisha was peddling. Trotwood investigators, who had already battled with Tanisha in the interview room, wanted a fresh set of voices to come at her from a different direction. That's why we were there.

As we walked to the interview room, my partner, the one who predicted from the beginning that Erick was dead and his mother would be the suspect, chided me.

"I told you," he said. "I'm always right."

"I believe her," I said.

"Yeah, right."

Tanisha sat in the interview room, staring calmly at the floor. She looked up at us as we entered the room. The Trotwood detectives introduced us, stressing that we were from the homicide squad. Usually, the parent of a missing child becomes horrified to learn that homicide investigators are taking over the case—because that means that they believe, or know, that the child is dead. Tanisha never flinched.

I reached out to her to shake her hand. "I'm Detective Burke from homicide," I said, making sure she understood I worked homicide cases. She shook my hand and said hello. My partner did the same. We took her to our car and drove to her apartment on Hoover.

When we arrived, we went over the consent-to-search form. A police search of a residence usually requires a search warrant, meaning that we needed a judge to agree that we had "probable cause" to believe that evidence would be found there. Given Trotwood's investigation, we knew we could meet that legal test. But to save time, we were asking for her permission to search without a warrant. Tanisha said she understood the form and her rights, and signed it.

We wandered around the apartment while talking with Tanisha. There were no signs of chaos. The apartment appeared clean and well ordered. This wasn't really a normal search. Usually, you know what you're looking for: something specific, like a weapon or blood-spatter evidence or signs of a struggle. Here, we had no idea. But our small talk opened her up a bit. Now it was time for reality.

My partner and I stopped looking around and sat down with her. It was over, we told her. She no longer had to live a lie. We needed to hear the truth. She needed to hear the truth. She needed to tell us the truth. And she did.

On December 26, Tanisha was giving Erick a bath. The water was running in the tub and the phone rang. It was Erick's grandmother.

At this point, Tanisha began explaining her feelings about her son. That he had "gotten on her nerves." "I couldn't never go anywhere," she said. "I couldn't never do anything." Then Tanisha told us what she did when she returned to the bathroom after the phone call. She held Erick's head under the water until he stopped moving.

"What did you do next?" I asked.

"He was just lying there," she said, adding that she had checked for a heartbeat but didn't find one.

"I put him on the bed and dressed him, then I wrapped him up in a big shirt," she said.

"Go on," I said.

"I put him in a plastic bag and put him in the closet," she said. "He was there for a couple of days."

"Where is he now?" I asked.

"I waited till it was dark one night and I put him in the dumpster," she said.

Tanisha showed no emotion during the interview, but you could tell that this time, she was telling the truth. She looked right at us as she spoke. She didn't appear to be thinking about what she needed to say. These words just flowed from her lips. It was as if she had justified her actions to herself. Satisfied she was telling the truth, we put Tanisha back in our car and drove to headquarters.

When we arrived, we saw a large crowd of people. They were clearly there in support of Tanisha and not us. News reports had already told of our involvement in the case, and people were angry. This is not surprising. Whenever a missing-person inquiry shifts to a murder investigation, people become upset. It would be nice if they would be upset with the right party. But I understood their anger. Tanisha was different from a lot of murderers, who come across as menacing or scary to the public. Tanisha was a mom, and on camera she appeared quiet, well spoken, and very respectful. Eric Nobles had garnered tremendous community support and concern. So, logically, had his mother. Now those people were furious, and they didn't know whom to lash out at.

We slowly backed away from headquarters and drove around to the front doors. A smaller group of Tanisha supporters were there. They expressed their anger at us, but offered no physical resistance, and we took Tanisha from the car and headed up to our office. Once there, we sat down with Tanisha again, this time in front of a video camera.

The videotaped interview began as most do. Tanisha and I were on camera while my partner operated the camcorder. I introduced the participants, then asked Tanisha if she recalled the rights waiver and consent form she had signed. She said she remembered. I then asked her to tell us what happened at her apartment on December 26.

Tanisha calmly faced the camera and began to repeat the confession she had given us just a short time ago. The words flowed. At first, she showed no emotion. *At some point, she will realize what she has done*, I thought. I didn't realize how soon that point would come.

Tanisha talked about the bath, the phone ringing, everything she said before. But she changed a key detail. Instead of stating that she had held the boy under the water, she said that the boy was splashing water all around and it was getting in his face.

"And I didn't help him," she said slowly. Her demeanor had changed. She was finally showing some emotion. She'd already acknowledged to us what she had done. This time, she was acknowledging it to herself, even as she was trying to put a spin on it for us.

I couldn't put words in her mouth, but I wasn't going to let her gloss over what she had done. I asked if she remembered telling us earlier that she had held Erick under the water until he stopped moving.

"Yeah, I couldn't never go nowhere," she said.

"I understand," I said. "You're young. You couldn't go anywhere. After you held Erick under the water, what did you do?"

Her moment of emotion was over. Tanisha returned to the story she told us at her apartment, about how she had dressed the boy, put him in a plastic bag in the closet, then later tossed him in the dumpster.

We had our confession, but the investigation was far from over. We'd suspected that Erick was dead, and now we knew where to look for his body.

The Ohio Revised Code states that to prove a charge of murder, you need to show a "purpose to kill." For example, if you shot someone, you could always argue that you were only trying to scare your victim. You had no purpose to kill. Purpose can be difficult to prove. Not in this case. Tanisha had held Erick's head underwater until he drowned. At any time, she could have stopped what she was doing and saved his life. She chose not to. She had a purpose to kill. We booked Tanisha on a murder charge, then started the search for Erick's little corpse.

It had been almost two weeks since Tanisha had thrown Erick's body away. Needless to say, we did not find Erick in the dumpster. We contacted the refuse company that serviced the Hoover Apartments. The dumpster's contents, we were told, had been taken to the incinerator and then the landfill. That was our next stop.

We were optimistic as we drove to the landfill, thinking that we had our confession and now we would find the body. Optimism quickly faded into desperation. We thought we would be directed to Thursday's pile, or the pile from two weeks ago. "That is not how the landfill works," the foreman told us. He explained that workers used graders to smooth out and level off what they called the "ash heap." As soon as a truckload of incinerated garbage made it to the ash heap, it was immediately spread out. Then it was covered by more trash, which was spread out again.

"You're talking about trash from two weeks ago or better?" the foreman asked.

"Unfortunately," I said. I looked out over the ash heap. It was huge—more than thirty feet tall and covering an area the size of several football fields.

"Could be anywhere," the foreman said. "Could be half a foot down or just a few inches. And it really could be in any part of the ash heap, not just this area."

"But we aren't looking for trash," I said. "We're looking for a little boy."

"It all looks the same up here," the foreman said. As if on cue, it began to rain. As the cold raindrops hit the warm, incinerated trash, steam began to rise from the ash heap.

"Looks like something out of a Dracula movie," my partner said.

"Now I know how Doctor Frankenstein felt," I replied.

There was no way we would ever find Erick's body. We all knew that. But human decency demanded that we try, so we did, digging through tons of molten garbage. After three days of searching, we gave up. We would not find Erick's body, ever.

If you have been around a criminal investigation, or even just read about one, you may have heard the term "corpus delicti." Though some assume this legal term means the corpse, it does not. In fact, it is Latin for "the body of the crime," and it is the set of facts that establish a crime has occurred. Concerning the murder of Erick Nobles, we had corpus delicti, but we didn't have a corpse.

To convict Tanisha for Erick's murder, we would have to prove not only that she killed him, but also that Erick was dead. This was not impossible. We had other cases where the victim's body was never found, and we still were able to convict those responsible. But those cases involved adults. It's easier to show that an adult is no longer alive: There is no more financial activity. Bank accounts and credit cards remain untouched. Bills are unpaid. They never work anywhere or file a tax return. They never use their Social Security number.

None of those things apply to a toddler. Though we had Tanisha's confession, the law required us to bolster it with other evidence. So, we would have to rely on two things: the fact that no one ever saw Erick after December 26, and that Tanisha lied repeatedly to several people about where Erick was.

The grand jury indicted Tanisha on charges of inducing panic, gross abuse of a corpse, and murder. The inducing panic charge stemmed from her lies about Erick's supposed abduction. "Gross abuse of a corpse" covered how she had disposed of his body. "Murder" speaks for itself. In February 1994, Tanisha Nobles went on trial for two of those charges.

Earlier, Tanisha had pleaded no contest to the inducing panic charge. A no-contest plea meant you were not admitting guilt but believed, based on the facts, that you would be convicted. It was similar to a guilty plea in that it would result in a conviction. This was a strategic move. There was no doubt she would be convicted of inducing panic, given that, by her own admission and her changing stories, she had falsely reported a missing child, causing days of searching and investigation. By pleading out on that one—the easiest conviction—that left only the two more difficult charges for the jury.

Given this, we started the trial knowing that the issue was simple: either the jury believed in us and Tanisha's confession or they didn't. One by one, our witnesses took the stand. We had Tanisha's neighbors, her friends, the bus driver, mall security, Trotwood officers, and more. The defense offered little or no cross-examination of any of them. As expected, their sole strategy was to discredit the confession. This made sense. We had no body. If the jury didn't believe the confession, we had no case.

The prosecution played the video of Tanisha's confession during my testimony. I watched the jurors as they watched the tape. I could see it in their eyes. They believed Tanisha had killed Erick. They believed us.

The defense attorney's closing argument held no surprise: it focused on Tanisha's hedging during her videotaped confession, where she tried to deflect blame toward the boy splashing the water, instead of the adult woman holding his head under it.

"Tanisha Nobles never confessed," the defense attorney said. "You all saw the tape. Detective Burke confessed for her. Tanisha never said she killed Erick."

It was a good strategy, but Tanisha *had* said she killed Erick. Prior to the videotaped statement, back in her apartment, she had admitted to killing Erick to my partner and me. In the videotaped statement, she could have recanted that earlier statement or denied making it. Instead, she acknowledged it. She didn't act surprised when I asked her if she recalled making that prior statement. Instead, she said yes. *Surely the jury will see that*, I thought.

I was surprised to get a call from the bailiff shortly after the jury started deliberating. "The jury has reached a verdict," the bailiff said. *That was quick*, I thought. We hurried to the courtroom. The jury convicted her on both remaining counts. A few weeks later, the judge sentenced Tanisha to eighteen months in prison for gross abuse of a corpse, six months for inducing panic, and fifteen years to life for murder.

For years, every time I drove past the ash heap, I would take a moment and stare at it. It increased in size as time went on. Somewhere in there was a little boy who never had a chance, a toddler killed by the person who should have been his protector. All because Tanisha "couldn't never go nowhere."

For twenty-four years, Tanisha couldn't go nowhere. She sat in a prison cell and the parole board declined to release her. There's no way to know if that brief expression of emotion— "And I didn't help him"—was an indicator of a larger sense of guilt, or whether she'd rationalized it all away. But on May 14, 2018, she exercised her only other option: she committed suicide.

14.
WHITE BOY

TO WRITE AN honest account of my career, or of policing in general, I cannot ignore the racial tensions that revolve around police work. Those tensions are there, they have been for decades, and sadly, they will probably be there long after we are gone.

We have seen a number of controversial police shootings on the news, particularly in recent years. In Dayton, I investigated three cases where Dayton police officers were shot to death in the line of duty. I've also investigated dozens of cases where suspects were shot by police, sometimes fatally. Sometimes, those suspects were white; other times, they were Black. A police-involved shooting is always tragic, regardless of circumstances.

Do Black lives matter? Of course, they do. I don't recall anyone—ever—during my four decades of police work ever suggesting otherwise. "Black lives matter" is now part of our American vocabulary, thanks to the 2013 social justice group of the same name. But this issue is even older than that. In Dayton and elsewhere, suspicion of the police in Black neighborhoods is a long-standing problem. The only solution is engagement with the public.

As police officers, we are trained to evaluate, assess, and react to a potentially deadly situation in an instant. This is never easy. The general public and the media have hours and days to examine the decision we were forced to make in a split second. And even though we do our best, we sometimes do not make the right decision. Or so it appears.

Sometimes, the weapon a suspect held is later found to be a toy, or an unloaded or inoperable gun. The key word here is "later." We have to act based on what we know or reasonably perceive at the time. Not what the investigation reveals later. Consider one case from the mid-1990s. An officer gets dispatched on a call: a drug addict is threatening his mother with a knife. When the officer arrives at the residence and gets out of the cruiser, the suspect comes out of the house, then runs toward the officer, who sees something shiny in the suspect's hand. What would you think? What would you do? Remember, you've got seconds, at best.

In that case, the officer fired, killing the suspect. Then it was found that the "knife" was actually a shiny cigarette lighter. This is tragic. But the officer made a good-faith decision based on prior information and the suspect's actions. That officer was under no obligation, legal or otherwise, to allow himself to be stabbed just to be sure that the suspect was holding a knife.

Controversial police shootings can bring protests or worse. In the above case, we may have avoided it because the suspect, like the officer, was white. But Dayton generally avoided those types of reactions, despite the racial divisions that permeate the city to this day.

What happened in the 1960s elsewhere also happened in Dayton. There were riots, and the scars are still visible fifty years later: Parts of the city's west side were never rebuilt.

Many people fled the city, and there was massive growth in the suburbs. Some returned. Others did not. But the Dayton Police Department was a pioneer in building community relations. In their book *Fixing Broken Windows: Restoring Order and Reducing Crime in Our Communities*, George L. Kelling and Catherine M. Coles write that Dayton Chief Robert M. Igleburger was "one of the most innovative chiefs of the 1970s," in terms of building trust and cooperation between police and the neighborhoods they policed.

That was a bit before my time, but Igleburger's influence is still felt today. I joined the force a few years after Igleburger retired, but I found a department in which city officials always tried to ensure there were open lines of communication between the police and community leaders. Officers were encouraged to walk their beats and talk to the residents there. By talking to the people whenever possible, violent confrontations and demonstrations could be avoided. Tensions sometimes ran high and tempers occasionally flared, but talk and cooler heads usually prevailed.

This was particularly important in dealing with the Black community. Despite massive recruiting campaigns, the police department remains overwhelmingly white. I can't recall a time that the percentage of white officers ever dropped below 80 percent, and this is in a city that is near evenly divided between whites and Blacks.

We had many good minority officers, including Blacks, Latinos, and even a few Native Americans, and trust between us developed naturally. My office was across the hall from the morals/juvenile squad. There was a Black female detective on that squad who was quite outspoken. She was a good detective and a good person, but not above having some fun. We had a little routine when we passed each other in the hallway.

"What up, witch?" I would say, never looking up from the papers I was carrying.

"White boy, I will fuck you up," she would reply, laughing.

Then we would go to roll call and discuss the news of the day, the weather, whatever. We were comfortable with each other. We trusted each other. We were friends, long before we got sent to the same mandated diversity training class.

We sat together and listened as the "expert" told us how we must all get along. Made sense to me. But he began to lose me when he said that we must "walk on the eggshells of race," using carefully chosen words and actions to treat people who are from different backgrounds. Okay, I'm totally down with not using ethnic slurs and trying to avoid thinking in stereotypes. But true communication requires honesty. So does trust. If someone can offer me a different perspective that will help me be a better officer or a better person, I'm open to hearing it. But that's not going to happen if we're all speaking in code. I wasn't buying it, and neither was my outspoken friend, who raised her hand.

"This white boy next to me is my friend," she said, motioning to me. "So, you're telling me I can't joke with him and he can't joke with me?"

The expert seemed startled and told her "most definitely not." Then he repeated his mantra: people of different races must choose their words carefully so as not to offend. My friend turned to me.

"Are you offended, white boy?" she asked me with a smile.

"No, I'm afraid of you," I replied.

Everyone laughed. She turned to the expert, as if to say, *There you go*. He was undaunted. It would make no difference that we were clearly friends, he said. Other people may not like it.

"Ain't that some bullshit?" my friend asked.

I agreed. I believed then, as I do now, that communication and respect are key. Truly treat everyone the same and no one can complain. I joked with my white friends. I jokingly called my white friends names. Why couldn't I do the same with my Black friends? And why couldn't they do the same with me? Why would I act differently toward one group of friends than I would the other? We left the training unaffected. The next morning, when I saw my friend, I decided to try out my new diversity-friendly greeting.

"Good morning, madam, how is your day going?"

"Fuck you, white boy," she said with a grin.

I laughed. "She must have flunked diversity training," I said.

There is no doubt that she and I have had different life experiences, some of them based on our demographic differences. I've never been Black, and she has never been white. But we were friends, and we got that way because we trusted each other, were honest with each other, and despite the jokes, genuinely respected each other. We didn't get there through carefully measured words.

I really believe that's why Dayton was, and still is, different from many other cities today. Spoken words are powerful. They can be used in anger. Words can also be used to soothe, reassure, and calm down. You had to honestly talk things out. And we did. But when we cut corners on community dialogue, we paid for it.

Vernon Geberth, a retired NYPD lieutenant commander, coined the phrase "We work for God." Though it certainly felt like that, it was the city that paid us—and the city did not like overtime. In 1996, our squad sergeant retired, and a new sergeant arrived. I had known him for a long time and really liked him, both as a person and an officer. It was clear early on though that his superiors had mandated him to cut overtime. Soon after he arrived in homicide, there was friction.

We had just cleared a strange case at a local hospital. Two security guards, both white, had attempted to arrest a disorderly woman whose bizarre behavior attracted their attention.

She was obviously high on something. She ran around the hospital flailing her arms wildly. The guards had patiently escorted her outside several times, only to have her return. That left arrest as their only option. She actively resisted, the guards wrestled her to the floor, and as they held her down, she died.

The cause was what we call "positional asphyxiation." The guards weren't sitting on her or applying a lot of pressure. We could see that from the security camera footage. The guards said they were just trying to prevent her from struggling and injuring herself, and it appeared to be true. As for positional asphyxiation, I had seen it before.

How can you suffocate when your airway, mouth, and nose are unobstructed? Actually, it's very simple. The respiratory system is like a car. Let's say the car has a full tank of gas; that's the air we breathe. The car's fuel line is the mouth, nose, and airway. Even with a full tank of gas and a clean fuel line, if you prevent the car's pistons from moving, the car doesn't go anywhere. The lungs are the car's pistons. If the lungs can't expand and contract, there is no breathing—and if this goes on long enough, death follows. That's exactly what happened to the woman in this case. With her chest on the hard marble floor, and the officer applying pressure to her back, it prevented her lungs from expanding and contracting.

This was a terrible case.

It was tragic, but it wasn't criminal, because the guards had no intent to harm her and it was not a foreseeable consequence of their actions. This was nearly a quarter century ago. At that time, many people working in security and law enforcement were not aware of positional-asphyxiation deaths. Now we are trained on how to avoid them.

We completed our scene investigation at the hospital then returned to headquarters. Though we cleared the case, the optics appeared quite obvious to me: we had two white men holding down a Black woman until she died. I told our new sergeant that we needed to meet with the west-side community leaders immediately to explain what happened and why there would not be criminal charges.

He decided not to, explaining that this was just the type of overtime assignment that needed to be quashed. So, we went home, and returned the next day to a community-relations nightmare. As I had predicted, leaders in the Black community were very suspicious. We did end up meeting with them, to handle questions that could have been answered calmly the night before. There was nothing calm about this meeting, and when it was finally over, I took my friend, our new sergeant, aside.

I explained that this was exactly what I'd been trying to avoid by meeting with the community leaders. Dialogue with community leaders was an investment. It helped prevent problems. It was worth the overtime cost.

To his credit, he understood. He also went on to be one of the best supervisors we ever had, and he learned quickly to fight valiantly for our overtime. It wasn't just in our interests. It was in the interests of the public we served.

Over the years, I have had several partners. Some were white. Some were Black. Most were male. Some were female. But we were all there for the right reason: We wanted to solve these cases. We wanted to speak for the dead. If you came to homicide and stayed there for any length of time, you were part of the team. Really, it was family.

Early in my homicide career, I had the good fortune to be teamed up with a veteran Black detective. Tony Spells grew up on Dayton's west side. I was east end. Tony was well respected as a detective, particularly in the Black community. I would get Tony into doors on the east end's white neighborhoods that would never open for a Black man. He did the same for me on the west side. The credibility he brought me in the city's Black neighborhoods would help me my entire career, long after Tony retired.

Tony and I worked together for years. So long that a lot of citizens thought we were one person. More than once I overheard mentions of "Detective Burkenspells." Tony would always joke, "Burkenspells, must be a Jewish detective." We would laugh, but Detective Burkenspells got results and people noticed, particularly in the neighborhoods.

People on the street trusted us. We made it a point to stop at the family-owned carryouts, the roadside BBQ stands, and the small businesses. These shops were generally run by hard-working people who desired good relations with police, and wanted safety and security for themselves, their employees, and their customers. We visited no matter how busy we were, even when we didn't need anything. That was important.

"You need to get to know people before you need them," Tony would say. "That way, when you do need them, they'll be there to help you."

By making friendly contacts, we gained acceptance. More importantly, I gained acceptance in the Black neighborhoods. I had my own friends and contacts on the east end, but that was only part of the city. It was immensely helpful to have friends and contacts citywide.

After Tony retired, I stopped in one of the small businesses we used to visit together. To my delight, I was given a warm welcome. They trusted me. White boy or not, we were still all in this together. It was a good feeling. Talk builds trust. But it wasn't just friendly banter. Consider it an investment: the time spent on these visits was minimal compared to the amount of information we received from those people whose trust we had earned. Those people weren't the television-stereotype snitches. These people lived and worked in crime-ridden areas of the city. They disliked criminals as much or more than we did. They were glad to help us, and we were grateful to them.

One of the most important friendships I ever had was with the chief investigator for the Dayton branch of the National Association for the Advancement of Colored People, General Mwesi Chui (pronounced "Chewy"). Born John Franklin Taylor, Chui changed his name after he became a five-star general in the Black Legion of the Republic of New Afrika, an early civil rights organization. An activist who lived through the riots, Chui was a veteran crusader for the underprivileged. Friendly and personable, he was also intelligent and street-smart. I found him sensible, a man who understood the nuances and complexities of race relations too much to reduce them to the literal black and white.

"The gray areas are where we can do the most good, my friend," he would tell me. I agreed. Chui and I hadn't yet met when the riots in Dayton occurred, but we both remembered them. Neither of us wanted to see Dayton in flames again. And we both did all we could to prevent it.

I spoke with Chui at least weekly—more often if something was going on—and used to stop by the NAACP office to have coffee with him regularly. People would come to him when they had issues with the police. If there was an issue that I could help him with, I did. If not, I tried to steer him in the right direction. When a violent confrontation occurred between the police and a resident, Chui wanted answers. I never lied to him and he never lied to me. You can't buy trust. You work for it and you earn it.

As noted earlier, we had dozens of officer-involved shootings during my time on the force. You cannot sugarcoat it—Dayton is a violent city. Those times when an officer was obligated to use deadly force were the times that most tested our credibility. Officer-involved shootings were always the focus of two investigations: one by the homicide squad and the other by internal affairs. The case facts were then reviewed by a grand jury to see if any criminal charges were warranted against the officer. At the police department, the command staff would review the Internal Affairs report and see if the officer had violated any policies or procedures. But neither of these reviews were the most critical or most important. That would be the perception of the public.

Consider this officer-involved shooting, which occurred outside a well-known bar on the city's West Third Street. Two rival gangs were engaged in a shootout in the bar's parking lot. There were plenty of innocent bystanders nearby. As two officers approached, most of the shooters fled. But two men from the same gang turned their attention, and their fire, on the officers. Those officers returned fire. The officers survived. The two suspects did not.

The use of deadly force was undoubtedly justified. Bullets were flying in a public place. Had the officers not neutralized the threat, they or someone else could have been injured or killed. And there was quite a crowd, which just kept growing. I don't know how that many people can appear at a tense and dangerous scene so quickly, but they do.

The first thing the crowd sees is two white police officers and two dead Black male suspects. Many don't know exactly what happened. This makes for a potentially volatile situation.

Most people in the crowd wanted answers. Some just came to watch. Others saw an opportunity to start trouble. As I pulled up to the scene, the crowd was growing in size and becoming angry. We had dozens of police officers securing the scene and keeping the crowd back as best they could. But it was a difficult job under tense circumstances. We had a Black police chief and a Black major at the time. Both came to the scene. I hoped this would help, but it didn't. I surveyed the crowd, looking for a familiar face, and found none. *This will only get worse if we don't do something soon*, I thought.

Thankfully, some of the Black community's leaders began to arrive. Some cities would frown on their presence at a scene like this. We welcomed it. Their voices would be heard by this crowd when ours would not.

I could see the president of the NAACP and my friend, General Chui. There were also some influential ministers from the Southern Christian Leadership Conference. I could see our chief, Ronald Lowe Sr., talking with them. To my surprise, it was a very brief conversation, and then the chief headed my way.

"Doyle," he said with a grin. "They want to talk to you."

He patted me on my shoulder as if to say good job. I liked and respected Chief Lowe, who was a decent man. I could tell he was proud that those Black community leaders wanted to talk to the white boy. It showed how far we had come, and how much was possible.

When I spoke to those ministers and community leaders, I told them the truth: It was early in the investigation but so far, there were no red flags. Two gangs were engaged in a gunfight. Our officers got caught in the middle of it. One group ran. Two men from the other group unwisely chose to shoot at our officers. It appeared our officers had no choice. There was a lot more work to do, but that was what we had so far.

Chui spoke for the group. "You'll keep us informed?" he asked.

"Absolutely," I said. "And you all have my cell number. Call me with any questions."

"Thank you, Detective," Chui said. They talked among themselves for a moment and then went to address the crowd. A short time later, the majority of the crowd dispersed. Those who remained watched quietly.

There would be no riots. There would be no looting. There would be no violent protests. That wasn't because of what happened that night, but because of everything, all of the talk and trust and relationship-building, that had happened before. We would have many more officer-involved shootings in my career. Some would involve white officers and Black suspects. Tensions would ride high, but talk and cooler heads would prevail. So far, Dayton has not burned since the late 1960s. As long as honest dialogue continues, we have a shot at making sure it never burns again.

15.
YOU FIGURED OUT I DID IT

FIRE DEATHS ARE different. The scenes are often partially or completely destroyed, obscuring evidence that usually would be instantly obvious. Bodies would be damaged postmortem. Cause of death was rarely apparent—which was why we were typically called out. A fire death was treated as a possible homicide until proven otherwise.

There were times when a space heater tipped over and started a blaze, or when someone was smoking in bed, went to sleep, and burned the house down around them. Although tragic, these were the simple fire deaths. We would be notified and respond to the scene as a safeguard. But most of the work would be done by the fire department's arson investigators and the state fire marshal.

These were highly trained professionals who could follow a fire's path through a residence the same way we interpreted blood patterns. Some had been firefighters, some had been police officers, and a few had been both. We worked well together, and I was always amazed at what they saw at these fire scenes that I didn't.

On the truly accidental fire deaths, our role was simple. We would respond, do some preliminary investigation while waiting for the arson investigators' opinions. Once it was ruled accidental, we would leave the rest to them. Still, an autopsy was conducted on every fire victim, and we would always attend. Many times, nothing of interest was found. We took over when the pathologist discovered a stab wound or bullet in the body—and that happened more often than you might expect.

Many criminals believe you can burn up a body, thus hiding your crime. Not true. In reality, a home fire, no matter how strong, will not reach a sustained temperature hot enough, nor long enough, to consume a body. A typical cremation requires intense direct heat for hours, and still leaves behind teeth and some bone fragments. In a city like Dayton, with a full-time professional fire department, it was rare that a fire wasn't extinguished in a timely manner.

Shortly before 2 a.m. on April 18, 1997, Dayton firefighters were dispatched to 39 Riegel Street on the report of a house fire. On the city's west side, Riegel was somewhat quiet and remote for a city street, isolated from the crime that plagued nearby blocks. Firefighters battled the blaze, and though the fire still raged, a few entered the residence to search for victims. A chilling scene awaited them.

On the first floor, they found the body of an elderly Black woman, lying in a pool of blood that spread outward from her head. A bloody baseball bat lay beside her. They hurriedly carried her outside, but she was already dead.

On the second floor, they found an elderly Black man. The house was filled with smoke, making it hard to see anything in detail, so they scooped him up and took him outside. He, too, was dead—and the firefighters noticed that their fire gear was covered in blood. The elderly man had been savagely beaten as well.

At that point, the fire's intensity prevented further searching. It would be two hours after the first call before it was safe enough for them to resume the search—"safe enough" being relative. It is never safe at one of these scenes. Ceilings, floors, and even walls routinely collapse.

In the first floor's center room, they found a third victim, this time a middle-aged Black man. The body was carefully removed and placed with the others. That's when we got the call.

The house was still smoking upon our arrival. Firefighters remained on the scene to douse any hot spots—those small outbreaks of fire that pop up among the smoldering ruins. The arson investigators were already there and working.

"Definitely an arson," one investigator told us. "We've got a trailer all through the house."

A "trailer" was arson talk for an accelerant, such as gasoline, that fueled the fire. When a liquid accelerant was poured through a building then set on fire, it left a trail in its wake.

This most certainly was a triple homicide—after all, at least two of the victims had been beaten before the fire was set. It was doubtful that the killer set that fire then stuck around to assault the victims, or that they stuck around in the fire voluntarily. The fire's purpose was to destroy evidence.

Step one in a case like this is pretty straightforward: you need to identify your victims. Sometimes in fire deaths, this is a difficult task. Not so this time.

A woman pulled up to the scene and approached us. She was crying as she surveyed the scene. I approached her.

"I'm sorry, ma'am. Did you know someone who lived here?" I asked.

"Yes," she replied. "My parents and two others."

"Let me take you over here and get a little information from you," I said. "Then maybe I can answer some of your questions."

I moved quickly, steering her toward a cruiser, facing away from the residence. She was already a wreck, but it would only get worse if she realized those sheet-covered mounds were the charred bodies of her family.

Inside the cruiser, she identified her parents as Ivory and Ophelia Franklin. This had been their home for many years.

Okay, I thought. *That accounts for the two elderly bodies.*

Two other relatives also lived there, she said. One was her brother Anthony, a middle-aged man, who was likely our third victim. The other was a nephew, the son of another sibling: eighteen-year-old Antonio Sanchez Franklin.

"Did anyone in the house have a car?" I asked.

"Yes, my dad did," she said. "He always parked it right in front of the house."

There was no car there now. I checked with the first-responding crews. "Nothing here when we arrived," they all said.

I obtained a description of the car and made a stolen-vehicle broadcast. The woman was getting anxious. She looked at me with a tear in her eye but said nothing. Neither did I. I looked directly at her and shook my head. She knew. She started crying as I tried to comfort her.

How many times have I done this before? I wondered. How many people had I told that their child was not coming home? That their spouse had been found dead? Or in this case, that their parents were gone forever? It was never easy and never routine.

In fire deaths, identification is usually made preliminarily through common-sense investigation, then verified through dental records or DNA comparisons. That's what happened here. We had three bodies that matched three of our residents. None of our bodies was an eighteen-year-old male. That left one person unaccounted for: Antonio Sanchez Franklin.

His aunt described a young man with a troubled background, a petty criminal drifting deeper into that lifestyle. Despite this, his grandparents allowed him to stay with them, but the relationships were getting strained. Ivory and Ophelia wanted him to get a job or go to school. They had just issued an ultimatum to him: you have thirty days to straighten up, or you will leave this house. It seemed obvious that Antonio had taken that ultimatum seriously—just not the way his grandparents had hoped.

Having answered my questions, the woman left the scene to contact the remaining family members. At this point, the deaths had not yet been officially ruled homicides, though that was clearly coming. I left it that way with her, telling her we didn't know the cause of death. I suspected she knew where this was going.

As the autopsies began, I added Antonio to the stolen-vehicle broadcast, listing him as a possible suspect, then watched the pathologists do their work. I was somewhat surprised at what we learned.

Ivory had been struck in the back of the head at least five times with a heavy blunt instrument. Anthony had been beaten about the face and head with a baseball bat.

"Could Ivory have been hit with the bat?" I asked.

"No, his wounds are rounded and smaller," a pathologist said. "A bat leaves a linear mark. Definitely not a bat."

Ophelia was the shocker. She had been struck in the head at least eight times with a baseball bat, but she had been shot in the head as well. The pathologist told us that either the beating or the gunshot would have killed Ophelia.

This was strange. This little old lady was probably the least-threatening victim to our suspect. Why shoot her and not the others? We needed to conduct more interviews and profile the scene, comparing those findings to the new information. First though, I upgraded the broadcast from grand theft auto to murder.

Next, we went to talk with the family. From them, we learned that a baseball bat was kept near the front door for protection. There was also a gun in the house, as Ivory owned a .38-caliber revolver, which he kept loaded in an upstairs dresser drawer.

I peered through the crime-scene photos. None showed a revolver. We had the bloody bat that had been found lying by Ophelia, which matched the injuries to Ophelia and Anthony. Presumably, both of them had been downstairs when they were attacked. But Ivory's body had been found upstairs, and his injuries were not consistent with the baseball bat. I looked at the pictures again, then called the coroner's office.

"Could a hammer have been used on Ivory?" I asked.

"Absolutely," the pathologist said. "A hammer would match perfectly."

I held on to the photo of a hammer lying in the bedroom at the top of the stairs—the same bedroom where Ivory had been found.

"It always bugged me that Ophelia was the only one shot," I told my partner. "But now it makes sense."

I played out my case for my partner. All four family members are on the first floor when Antonio becomes angry, presumably because his family is tired of his antics. The bat is there by the door, so Antonio grabs it and attacks Anthony, who poses the biggest physical threat to Antonio. He takes out his uncle first, probably by surprise.

Next, he turns his attention to his grandparents. Ivory runs upstairs to get his gun. Antonio beats his grandmother with the bat, then drops it to chase his grandfather upstairs. At the top of the steps, he finds a hammer, which was there because Ivory had been doing some work on the stair railing. As Ivory frantically tries to obtain the gun, Antonio strikes him repeatedly from behind with the hammer, killing him. Antonio now finds the gun and takes it downstairs, where he fires a round into Ophelia's head.

"Why just her?" my partner asked.

"Maybe she moved," I said. "Who knows?"

But where was Antonio? We found out two days later—through an unexpected phone call from police in Nashville, Tennessee. That was where Ivory's car was involved in a hit-and-run accident the morning after the homicides, and where our suspect was now in custody.

"Well, at least we know where he is," my partner said.

"It's a start," I said. "We may as well plan a trip to Nashville."

By car, Nashville was just about five hours from Dayton. After the accident, the driver fled on foot, abandoning Ivory's car. A few hours later, the evening after the homicides, Nashville PD responded to a suspicious-person call. They found a young Black male. The officers asked his name and he gave a false one. They asked his age and he lied and said he was seventeen. They asked for some identification, and he said he had none. It was all too weird, particularly after one of the officers noticed a bulge under the young man's jacket. When the officer drew closer to frisk him, the suspect ran. After a short foot chase, he was apprehended.

The young man had jewelry, including some rings, stuffed in the soles of his shoes. He was also carrying a loaded .38-caliber revolver. Police booked him into the jail for carrying a concealed weapon and fleeing the police. His clothing and the jewelry were placed in his effects, and the revolver was tagged as evidence in the weapon's charge.

It wasn't until the next day that Nashville police positively identified the young man through fingerprints as Antonio Sanchez Franklin. After they made the connection, they called us.

One day after that, my partner and I arrived in Nashville. From our prior discussions with Nashville police, we knew that Antonio certainly had enough time to kill his family, burn down their home, then arrive in Nashville in time for the hit-and-run accident—though he likely hadn't stayed in Dayton long after committing his crimes.

"He probably hit the freeway the minute he torched the house," my partner said.

"Probably," I agreed.

The jail that housed Antonio was inside a police building. As we entered, we stopped at the front counter. Ahead of us was a Black family leaving money for an inmate's commissary and retrieving his effects. We paid little attention to them. When they were done, we identified ourselves to the person behind the counter. Minutes later, we were meeting with a Nashville homicide detective. He had Antonio removed from his cell and placed in an interview room.

"You need anything, let me know," the detective said.

"We're good to go," I said. "Thanks."

Unlike most professions, there are no strangers among police officers. Firefighters and military personnel have a similar bond. Anywhere in the country that you traveled, if you found a cop and told them you were a cop, you were instant friends. We all fought the same battles. Later in my career, I would learn that this bond extended beyond international borders. We were all family. I was grateful for the help of the Nashville police and more than happy to help them if the need arose, wherever or whenever I could.

As we entered the interview room, I was ready for the interview. This was an important case, a triple homicide, which would probably be a death-penalty case. A confession would be particularly important here. What I wasn't ready for was what I saw as we opened the door.

Antonio was seated facing the door. He had several home-made tattoos on his arms. One said "CCP," which stood for "Chelsea Court Players," a small-time gang of thugs. Another said "URTRU SOLDIER," which was another street-gang phrase: "you're a true soldier." *Pretty common fare*, I thought.

It was the new tattoo that caught my attention. The words "Bout it Bout it" were emblazoned across his upper arm. Under these words was a crude drawing of a tombstone. Written inside the tombstone was "RIP Franklins." It was like he'd tattooed his confession on his arm.

People drawn to street gangs often have troubled relationships with their own families. For them, bonds with fellow gang members surpass or even replace those with blood relatives. I wondered if this had happened to Antonio. While I doubted that the murders were gang-related, perhaps being in a gang may have empowered him to kill his family.

I chose not to acknowledge the new tattoo. I didn't want to do anything to jeopardize the interview. There would be plenty of time to photograph it later.

I read Antonio his rights using our standard form. He stated he understood and signed it. Cautious at first, he chose his words carefully. He was talking freely; he just wasn't admitting anything. We weren't really getting much, but we were patient and we had time. Antonio wasn't going anywhere.

After a short while, my partner and I left the room. "Be right back," I said to Antonio. My partner and I chatted briefly, then he went outside to smoke. I walked back to the room to check on Antonio. As I opened the door, Antonio motioned for me to come in.

"I want to talk to you," he said. I sat down and Antonio looked at me from across the table.

"You figured out I did it," he said.

"Yeah, we're good like that," I said. "And yes, we know you killed your family."

I wanted it to be perfectly clear what we were talking about here. I didn't want him saying later that he thought I was talking about him stealing Ivory's car. But Antonio nodded, acknowledging my statement. This was going to be easier than I thought.

"Why?" I asked, and Antonio gave me his lie-fession.

Antonio claimed a life of abuse and mistreatment by Ivory and Ophelia. They were always "bumping heads with him." Their sins included not letting him use the phone as much as he wanted to and, even more horribly, telling him to clean up his act or get out of the house. I listened intently and tried to hide my disgust. It's not that you anticipate a valid excuse from a murderer, ever. But even by those low expectations, his confession was incredibly lame.

Antonio must have sensed how I felt. As an afterthought, he added that his uncle Anthony had sexually assaulted him four years earlier.

"Son of a bitch raped me, that's why I killed 'em all," he said. "He raped me when I was fourteen and the old man knew about it, but that was his son, so he didn't do anything about it."

If that wasn't justification enough for a triple murder, Antonio added that on the day of the murders, his uncle had accused him of being gay. It struck me as nonsense. But then Antonio detailed how the slayings occurred—and that was just as we'd theorized. I left the room and briefed my partner.

"We'll be on the road home in the morning," my partner said.

"Still a couple of loose ends," I cautioned.

The property room was closed. It was Sunday and it was late. We would have to pick up the revolver later. But the Nashville detective offered to get us the rest of Antonio's effects tonight.

We approached the window in the lobby where we had first come in. The same officer was on duty, and we waited as he searched the computer for Antonio Sanchez Franklin.

"Yeah, got them right here," he said. "Some rings and his clothes."

"Okay, I'm seizing his effects as evidence in a homicide," I said. "Do you have a form I need to sign?"

"Wish I still had them," he replied. "We already released everything a few hours ago."

"What?" the Nashville detective asked. "To who?"

"His family," the officer replied. He looked at us and added: "It was the Black family who was at the window ahead of you when you first came in. There was no hold on it."

That explained why Antonio had fled to Nashville: he had family here and he knew the place. But now his family members had taken his property. They probably had no idea what Antonio was really involved in—the slayings of three other relatives.

It was really no one's fault. At the time of the booking, Antonio had not yet been charged with the murders. He was booked on a weapons charge with a hold for Dayton police. But the hold didn't extend to his property, just him. The clothing and jewelry had nothing to do with his local charges, so it had been released.

"Looks like we're here for the night," I said.

"Let's get a drink," my partner added. We rented a hotel room and headed for a bar with food.

My partner on this case was an experienced Black detective. He had worked narcotics and vice for a long time but had been on homicide for only a few months.

"Are they always this fucked up?" he asked.

"What? The cases or the suspects?"

"Both."

The waitress interrupted us. My partner ordered two "Negra Modelos" and she walked away.

Many police officers drink socially. But I rarely drank. The easy explanation is that I was constantly on call. But there was another reason. I had grown up watching my father slowly drink away his life. In most ways, he was a good man. He always worked, and we always had clean clothes and food on the table. But we could have had so much more.

After I was born, doctors discovered that my mother had cancer. That's why I'm an only child. She fought it for many years, finally succumbing when I was twenty-five. After her death, my father spiraled further into the bottle. I checked on him frequently, but it was painful. He lost the house and moved into an apartment.

One day I stopped by and his apartment door was ajar. I entered and found his body on the floor.

Years of alcohol abuse and cigarettes had taken their toll. He died of a heart attack. I already had a young son and soon would have a daughter. I vowed to myself that I would not end up like this. My children would never have to go through this.

So, I rarely drank to excess, but wasn't above having an occasional beer. Still, I didn't know much about booze, particularly for a streetwise cop.

"What's a Modelo Negras?" I asked my partner. He laughed.

"As long as you've worked the west side, you still don't know what a Negra is?" he said. "It just means dark beer."

We both laughed. We ate, drank a few beers, and returned to our hotel room. Though we'd taken a few moments to relax, it was still an early night. We had just solved a triple homicide and obtained a confession, but we weren't done yet. Tomorrow would come quickly, and we still had a lot to do.

That next day, a Nashville officer drove us from address to address as we tried to find the family member with Antonio's effects. Eventually, we ended up at a Baptist bookstore. The Nashville officer explained that one of Antonio's relatives worked there.

"That's a good sign that it's a Bible store," I said.

"I hope so," he said.

We went in and found Antonio's relative. I recognized her as one of the people I had observed at the jail the day we arrived. I told her why we were there. She hadn't heard about the Dayton homicides, and she immediately agreed to cooperate. We followed her home and retrieved the effects package. It was still unopened.

"I cannot thank you enough," I told her.

The woman seemed genuinely shaken by the murders. "I'm sorry we had to meet this way," she said.

We hurried back to the Nashville police station and inventoried the bag of effects. All of the jewelry was there. We then turned our attention to the clothing. There was blood on the shoes, pants, and jacket.

"That seals it," I said.

Our next stop was the property room to pick up the revolver. We arranged to have Ivory's car towed back to Dayton. Next, we headed home, leaving Antonio behind. Moving him would be more complicated than towing the car.

Not that we didn't have a good case. Our crime lab would ultimately match the revolver taken from Antonio in Nashville to the bullet removed from Ophelia's head in Dayton. The blood on his clothing would also be matched to our victims. The car Antonio had wrecked in Nashville belonged to Ivory. And to top it all off, we had a damn good confession.

The thing that haunted me the most though was that tattoo. He had actually tattooed a tombstone on his arm with "RIP Franklins" on it. Work homicide, and you will meet ruthless people: cold, calculating, violent, and deadly. But even among them, there are standards. For example, many of the most hardened criminals detest people who prey on children. There are many vicious gangsters who love their grandparents.

But it was truly rare to meet a suspect who had no conscience whatsoever. Antonio was proud of what he had done. He had to be. He tattooed it on his arm. Clearly, he was more dangerous than most. We would have to be careful when we brought him back to stand trial.

Extradition of a prisoner requires what's called a "governor's warrant." It's basically a document that outlines the charges and the reason we would like to have the prisoner transferred from another state to Ohio to stand trial for their crimes. The prosecutor's office approved seventeen counts, including aggravated murder charges, which carried the possibility of the death penalty. Afterward, we got the extradition papers approved. The process took several days, and then we returned to Nashville to bring Antonio back to Dayton.

Six hours in a car is a long time, particularly when transporting a murderer facing possible execution. Antonio was violent and an escape risk as well. To ensure our safety, and his, we took the usual extradition precautions. He was placed in shackles, which would allow him to move his feet just far apart enough to walk, but not run. A large, heavy leather belt was placed around his waist. Two heavy steel rings protruded from the front of the belt. He was handcuffed in front and the handcuffs chain was looped through the rings. This would allow him to have some limited movement of his hands. Finally, we fastened his seat belt—with his hands secured, he couldn't reach the buckle.

During the drive, we would have to stop for food and a restroom break. If we didn't, it would certainly be an issue at trial. He had been charged with several crimes and now his welfare was our responsibility. That meant we had to feed him. We searched for an isolated location and found a small mom-and-pop diner/gas station with one car in the lot. My partner went in to order the food and to explain who we were and what we were doing. The plan was that we'd order the food to go, but that I'd also take Antonio inside to use the bathroom. The diner's owner said he understood, and we started to take Antonio from the car.

A school bus loaded with children pulled up as I was taking Antonio from the car for his restroom break. It was routine for us but must have been quite a sight for them: a visibly armed plainclothes detective escorting an orange-clad, shackled prisoner into the building.

"Bet they don't see that every day," my partner said as he returned with our food.

"Maybe it's good for them to see," I said.

We continued back to Dayton. As we approached the city, Antonio had one request. "Can we drive by the house?" he asked.

"Sure," I replied. This was great. I wanted to see his reaction to what remained of the house where he had killed his family.

Slowly, we pulled onto Riegel Street. The charred remains of the house came into view. I was not surprised by Antonio's reaction: He was in awe. He showed no remorse, and instead appeared almost excited. His face beamed, as if with pride over some major accomplishment.

In a capital case, you actually have two trials. The first part concerns guilt or innocence, just like any other trial. Should the jury vote to convict, there will be a second phase, in which the jury must decide whether to recommend the death penalty. In Antonio's case, the first phase was fairly straightforward, as the evidence was overwhelming that he was guilty of all charges.

We did get a chuckle, however, on the trial's first day. One of the fundamental concepts of our legal system is the separation of witnesses—witnesses are not allowed to watch the testimony of others. The lone exception is the state's representative, a detective who is allowed to sit with prosecutors during the entire trial, in part to assist prosecutors with their case. Prosecutors selected my partner, who was new to homicide and had worked undercover for years. News reporters did not yet know him.

Ordinarily, the defendant sits up front with his attorneys. Not Antonio, who was so potentially disruptive that the defense table had been moved from its usual position to a more secure corner of the courtroom. So, when the news cameras focused on the "defendant," they chose the only Black man seated up front.

"They think you're the killer," I told my partner as we watched the news that night.

"I told you we all look alike to you white people," he said. We had a good laugh and the videographers figured it out the next day.

After the jury convicted Antonio of all counts, the trial moved into the second phase. The prosecutor's case argued for the death penalty and submitted to the jury the facts of the case they had just heard.

The job of the defense during the second phase is to present mitigating factors that argue against execution. They presented witnesses who testified Antonio's mother hadn't wanted him, even trying to induce an abortion by sticking a pencil into her womb to "dislodge the thing."

Doctors and other experts testified that Antonio exhibited classic symptoms of mental illness. However, our experts testified that Antonio was only feigning a mental illness, and that he clearly knew right from wrong and understood the consequences of his actions. After all, he had burned down the house to try to conceal the murders. The jury believed us and recommended the death penalty.

The judge agreed with the jury. Antonio Sanchez Franklin was sentenced to death for each of the family members he had murdered. He was also sentenced to an additional ninety-one years for the other crimes he had committed. Antonio still sits in prison today, all conceivable appeals having been exhausted, awaiting execution. Yes, Antonio, to use your words, we figured out you did it.

Many times, if I am in a certain area, I will seek out a specific house, usually one tied to a specific case that I can never forget. More than once, I have driven down Riegel Street to remember the Franklin family and what was done to them by their own kin. But I try not to dwell on the past. One of my old partners once told me that a homicide detective is like a fish. Fish have to keep moving to circulate life-sustaining water through their gills.

"Never slow down, always keep moving," he said. "If you slow down, it gives you too much time to think, too much time to remember."

I remember my past. How can you not? But I try not to be controlled by it. I tell myself to keep moving forward.

16.
YES, HONEY, THE ROPE TOOK HIM TO HEAVEN

I REMEMBER A night during a long, hot summer, a very busy summer for us. As I got out of bed and put on my suit, I noted that it was 3 a.m., then grabbed my badge and gun and headed out. I was driving far from home when I realized I had forgotten the location of the call, so I phoned dispatch.

"Good morning, this is Burke," I said. "Hey, what's the address on the callout?"

There was a moment of deep silence and the dispatcher replied, "There is no callout."

I was confused for a moment. Then I realized that I didn't remember the pager going off or talking to dispatch. I just woke up, got dressed, and started driving, completely on autopilot.

I'd like to think that this job didn't affect me. But it did, in ways that were obvious and in ways that I'm still figuring out. When you're waking up in the middle of the night assuming there is a callout when there isn't one, you know the job is affecting you quite deeply.

It never leaves you. Even when you are alone, at home, you find yourself haunted by certain incidents that just stay with you. But home alone is often better than going to a party. It's hard to talk about this stuff with people who don't experience it firsthand.

The hours didn't help. Some people punch a time clock at work. You won't find a time clock in a homicide office. Our scheduled hours were 8:45 a.m. to 4:45 p.m., but you might as well have called that a suggestion. We were always in early and usually worked late. When you get a promising lead, you follow it. You don't yell "time-out" and go home, even if it's 9 p.m. and you're already three hours late for dinner.

Then consider the call load. We investigated dozens of homicides a year—but we also handled hundreds more cases where the victims survived. Most of those assaults did not happen at 9 a.m. on a weekday. We were always on call. Even if you were already working a half dozen cases, when a body dropped, you headed that way. There's an old cliché about not knowing if you were coming or going. For us, this was the truth, and sometimes, as I discovered that evening when I must have dreamed about a callout, there was nowhere to go.

Our squad agreed that we had to give every victim our best effort. Victims vary. Some are completely innocent, like a four-year-old bystander to a drive-by shooting. Others are criminals themselves. But all of them have a loved one out there. Even when it wasn't easy, we told ourselves that every victim deserved justice, and so did their loved ones.

The line between hero and scapegoat turns out to be quite thin. At times, victims' families were so grateful that you could really feel a bond develop with them, sometimes almost instantly. Others hated us because a case went in a direction they didn't like, perhaps revealing something they didn't want to face about the victim's lifestyle. Even when the victims were criminals themselves—and homicide is an occupational hazard for those in the drug trade—some families accepted the truth and others were in complete denial. Regardless, you had to put their reactions aside and investigate to the best of your ability.

One of my partners said it best: "We only walk on water because we can't swim."

You needed to resist all temptation to become personally or emotionally involved. You had to be above the case. You could never "swim" in the same water as your victim or suspect. If you did, you wouldn't last long on this squad. Those who tried didn't.

This job changes you, period. You cannot deal with tragedies on a daily basis and remain unscathed. To survive, you learn to work through it in your own way, or you move on to another line of work. It wasn't that we didn't care, because we did. But you had to compartmentalize it, to separate personal feelings so that you could do the job. As one of my academy instructors said, "You can't save anyone if you can't save yourself."

Some years ago, all Dayton police officers were ordered to attend a mandatory day of stress-relief training at the police academy. This was an obvious reaction from the brass after several officers retired on stress disabilities.

We were given a questionnaire to fill out. Each event you checked carried points. Events included things like the death of a relative, a divorce, a bloody crime scene. The instructors would tally up the points to show you what your perceived stress level was, so the more points you had, the worse off you were. I filled out the form and added up my points.

"Excuse me, is this checklist for the last few months, a week, or what?" I asked.

"Oh no, this is for your lifetime," the instructor said.

Well, I'm screwed, I thought. *Hell, I've got enough points from last week to put me in the crazy range.*

I kept my mouth shut as I erased some of the boxes I had checked.

This was an upsetting process. At one point, an older sergeant became angry, noting that the psychologist had never been a police officer, and couldn't understand what the job entailed. He balled up his survey, tossed it in the trash, and walked out.

After reviewing my checklist, the instructor asked, "Do you ever see dead people at night?"

"Yes," I replied.

"In your dreams?"

"No, only on overtime," I said. But I didn't tell him about the imaginary callout. I simply didn't want to talk about it.

Not long after that, I was watching a movie, *8mm*, which had a line in it that I often remember: "When you dance with the devil, the devil doesn't change. The devil changes you."

It was true. It was impossible to go where we went, see what we saw, do what we did, and think it had no effect on us. It did and it still does. You just have to control it.

* * *

It was late November 1987, and one of Dayton's strangest murder cases was developing—and we didn't even know it. It started as a standard missing person's case, involving an adult woman who had every right to disappear, and as it turned out, every reason to want to. But it was not the type of case to attract our immediate attention.

Ted Sinks, forty-nine, phoned the Dayton Police Department on November 23, a Monday, to report that his wife had been missing for more than twenty-four hours. Judy, forty-four, had been married to Ted for two years.

Uniformed officers responded to the house and took notes. There were no signs of a struggle. Judy Sinks had not left a note or any other clue as to her whereabouts. Her purse and all of its contents—identification, credit cards—were gone. Early bets had Judy leaving to start a new life somewhere else—which adults do—and though there was no sense of urgency, officers did do routine checkups.

The vast majority of these situations end with the missing person showing up later on. Plus, in the age of computers and the Internet, it's not as easy to voluntarily disappear as it once was. Detectives will check for activity on the missing person's bank accounts, credit cards, and even their Social Security number. Usually, the missing person is quickly located in another city or state.

Today, a credit card check would be instant. Back in the more technologically primitive time of 1987, it took a day. So, the next day, detectives learned that those cards had not been used. But that same day, they learned that the purse and all its contents had been found—stuffed in a mailbox, just blocks from the Sinks' home in the city's Belmont neighborhood. Belmont is one of those "last built" neighborhoods that cities have on their borders. Most of the homes date back into the late 1940s, early 1950s, and the neighborhood blends seamlessly into the suburbs of Kettering and Riverside. Not the kind of place where homicide detectives are routinely dispatched.

This was particularly odd. If a stranger had abducted Judy Sinks, why would he leave the purse in the mailbox? If a thief had stolen the purse, why wouldn't he take the credit cards?

That's when we knew this would not be a standard missing-adult investigation. But we had no good clues. We had the absence of clues, or clues that made little sense.

Both Ted and Judy worked at the *Dayton Daily News* building on Ludlow Street, in the heart of downtown. Ted was in maintenance, primarily working with the building's heating, ventilation, and air-conditioning systems. Judy was a clerical worker in the circulation department. Detectives interviewed coworkers, friends, and relatives, and learned that Judy had not been at work the Friday before Ted called police. There was no explanation for her absence. Ted said he didn't know about that.

Interviews with coworkers gradually painted the picture of an unhappy marriage. Ted clearly wanted out. Judy might have too. Some of Judy's friends didn't like Ted. But no one reported any signs of domestic violence or abuse. The entire situation was suspicious, but of what? We had no proof that Ted had harmed Judy. In fact, there was no proof anyone had harmed Judy. We needed to find her. We had no idea how long that would take, or how bizarre this case would become.

With no evidence to point in any particular direction, the investigation stalled out. Obviously, we were looking at Ted. In this type of situation, you always look close to home, and Ted was not only the unhappy husband, but also the person who had reported her missing. But there were other possibilities as well. Five months after Judy disappeared, we decided to rein-terview several people, to see if any new angles shook loose.

As part of that process, we spoke with a maintenance worker at the news building, and he provided us with some very interesting information he said he'd just recalled.

On November 20, three days before Ted reported Judy missing and the day of Judy's unexplained absence from work, Ted had asked for his help. Ted was working on a concrete ped-estal for a water-purifying unit at the news building. He told his coworker that he needed help moving a fifty-five-gallon barrel of asbestos to the seventh floor, and the man agreed to help. The coworker drove to the Sinks' house and helped Ted move the barrel from the garage to Ted's truck. When they returned to the news building, they carried the barrel to the seventh floor, which was not accessible to nonmaintenance employees.

The coworker said that he thought it was odd that the barrel was very heavy, when asbestos should be very light. When asked if Judy was there when he helped move the barrel, he thought for a moment and then answered, "No, she wasn't there."

The worker had not put it all together. We hadn't either, but we were starting to. There was no doubt in our minds that the "asbestos" in that barrel was in fact Judy Sinks. She had to be somewhere in the news building, and we had a good idea where. We obtained a search warrant and headed for the *Dayton Daily News*.

Up on the seventh floor, the pedestal for the purifying unit was larger than I had expected. It was about two feet high and four feet wide.

"Looks like a tomb," I said.

"I think it is," my partner replied.

We were armed with more than a search warrant. We also had brought several city maintenance workers who were equipped with the tools to crack this pedestal open. And that is exactly what we did.

The work was painstakingly slow, but it had to be to insure we didn't damage what—or who—we thought was inside. Eventually, the crew penetrated the top of the concrete, and once that seal was broken, there wasn't a person on that floor who didn't know where Judy Sinks was.

Now, I have worked through some extremely foul-smelling scenes. I have been on cases where people hadn't been seen for weeks, months, and longer. But this was much different. Judy's decomposing body had been sealed in an airtight concrete pedestal for five months. I had never, and still have never, smelled anything quite this foul. People ran gagging from the scene. But we still had plenty of work to do, right there.

Hours later, after all the photographs had been taken, we pulled the badly decomposed body of Judy Sinks from her tomb. It was ghastly. What flesh remained was clinging to her bones. There were remnants of her dress still on her body and a watch on her left wrist. A rope was still tied around her neck and torso. The autopsy would show that Judy had been beaten and strangled. Though it would take more time to positively identify her through dental records, we knew it was her. We had a homicide, and we knew exactly who our suspect was.

We arrested a remorseless Ted Sinks and charged him with the murder of Judy Sinks. Ted was subsequently convicted and sentenced to a term of fifteen years to life in prison. He died there in November 2016 at age seventy-seven, having never admitted what he did to his wife.

Anyone can kill. Ted Sinks is living proof of that. Sinks was a middle-aged white man without a criminal record. He was a creature of the middle class, a homeowner with a steady record of solid employment. Of course, this was a domestic-violence murder, and domestic violence can and does happen everywhere, in all communities, whether or not we like to admit that.

In 2013, the news building on Ludlow Street, vacant since the company had moved operations to a newer facility in 2007, was imploded. Had it not been for the maintenance worker and his memories of that heavy barrel, coupled with the hard work of the detectives who refused to give up, Judy might never have been found. Prior to the news building being imploded, it was listed as one of the ten most haunted sites in Dayton. The ghost of Judy Sinks was said to roam the seventh floor of the building routinely.

Whether or not Judy haunted that building, she certainly haunted my partner, who was one of my mentors. He had years of experience working numerous tough cases. He was there to investigate Samuel Moreland's massacre a few years earlier. But Judy's case bothered him more than most. You never know which ones will hit you the hardest.

My colleague decided to take a break and go fishing at a nearby lake. While he and some friends relaxed in their small boat, he went to check one of the fishing lines and fell into the water, then vanished underwater before he could get back in. It took several days to find his body.

His son was also a detective, assigned to the assault squad. We spoke while they dragged the lake, but there was little to say. No one doubted that it was an accident, but I couldn't help thinking that stress had finally worn him down. If the job hadn't killed him, it was certainly an accomplice in his death, and the deaths of many others. He had planned to retire soon, but never made it. The fates of some who did make it to retirement were not much better.

I watched several of my partners retire from this job. There was always a party. They would receive a retirement badge and a gold-colored watch. We would all wish them well and pat them on the back for a job well done. But this is a hard job to leave. Death investigation takes over your life, and it never truly releases it. I am convinced it is almost impossible to fully leave this job. The job follows you everywhere you go. You can never leave it because it never leaves you.

One study showed that, though police officers generally retire younger than most other workers, the average officer dies within the first ten years of retirement. It's really not that surprising. In twenty-five to thirty-five years on this job, you gain several lifetimes of experience, many of which are traumatic and take a toll. I would watch my friends and partners retire and walk out that door one last time. Some would stay in touch for a while. Others would instantly vanish from our lives. Some would come back around the old office. Others would never step back through those doors. One by one, we would hear of their deaths. Some had been retired for a few years, some for many years, others for only months. Some of them drank heavily before they retired. The job limited how much they could drink and how often. Without the job, they drank themselves to death. I firmly believe they were trying to drink away some of the horrors they had seen. I hope they were able to.

Some needed a quicker escape. There is almost nothing sadder than suicide. Death is painful enough for survivors. Suicide leaves additional guilt, anger, and confusion.

* * *

One of the hardest scenes we ever dealt with involved the suicide of a brother officer. We all knew him. Though he was not permanently assigned to our squad, he had been working with us for the past few months. He and his brother were both uniformed Dayton officers, but he had been temporarily placed in the detective section as clerical support.

It was a stress transfer. When officers show signs of succumbing to stress, they are placed "inside," where they don't have contact with the public and aren't generally in dangerous situations. Typically, this means dispatch, property room, records, or a clerical role in our section. This gives the department time to evaluate their options. And hopefully help the officer.

This officer was a great guy with a loving family. But he was clearly troubled. It seemed he had found his way out. He had taken a rope and hanged himself in his garage.

The four of us pulled up to the residence. Typically, three detectives from homicide squad responded to a callout. If there were a lot of witnesses or a huge scene, we would call out more. Four of us responded to this death solely because of who it was.

We split up to get this over with as quickly as possible. It's tough to investigate any death. But it's horrible to have to investigate a brother officer's death. This was not a line-of-duty death, but certainly it was the job that killed him. Stress had taken its toll.

I reviewed the death scene. A rope had been affixed over a joist. The rope marks on our friend's neck were vertical, not horizontal. In a homicide, the marks were almost always horizontal. No one ever choked someone on an angle. But in a hanging such as this, the marks would be vertical because of the higher suspension point. No doubt: our friend had hanged himself.

As the coroner's office arrived to transport our friend to the morgue, I took one last look at him. I didn't know him as well as some others did, but in the short time we had spent together I had grown fond of him. He was a likable guy. *Why did it have to end like this?* I wondered as I left the garage and headed for the house.

A priest was inside talking to the family. There were three small children listening to him. I guessed they were elementary-school age. I spoke with the officer's wife. She was upset but composed. You never expected something like this to happen, no matter what the warning signs were. I wanted her to be at peace with herself, as much as possible. Those children would need her.

It was important to her that the priest would be allowed to administer last rites. I hurriedly stopped the van and ushered the priest over. As the priest gave that final sacrament to our friend, I continued speaking with his wife.

She was concerned about the children. They had discovered him together as they returned home in the family car and she pressed the garage door opener. As the door went up, it began to reveal his body. She'd gotten them away from the garage as quickly as possible but wasn't sure how much the children had seen.

I thought for a moment. All of the children were young enough to be in that gray area of comprehension. They may have seen a little or a lot. But how little or how much they saw didn't matter. It was how much they understood about what they saw.

"Should we ask them now or should we wait?" she asked.

"It never gets any better than now," I reluctantly answered. She nodded. Over time, I became friends with this woman, and we remain friends to this day. But on this evening, we were total strangers. Yet, I trusted her, and more importantly, she trusted me.

"I'll take care of it," I said, then I went to talk things over with the other detectives.

"We need to talk to the kids," I told them.

"For what?" one asked.

"To see what they saw," I replied. "More for them than us."

They understood now, but no one wanted to be the one to handle this. And it would have to be just one of us. Too many detectives could be intimidating to these children, who were already confused and traumatized by the day's events.

I was now the squad's most experienced member. "I'll do it," I said quietly.

I gathered up the children, and as they huddled around me, I knelt down to their level. I introduced myself to them, but not as Detective Burke from homicide. Instead, I was Doyle, and I was Daddy's friend. I told them he was a great man, but that even great people have problems.

"Your daddy was sick, but not like when you have a cold," I said, pointing to my head. "Daddy was sick up here. Do you understand?"

They all nodded in agreement. They had known for some time that something was wrong.

"Whatever you saw today makes no difference," I said. "What's important is that your daddy loved you all very much. Daddy is in heaven now and in heaven he isn't sick anymore."

They quietly nodded again. Then the little girl spoke. She moved a little closer to me and looked right into my eyes.

"Did the rope take Daddy to heaven?" she asked.

Any moisture in my throat evaporated just as water flowed to my eyes. I felt as though I were choking. I gave the most reassuring smile I could muster and placed my hand gently on her shoulder.

"Yes, honey, the rope took him to heaven," I said.

She hugged me and then took her place with the other children. We had done all that we could. It was time to go to headquarters and write it all up. But I didn't.

"I think I'll write my report in the morning," I said. "I'm going home."

The others agreed, and we went our separate ways. I have always loved the camaraderie of our squad, but sometimes you just needed to be alone. This was one of those times.

A few short years later, one of those partners retired. We talked before he left headquarters one last time. We talked about that case, and about the little girl who died after being stuck in the elevator. Those cases had affected all of us. He shook his head.

"I can still see you talking to those kids," he told me.

"I know," I said. "I'll never forget that either."

I hated to see him go. We had worked a lot of cases together. I really liked him, and he liked me. But I was glad he was getting out.

"I hear there is life after the DPD," I joked.

"I'm going to find out and let you know," he said.

We all stayed in touch with him for a while, though he gradually drifted away. But over time, we heard things: that he'd lost his house, that he was living in a run-down apartment, that he was drinking too much. We intervened, but we couldn't help him.

He died only a few years after retiring. Another friend lost. Another name that would not be read aloud at the annual memorial ceremony for officers killed in the line of duty.

This was not a line-of-duty death and does not belong in the same category as an officer killed while doing the job. But the job killed him, just as surely as it killed our friend who hanged himself in his garage. The job is exciting. The job is gratifying. But the job is dangerous, and not just in the obvious ways. A bulletproof vest gives you a fighting chance against an armed suspect. But there is no emotion-proof vest. Police officers try to support one another, but ultimately each officer deals with the stresses of the job alone.

When it came to the emotional dangers of the job, you were on your own.

17.
WHAT IS IT ABOUT CHRISTMAS?

CHRISTMAS REMAINS A special time for me. Growing up in Dayton, I looked forward to the bus ride from my neighborhood to downtown. The inner city was thriving, though in a few short years, businesses would begin their migration to suburban malls. But back then, downtown Dayton was the regional commercial center. If you wanted it, you could find it downtown.

All of this was magnified during the Christmas season, which I remember as magical. NCR—short for "National Cash Register"—had their world headquarters in Dayton back then. They would decorate lengthy blocks with wreaths and colorful lighting. Animated displays adorned the department-store windows. Everything was decorated, and we always had a giant Christmas tree in the center of town. To a small boy, it made Dayton feel like New York City or Chicago.

The main attraction, however, was the Arcade—an indoor shopping complex and architectural marvel, whose ceiling was a stained-glass rotunda. The Arcade, which housed several restaurants and stores, was beautiful in any season, but took on an even more brilliant character during the holidays. And the people came in droves.

What happened in Dayton is the same story of what happened in urban areas across the nation. Gradually, sadly, businesses moved away. Downtown retail mostly vanished. The department stores emptied out. By the 1990s, downtown Dayton was a shadow of what it had been.

But downtown was still important. Many people still worked there, and the police department needed to be visible. We had uniformed officers on foot, known as "the walking squad," who worked the downtown area along with regular patrol officers. We even had a mounted unit that worked downtown, which was very popular. Quietly commanding, but never intimidating, the mounted squad was a good public relations tool that also led to very effective policing. All of these innovations were designed to make people feel safe and secure so they would return to downtown. Though Dayton still had that big-city feel—particularly to those who had relocated to the suburbs—it had a hometown ambiance as well. Despite the challenges, downtown was still attractive to a lot of people. Not all of them were good people though, and for Dayton residents, Christmas 1992 would be unforgettable for all of the worst-possible reasons.

It was cold and snowy, and I was looking forward to the holiday. My young son and daughter were excited, and that excited me even more. But on this job, you never knew if you would be home for Christmas or not. After I graduated from the Dayton Police Academy in late 1978, I was assigned with a training officer who had Christmas off. I was on the same schedule as him, so in my very first month of police work, I had Christmas off. It would be three decades before that happened again.

My kids got used to it. Common Christmas phrases in our house included "Daddy will join us a little later" or "Daddy will be right back." Bad things still happened, after all. But nothing could prepare us—the detectives or our families—for the events that would be eventually known as the "Christmas Killings," and my family barely saw me during the 1992 holiday season.

It didn't start off so bad. On Christmas Eve, my family and I were visiting my grandmother, who lived with my aunt and uncle in a Dayton suburb. My wife and I always drove two cars when we went somewhere, so that they could stay if I got called out. That night, the turkey in the oven smelled great. As we sat down for a fantastic meal, my pager went off. I called dispatch.

"Got one shot in a phone booth," the dispatcher said. "Merry Christmas."

"I got it," I said. "Merry Christmas." I left my family and drove to Dayton's northwest side.

The glow of Christmas lights danced off the yellow scene tape. Danita Gullette, an eighteen-year-old single mother, had been shot to death as she used the pay phone.

"What is it about Christmas?" one of the uniformed officers asked me.

This was certainly the worst. Christmas lights and the marked cruisers' overheads flashed across the blood, making an eerie scene. It was obvious Danita had been completely defenseless in the phone booth.

"Her shoes are gone," my partner noted.

"She didn't walk here in her socks," I said.

"Do you think someone killed her for her shoes?" an officer asked.

"Anything is possible," I said, though that wasn't a satisfactory answer, at least not for a normal person. Killed for a pair of shoes on Christmas Eve. It boggled the mind.

Our attention quickly turned to the bullet casings our E-crew tech was collecting. The casing is the part that holds the actual bullet. In a revolver, those casings stay inside the gun until someone empties it. When a semiautomatic handgun is fired, the gun ejects the spent casing after the bullet leaves the chamber.

"Got about seven casings," the E-crew tech said. "All .25 auto, and all Blazer."

This was unusual. First off, a .25-caliber semiautomatic is not usually a weapon of choice for assassins. It is a very small caliber and while obviously potentially deadly, not nearly as powerful as larger-caliber weapons.

Even stranger was the ammunition choice. CCI's Blazer ammo was a relatively new product, generally used for practice. The casing was made out of aluminum instead of brass, making it easy to visually identify. You usually saw it at shooting ranges. This type of ammunition was rarely used in a homicide.

"Interesting choice of ammo," I said.

"Probably all they could afford," one officer said.

"Or steal," another added.

Danita had been trapped in a phone booth, unable to fight back or flee, when someone fired seven shots at her. The crime appeared particularly sadistic. But this was just the beginning. Later on, the sadism of the killings would shock even veteran detectives, while garnering international attention.

After we finished processing the scene, we returned to headquarters to file our reports. When that was done, we all headed home.

"Maybe we will get a little Christmas after all," one of my partners said before he left. *Maybe we will*, I thought as I drove home. We were both wrong. The next call came in on Christmas Day.

"Got one in a car crash," the dispatcher said. "Shot in the head."

We were back in northwest Dayton, not far from the Gullette scene. It was late evening, and the streetlights glistened off the white snow and the yellow scene tape. The overhead red and blue lights of the marked units added some color.

"Looks like red, blue, and yellow are going to be the only Christmas lights we see this year," I said to a uniformed officer, who laughed.

"I know what you mean," he said.

On homicide cases, you had a lead detective and a backup detective assigned. We all worked one another's cases, particularly the hard ones, but you had to have someone ultimately responsible for each case and its outcome. I had taken the Gullette homicide, so one of my partners took this one. There was nothing at either scene to indicate we were actually working the same case.

This second scene was not complex, though it also appeared senseless. There was only one person in the car, the now-deceased driver, whom we identified as Richmond Maddox, a nineteen-year-old Black male. Cause of death seemed obvious: the visible gunshot wound to his head. Apparently, he'd been shot while driving, then crashed into a tree. We searched the scene for any spent casings and found none.

"Looks like he was shot from the passenger side," my partner said. "Windows are all up."

"So, the shooter had to bail out of the car," I said.

My partner nodded in agreement. "That's a gutsy move," he said.

"And a risky one," I added. Jumping from a moving vehicle where the driver is dead is obviously very dangerous.

"Killer must be one badass," an officer said.

"Probably, probably," I replied.

The following morning, the autopsy revealed Maddox had been shot in the head with a .32-caliber handgun. I was relieved.

"At least it isn't a .25 auto Blazer," I said, thinking the cases were unrelated. I couldn't have been more wrong. In Dayton, the bodies would continue piling up.

On December 26, we received another call. "Shooting with multiple victims at the Short Stop Mini Market on West Fifth," dispatch advised.

This time, we were in the inner west side, not far from downtown's central business district. Our other cases would have to wait. So would holiday celebrations.

The market was a family-owned mom-and-pop store common to the inner city. There were two victims and a living witness who had escaped unharmed. One of the victims was Jones Pettus, a customer who had been shot and taken to a nearby hospital. Pettus would survive, but the store owner, Sarah Abraham, thirty-eight, was not so lucky. She died at the hospital five days after she was shot.

This time, we did have someone who could be interviewed immediately, seventy-one-year-old Jimmy Thompson. He told us that a Black female had entered the store to buy a soft drink but was a nickel short. Thompson gave her a nickel. But as he handed it to her, two young Black men burst through the door. They brandished guns and demanded money, which Abraham gave them without resistance. Abraham handed over all she had, which was thirty dollars.

The gunmen left, but not before shooting at all three of these innocent people. Somehow, they missed Thompson, who said he played dead and lay on the floor. Then the gunmen fled the store, accompanied by the woman to whom Thompson had given a nickel. There was no reason to kill any of these people, unless you were doing it because you liked it.

"You need to see this, Doyle," our E-crew tech said. I walked over to him as he motioned toward the floor.

At this point, I'd been a police officer for fourteen years, with seven on homicide. I'd observed many scary things, but what the tech pointed to frightened me more than anything I'd seen yet. The tech was pointing to the casings scattered across the floor. All of them were from .25-caliber Blazer bullets.

"Holy shit," I gasped.

"Not good," my partner chimed in. It hit us now. We were searching for a group of spree killers, a type of serial killer, and like all serial killers, they would continue killing until someone stopped them. It was chilling.

There are distinct differences between different types of multiple murderers. A mass murderer kills multiple victims, but usually in one occurrence and in one location. A serial killer also kills multiple victims, but usually over time, with different victims in different locations. They often prey on strangers but show a pattern or method of operation that links the victims. For example, some target only prostitutes, others only the elderly. While the victims may not know the killer or one another, there is usually a common link.

Spree killers are like serial killers on steroids, or crack cocaine. They are the most violent, their victims are the most random, and they generally don't have cooling-off periods like serial killers. They just keep going, indiscriminate, simply because they're hopped up on the adrenaline and are doing what they enjoy most: killing other people.

"We've got our work cut out for us," I said.

In three days, we'd picked up three senseless, sadistic homicide scenes. The Abraham and Gullette cases could be linked through the similar—but unique—ammunition. We strongly suspected that Maddox had been a victim of the same group, though the ammunition was different.

"Both Black males were armed at the mini-market," my partner said. "The .25-caliber Blazer ammo helps link the cases, but we know now they have at least one other gun."

We were convinced he was right: all three cases had to be connected. We started going through other recent reports, and quickly found more alarming information.

I found one report dated December 24, the same day as the Gullette slaying. A man driving through northwest Dayton had stopped to pick up a young Black woman. As he did, two Black men approached his car and started shooting, and the girl fled from the vehicle. But the driver wasn't hit and was able to drive off.

"Sound familiar?" I asked.

"It's the Maddox homicide all over again," my partner said. "Only this guy lived."

Another report from December 24: a young Black male shot at several times by two Black men, accompanied by a Black female at a housing project in northwest Dayton.

"That's victim number six," I said.

The day after Christmas, in the same area, a young woman was putting air in the tires of her car at a local gas station. Two Black males approached her, both armed with shiny handguns. "Shoot her," one yelled as she fled. She escaped unharmed but the two suspects stole her black Dodge Shadow and drove away.

We still didn't have any suspects, though we did have a possible suspect vehicle. We also didn't have much time. We were certain this group would kill again. We didn't know that they already had.

You work every case hard. This one was no different, but it had a greater sense of urgency. The victims were random innocent people. That meant that anyone could be a victim—and no one was safe. We were all exhausted. We had pursued every possible lead and still had not identified even one suspect. Sometimes you need a lucky break. We were about to get one.

Nicholas Woodson, seventeen, was a young man who had a lot to say. He knew who our shooters were and what they were doing. In fact, he'd been okay with it, to a point—until he became afraid that he would make the victims' list. He'd seen that the gang was already turning on itself, eliminating people who knew too much. So, he called dispatch on December 26, and the call was routed to our sergeant.

During that call, Woodson gave us names and told us that the group called itself the "Downtown Posse." We were already aware the gang might have the stolen Dodge Shadow, but Woodson also told us to look for a blue Pontiac Grand Am. That information was broadcasted to all police officers across the city.

It wasn't long until a uniformed crew found a blue Grand Am parked in a part of northwest Dayton where Woodson said the gang members frequented. The stolen Dodge Shadow was also parked nearby. The officer alerted dispatch, and everyone, including us, headed that direction. It happened fast, like it often does.

Before we could arrive, four people left a nearby house and started toward the cars, then saw the police officer. One of them, later identified as seventeen-year-old DeMarcus Smith, fled on foot. The other three people jumped into the Dodge, and the officer contacted dispatch, which dropped a tone.

A tone is a short, siren-like yelp, only used in emergency situations. It indicates that crews are to use lights and sirens, and get to a scene as quickly as they safely can. It worked. As officers were pulling out behind the Dodge Shadow, others, including my homicide partners, pulled into place to block the Dodge. The three suspects emerged from the car with their hands in the air. They surrendered. Sometimes timing is everything.

"Kind of anticlimactic," one of my partners said. I thought about that. I'd figured they'd be like Bonnie and Clyde, bad-asses to the end, and go out in a blaze of glory. But they didn't. These vicious spree killers were also cowards. They had preyed on and killed defenseless, innocent people. But when they came up against us—trained, armed police officers coming to confront them—they surrendered peacefully.

Meanwhile, DeMarcus Smith ran to a house on Kumler Avenue, not far from where the other three suspects were arrested. Woodson's aunt lived at the Kumler house, and our new snitch was watching from inside.

"They got 'em," Smith yelled to Woodson, who saw his chance. He fled the house and surrendered to a nearby police crew.

Woodson gave the address to police, and two of my partners went to the house on Kumler. Woodson's aunt, Sandra Pinson, answered the door. As they entered the residence, Smith came down the steps. He told them his name was Deon Pinson, but a records search quickly revealed his true identity.

After arresting Smith, my partners gathered up his clothing and found a pair of shoes. We'd obtained a description of the shoes Danita Gullette had worn when she was gunned down. These appeared to be hers.

"All for a pair of shoes," my partner said.

"The shoes were an afterthought," I replied. "It was about the fun."

We decided to check on "Deon Pinson," the alias Smith had tried to use. We quickly found there *was* a Deon Pinson in the county jail. He'd been arrested earlier that day, while driving a red Buick Electra. It wasn't his car, and though it hadn't been reported stolen, we suspected it was. The car was registered to a name and address we were unfamiliar with: Joseph Wilkerson, thirty-four, a white male who lived right in the neighborhood where the Downtown Posse had prowled.

My partner and I drove to Wilkerson's house. The door was closed but unlocked. As we entered the house, we announced who we were, but no one answered. We could see that much of the furniture was overturned. Some of the items in the house were broken, and others appeared to be missing.

"Something happened here," my partner said.

"And it wasn't good," I said. We worked our way through the living room and kitchen area toward the bedroom. The door to the bedroom was closed.

"You go high, I'll go low," my partner whispered. I nodded in agreement. In an area this tight and cramped, we could easily shoot each other if not careful. I would stay high on any potential target and my partner would crouch down and stay low. Hopefully this would keep us from hitting each other, should we be forced to fire.

I kicked the door open. "Dayton police," we yelled again. But there were no suspects hidden in this room—just another victim.

"Oh my God," my partner said. "Look at this." I was. I was taking it all in.

There on the bed lay Joseph Wilkerson. His arms were spread above his head and tied at the wrists to the headboard. His body was covered in dried blood, and there were visible gunshot wounds to his head and chest.

"Been here a few days," my partner said.

"Looks like it," I said.

Some bloody bedding partially covered the body. Then we saw it: a .25-caliber Blazer casing. There could be no doubt. We quickly called our partners at headquarters. We had yet another homicide to ask our suspects about.

While we were busy at Prescott, the other detectives were talking to our suspects. In addition to Smith, we had the three who had surrendered from the Dodge: Laura Taylor, sixteen, Heather Matthews, twenty, and Marvallous Keene, nineteen. Eventually, all but Taylor would confess. The details the other three offered were chilling. While Gullette was the first victim we had found, she was not the first victim. Wilkerson was.

Interestingly, the gang was somewhat racially mixed, in that Heather Matthews is white. The others were Black. That composition reflected the neighborhoods they used as hunting grounds.

According to our suspects, the Downtown Posse drifted between downtown and northwest Dayton. All of the members were estranged from their families, and so the gang became a substitute family for them. The leaders were Keene and Taylor, who had recruited the others. Taylor's recruiting pitch was that they needed to "put some drama in their lives." The drama began with Wilkerson, an acquaintance of Taylor.

On December 24, Taylor, Keene, and Matthews walked to Wilkerson's home, where the girls enticed Wilkerson into letting them in by promising him an orgy. In the bedroom, they bound his wrists with electrical cords and secured them to the headboard. Meanwhile, Keene ransacked the house, finding a .32-caliber derringer. With Wilkerson secured and defenseless, Keene entered the room and shot him in the chest. Next, Taylor shot Wilkerson in the head, using the .25-caliber handgun, which ejected the telltale casing. Leaving his lifeless body to decompose, the three stole Wilkerson's car and drove downtown.

In the city's center, the group spent time bumming money from downtown patrons, but didn't get much. They decided to use Taylor's sexuality to attract another "trick" to rob. The group, now four—DeMarcus Smith, who was Matthews's boyfriend, had joined them—returned to northwest Dayton, where Taylor flagged down a male driver.

As she entered the car, Keene and Smith approached with guns drawn. The victim sped off as the two fired their guns at the car, though the driver was unhurt. So was Taylor, who jumped from the speeding vehicle.

That same day, Christmas Eve, the gang shot two people. One was Danita Gullette, a stranger in a telephone booth they were walking past. As the others coldly shouted, "Merry Christmas, bitch," Keene pulled out the .25-caliber handgun and emptied it into her. As she lay dying, the gang stole her shoes.

Next was the man who was shot in the housing project and survived. We learned that he was Matthews's ex-boyfriend. Smith, her current boyfriend, shot him four times but amazingly, the victim was still able to run away.

As the mayhem continued, the gang kept attracting recruits. Nicholas Woodson, who was already acquainted with some of the members, was one. The day after Gullette's homicide, the gang hung out at Woodson's aunt's house on Kumler. Sandra Pinson prepared a big meal for Nicholas and his friends. It was, after all, Christmas Day. During the meal, Matthews showed off her new shoes, even bragging to Woodson's girlfriend that she had pulled them off a girl they had killed earlier in a phone booth.

After dinner, the gang returned to Wilkerson's house to plan their next robbery. They partied some more, eating and drinking while their host lay dead in a nearby bedroom. During their bash, someone decided to cover Wilkerson's body with blankets to lessen the smell of his decomposing body. For their next crime, they decided the target would be another stranger, this time at an ATM machine.

They took Wilkerson's other car, the blue Grand Am that Woodson mentioned, and staked out a nearby ATM. But it was Christmas and most people were home with their families. After waiting several hours, with no one stopping by the ATM, they changed plans. Taylor called her ex-boyfriend, Richmond Maddox, and promised him sex in exchange for a ride.

Maddox picked her up, but as he drove away, he spotted the Grand Am following him and got spooked. He accelerated, perhaps not realizing that one of his attackers was in the seat beside him. Taylor then pulled out a .32-caliber derringer and shot Maddox in the head. She jumped from the car before it crashed and Matthews, driving the Grand Am, picked her up.

Back at Kumler, they found two new visitors: Marvin Washington, eighteen, and his sixteen-year-old girlfriend, Wendy Cottrill, who is described in later news reports as a close friend of Taylor. Reflecting the mixed race of the gang, Washington was Black and Cottrill white.

The next day, December 26, the gang was out trolling ATM machines when they spotted the young woman putting air in the tires of her Dodge Shadow. After terrorizing her and stealing her car, they returned to Kumler. They now had three cars, but little money. No longer patient enough to wait at ATM machines, they decided to rob a store.

The attacks at Sarah Abraham's mini-market happened just as Jimmy Thompson described them to us. Taylor was the girl who cased the store, and Keene and Smith were the men who robbed it, then shot at everyone in sight. Matthews drove the getaway car, which was the Grand Am.

By this time, Woodson was becoming wary, wondering about the endgame. As the others spoke about "snitches" that would need to be taken care of, he wondered if he knew too much. Worried about becoming the next victim, Woodson elected to call us. He would help us, eventually becoming our star witness, and for this he would get to stay alive. Woodson was probably the best of a bad bunch. Though he had been aware of what was going on and even participated in some of the activities, Woodson hadn't robbed or killed anyone.

The Christmas nightmare was nearly over, just days after it began. We had all four suspects in custody, and all but Laura Taylor had confessed. She never did. Keene may have been the visible leader of the gang—the muscle, really—but Taylor was the brains. She was cold and heartless. All of us took a shot at interviewing her. None of us were able to get her to talk.

At one point, my partner asked Taylor if she needed to use the restroom. She looked at him and urinated on the floor. At the young age of sixteen—still legally a child—she was a hardened criminal. How this happened would remain a mystery. We would later learn that she came from a good home with what appeared to be supportive, middle-class parents. Taylor had participated in her high school's ROTC program for the Marines and was a good student until her junior year, when she started skipping school and hanging out with Marvallous Keene. At that point, her parents told us, they could no longer control her.

So, what happened to her? Did Keene really have that kind of influence on her, to change her so much? Or was she a budding sociopath hiding in plain sight until the conditions were right for her true self to emerge? I still don't know, but as always, I remind myself that anyone can kill, regardless of background. Laura Taylor was proof of that.

"It's good we got this one early," I said.

"No shit," my partner agreed.

We booked Keene and Matthews into the county jail and Smith and Taylor into the Juvenile Justice Center, but there was still a tremendous amount of work to be done. The gang had kept us running. We hadn't even started on any lab requests or additional reports. We hadn't even had time to review the evidence gathered at the scenes. But we did have the Christmas Killers, as the news media had dubbed them, in custody. We thought it was over. It wasn't.

December 27 was a Sunday, and with the killers in custody, people across the city felt safe enough to leave their homes and worship. After services at a small West Dayton church, Reverend Bill Head learned of the arrests and was shocked to learn that one of the accused killers was a sixteen-year-old girl. Though Head did not know Laura Taylor, he felt compelled to visit her in juvenile detention and minister to her.

I'm glad he did. Reverend Head was one of the west-side religious leaders who I frequently talked to. I had gained his trust and that day, it paid off. I was at home still trying to catch up on some much-needed sleep when my cell phone rang. It was Reverend Head, who was panicked.

"You can never let anyone know where this information came from," he said.

"Okay."

"I've been talking to Laura Taylor."

"Okay, you have my attention," I said, now fully awake.

"There are two more victims," Reverend Head said. "She told me where the bodies are."

The girl who none of us could break opened up to a man of the cloth. I still wonder why she talked so freely, even bragged, to Reverend Head. Much later, I would talk with him about the interview. I could tell it haunted him. He had gone to Taylor believing, or hoping, that she was innocent. He left the interview with the realization that she was not, and it affected him deeply.

That morning, I took the information from Reverend Head and called the rest of the squad. We met at headquarters, then headed to a local gravel pit. The fence there was open, so we walked inside and, after a short distance, found the bodies of Marvin Washington and Wendy Cottrill. They had made the mistake of tagging along with the Downtown Posse, but didn't have the realization that saved Nicholas Woodson's life.

"Does it ever end?" one of my partners asked.

"It never ends," I said.

"Looks like Woodson was right," my partner said.

"Woodson was probably next," I said.

"He was lucky to get out alive," my partner said.

This was a somber scene. The gravel pit resembled a graveyard. Ironically, we later learned that Marvallous Keene's brother, who had been shot to death in a robbery a year earlier, was buried in a cemetery nearby.

By now we were numb: so much death, all for nothing. Sure enough, there were .25-caliber Blazer casings next to the bodies. Washington had been shot seven times. Cottrill had been shot three times, including once in the mouth.

"So young," my partner said. "So young."

We all stood there silently for a moment. It made no sense. It still doesn't. Then we processed what we hoped was our last scene from this crime spree.

Through further interviews, we later learned that Smith shot Washington because Keene couldn't—because at the time he had his gun in Cottrill's mouth. These two were the gang's last victims.

The final tally was this: this gang had killed six people over a seventy-two-hour period. Marvallous Keene shot four of them, though Wilkerson was also shot by Taylor. Smith killed Washington and Taylor killed Maddox. Thankfully, it was finally over.

The trials occurred in 1993 and 1994. Heather Matthews entered into a plea agreement and testified against the others, thus sparing her the death penalty. She is currently serving in excess of one hundred years in prison.

So are Smith and Taylor, who were both juveniles at the time of the killings. Though they could be tried as adults, and were, they were not eligible for the death penalty due to their age.

That left only one, Marvallous Keene. Keene was convicted and sentenced to death. He received his well-earned lethal injection in July 2009.

"I'm glad Marvallous Keene is dead," I told news reporters after his execution. "He deserved to die."

During those interviews, I was asked the standard questions about the death penalty. I respect the opinion of those who oppose the death penalty, though I disagree with them. Experts say that the death penalty is not a deterrent to other killers, and I'm inclined to believe that. I have no expectation that the death of this Marvallous Keene will prevent the next one from rising up and killing. But this Marvallous Keene deserved to die.

"There have to be consequences for your actions," I said. "And grave actions bring grave consequences."

If Marvallous Keene doesn't deserve the death penalty, who does? Keene had no compassion for his victims. I have no compassion for Keene. I cannot.

At the time of his execution, Keene was asked for a final statement. Keene responded, "No, I have no words." Neither do I, beyond what is written here. The actions of the Downtown Posse were simply beyond words, even for their purported leader.

18.
DON'T TELL ME

THE LIFE-CHANGING CALL from dispatch came in the summer of 1980. I'd been a police officer for almost two years, and my partner and I were having our usual active night.

We both loved working the midnight shift and we made a great team, complementing each other's skills and temperaments perfectly. More experienced than I was, he was also more patient. Except for the paperwork involved with a busy night. We became great friends and I learned a lot from him.

The voice came over the radio: "Crew 111A?"

"Go ahead," I answered, and the dispatcher instructed us to drive to the rear of headquarters.

"We just cuffed one," I said.

"Charge?"

I explained that it was a public intoxication. The dispatcher ordered me to release our prisoner and get to headquarters.

"Okay, buddy, you're free to go," I said as I uncuffed our drunk.

"Get some coffee," my partner added.

"Yesh, shirr," our drunk replied.

As we drove to headquarters, our thoughts were with my partner's wife, who worked at the dispatch center in headquarters as a civilian call evaluator—the folks who answered the phones. The evaluator would obtain details from the caller, then issue a priority level on a scale of one to four, one being an emergency and four being a routine call. They then gave that information to a dispatcher, who would send police officers on the calls.

We weren't concerned about her job. My partner's wife was pregnant with their first child. Dispatchers didn't routinely tell us to release prisoners. Something was up and we were both concerned something had happened to her or their unborn baby. We hurried to headquarters.

The dispatch supervisor, known as Sergeant Al, was waiting for us, pacing in the back lot as we pulled up. As we left the cruiser, he walked toward us. To our surprise, he walked right past my partner and placed his hand on my shoulder.

"Doyle, I'm sorry," he said slowly. "Your mother has died."

I let those words sink in for a moment. My mother had been battling cancer for several weeks at a local hospital. I knew it was a battle she wouldn't win, but I wasn't prepared for it to end so soon.

"She's been real sick," I told Sergeant Al when I could finally say something.

"I know, son. That doesn't make it any easier."

He was so right. Death is final, whether it's sudden or slow, expected or a complete surprise. There was always some hope, until death. I would remember this night every time I made a death notification myself, and in the course of my career, I would make a lot of them. And every one of them would be different.

As a homicide detective, I tried to make the death notification myself, whenever possible. Not because it's pleasant, because

obviously, it's not. But a lot of information can be obtained while people are grieving. You might as well get plugged in as soon as you can.

Crowds follow bodies, I have told many rookie homicide detectives. When victims are removed from crime scenes and taken to hospitals, their loved ones follow them. And those people are usually mad. Angry people talk freely.

I can't tell you how many times I've walked out of the emergency room into the waiting area to make a death notification. I would start by speaking about the deceased in a positive way.

"No one deserved this," I would say.

"That's right," the crowd would answer.

"I'm very sorry but [insert name] didn't make it," I would slowly add. Then I would sit back and listen.

Invariably, the people who were closest to the deceased would turn to the people who he ran around with.

"What happened?" they would ask them, shouting. "Tell the policeman what you know."

This might seem harsh—catching possible witnesses at a particularly emotional moment—but it isn't, and it works. Those people with information were much more likely to share it immediately after learning about the death, as tempers were flaring and people were crying. Give them a day to adjust to the emotional landscape, and they would shut down, often finding it in their own best interest to keep the details to themselves.

But you never knew what you'd experience when making a death notification. Sometimes you didn't get the anticipated reaction at all.

I remember a fatal stabbing in the city's east end, on a hot summer night many years ago in the late 1980s. Two men started to argue, then the argument escalated into a fight, which then escalated into a homicide.

"Pretty cut-and-dried," my partner said.

"Nice tight scene, lots of witnesses, suspect already in custody," I said. "I'll take this one."

"Oh no, you don't. You had the last easy one."

We laughed. "You can have it," I said. "Sounds like your deceased was the troublemaker anyway. I'll go with the doctor to make the notification."

The "doctor" was, in fact, not a real doctor. He was a veteran coroner's investigator who always dressed in a nice suit and tie with a matching hat. To complete the ensemble, he carried his notebook and a flashlight in a traditional doctor's bag. Hence the nickname.

"Doctor, you drew the short straw tonight. I'm going with you to make the notification," I said. He laughed. We got into my car and headed a short distance to the apartment of our deceased's father. Witnesses at the scene told us that our deceased had lived with his father and no other living relatives. I knocked on the door.

"Who is it?" came a male voice from inside.

"Dayton police," I said.

"Fuck you. I didn't call the police," the voice said.

"I'm Detective Burke from homicide."

"Then fuck you too. I damn sure didn't call about no homicide."

"Sir, it's about your son," the doctor added.

"Fuck off and leave me alone."

"I don't think he likes us," I said to the doctor. We both laughed.

"Well, his mood is not going to improve," the doctor said to me. "I came here to make a death notification and I'm making it."

The doctor raised his voice so it could be heard though the door. "Sir, I'm from the coroner's office," he shouted. "Your son is dead. And if he was half the asshole you are, I can see why he got killed."

I chuckled. "Nicely done," I said.

"Yeah, I think that went well," the doctor said. With that, we left. The notification had been made.

Every notification was different. Some people were too emotional. Some were not emotional at all. Some cried too much. Some cried too little. Some even laughed out loud. Others sat quietly. We had to determine who was genuine, and who was putting on a show. And make no mistake about it: to some, this was their time to shine. Just because you were related to the deceased didn't mean you cared about them.

Obviously, this is delicate business, but sometimes it was hard to keep a straight face. On one occasion, I was getting ready to tell an elderly lady that her grandson had just been killed in a west-side shooting. I tried to soften the blow by saying he had "passed."

The tired old lady looked up at me and asked, "Passed what?"

"Ma'am, I'm sorry. He's dead."

"Praise the Lord!" she exclaimed, rising to her feet. "I knew he never passed no job interview, or passed no GED test, or anything else good."

"I'm sorry, ma'am," I quietly said.

"Why?" she asked. "You kill him?"

"No, ma'am. I didn't kill him," I said, trying hard not to crack a smile.

"Don't you judge me," she said, now pointing her finger at me. "That little piece of shit ain't nothing but a street thug. He's better off dead."

"I understand," I said, and I left the house.

"Thank you, Detective! You have a blessed day!" she yelled from her doorway as I pulled away. I went back to the scene of the shooting.

"How did it go?" my partner asked.

"She took it pretty hard," I said.

"Really?"

"Not really," I said, laughing. He knew. We had all experienced this type of reaction. You just never knew.

Some of the worst ones happen when the family is at the death scene, watching you work from behind the yellow tape. A homicide scene can take some time to process. Obviously, the body is a crucial piece of evidence, which means it must remain there until we are satisfied it can be moved. Sometimes that can occur quickly. Usually, it doesn't. Uniformed officers do their best to keep the crowd behind the tape and the scene secure. But as time goes by, this becomes increasingly more difficult, if not impossible.

"He moved!" someone in the crowd would scream. "Look, look, he ain't dead!"

This would start the domino effect. People screaming, asking why we aren't calling a medic, why does he have to lie there like that? There are good answers to all of these questions. But the crowd, feeding off itself, doesn't want to listen.

"Sir, he didn't move. He has been shot in the head," I would say. Didn't matter.

"Don't tell me," they would say. "Don't tell me."

The longer we took, the more volatile the crowd became. The more volatile the crowd became, the longer it took us to get the work done—work that needed to get done properly if we were going to have a chance of obtaining a successful conviction. They should have focused their anger on the suspect, or the situation itself, but it was easier to lash out at the police. After all, we were there, even though we were trying to do something productive for the deceased.

"If you would help us by telling us what you know, we might find out who killed this young man and prevent it from happening again," I would say. Sometimes that helped, and sometimes those words didn't resonate. Yet we still did our jobs. As dangerous as some of these neighborhoods were, they would have been much worse if we didn't care. And we do care.

Sometimes, later, people from the crowd would apologize. Sometimes they wouldn't. It didn't matter to us if they didn't. We would remind ourselves that we were seeking justice for the victim and the family, not trying to please the crowd.

* * *

Still, in most cases, death notifications led to the expected response: pain and sadness. People who were too stunned to speak or who immediately broke down and wept. This is a difficult duty, but it's important that it's done right, for two reasons. The first is that all victims, regardless of how they lived, have loved ones who still care for them, and they do deserve the courtesy of a professional notification.

The second reason is that their reactions are part of the investigation. Sometimes their reactions alone can lead you to eliminate them as a suspect: their shock and grief is just so obvious that you know they had no prior knowledge. But sometimes a death notification can lead you directly to a suspect.

This happened on a cold December night in 1988, when an officer on patrol saw a car parked along the river levy on the city's west side. Upon closer observation, the officer saw there was a body inside. We received the call shortly after midnight.

"One down by the river," the dispatcher said. "Dress warm."

I wore as many layers of clothing as I could and still move. The temperature was seventeen degrees and I knew it would feel even colder along the river. It did.

For the purposes of this book, the names of the victim and her family members have been changed. The victim, who we'll call Patricia Anderson, was a white woman in her thirties. She appeared to have been shot several times in the chest. Patricia had been sitting in the driver's seat but was slumped over toward the passenger's side.

"Is it her car?" I asked.

"Yeah, the vehicle is registered to her husband, Steven Anderson," an officer replied.

"No casings. Must have used a revolver," my partner said.

"Not much of a scene at first glance," I added.

The scene was predominately contained inside the vehicle. Given the cold, the ground was too hard to preserve any footprints or any tread marks from a suspect vehicle. The vehicle didn't have much either: just the usual sandwich wrappers and soft-drink cans.

"Really nothing of note, except for the body," my partner said. I agreed.

I stayed to help process the scene while other detectives went to notify the deceased's family, which would provide our first substantial clue.

My partner drove to Patricia's suburban home, where she lived with her husband and her two teenage children. Steven was almost robotic, as if he were acting off a script. His wife worked at a fast-food restaurant about twenty minutes from their home. He told my partner that he had reported her missing earlier that night after she had been late coming home from work. He'd also searched all the areas she might frequent but had no success.

"Who reports their wife missing if she's just a little late coming home from work?" my partner would ask me later.

"The murderer," I said.

It was true. Steven had done all the right things—just a little too quickly. He was also fanatical about wanting to know the exact time of death, my partner said.

"What difference could that possibly make?" I asked.

"Probably setting up his alibi," he said.

It made sense. Here was Steven playing, poorly, the part of the grieving husband. He was acting out scene two of the play we were sure he had scripted. Scene one was most definitely the murder, and it turned out he wasn't the only player in that scene. But Steven might have done a better acting job had his accomplice not skipped a few pages in the script.

While our detectives were talking with Steven, Patricia's daughter was on the phone. The call had come from Steven's nephew, one William Campbell. After she hung up the phone, she asked Steven—what did Campbell mean?

Campbell had called to tell Patricia's daughter that he was sorry to hear about her mother's death. That's how she learned about it—from the call. The detectives were talking with Steven, but neither they nor Steven had the chance to tell her.

So how did Campbell know? Names of victims are never released to the media until after family members have been notified. Obviously, Campbell either heard about it from someone involved in the murder, or he was involved himself.

Our detectives quietly noted that but continued talking with Steven—the man most likely to have a motive. They asked how many firearms were in the house. Steven said there weren't any and explained that he was on probation for a robbery conviction and wasn't allowed to have any. We quickly learned that both Anderson and Campbell had extensive criminal histories, most involving elaborate thefts.

Patricia's children told us that there was an old .38-caliber revolver that Steven kept in the house. They took us to retrieve it and discovered it was gone. We did take a partial box of

.38-caliber ammunition that sat in the same cabinet where the gun had been kept. These bullets were not the common .38 Special rounds that dominated the revolver market. Instead, they were an older, less powerful type of round.

Later, the crime lab would note that those rounds had the same class characteristics as the five .38-caliber rounds taken from Patricia's body. It was the best they could do without the gun.

"Not a lot of these old .38s still out there," the lab tech told us.

It has to be more than a coincidence, I thought.

Follow-up interviews always produce interesting insights into the lives of both the deceased and the potential suspect. From Patricia's father, friends, and coworkers, a clear picture of Steven Anderson emerged. Steven beat her regularly. He was forty-seven, much older than Patricia, and insanely jealous of any friends she made. At one point, Steven forced Patricia to take a private polygraph exam to prove she was not having an affair. She passed the exam, but he insisted that she'd beaten the polygraph. It seemed that nothing satisfied him.

Some friends had photos of Patricia's bruises, which Patricia had given them in confidence. "If anything ever happens to me, give these to the police and tell them about Steven," she had told them.

We already knew Steven was a criminal on probation. But we soon learned he was a suspect in several high-profile thefts. His accomplice in those thefts appeared to be his thirty-three-year-old nephew, William Campbell, that same caring relative who offered his condolences to Patricia's daughter before he should have known Patricia was dead.

Patricia's coworkers also reported that she had an almost unnatural preoccupation with being robbed. Patricia was supposed to make the nightly bank deposit. She made sure that everyone knew that she dreaded this task. The staff found this to be very odd.

"No one has ever been robbed making a bank drop," one employee would tell us. But Patricia Anderson had, just not while working at this restaurant. Before, Patricia worked at another local branch of this same restaurant chain. Sure enough, she'd been "robbed" of the nightly deposit. We checked the police report and it was clear that, though she reported the crime, no one believed her version. She gave a vague description of events that made little sense and offered up a generic description of a Black male robber. Eventually, Patricia was transferred to the other location, where she kept talking about how worried she was. Was she a true robbery victim, so traumatized by the experience? Or was something else going on?

"It was too much," one employee told us. "She just kept saying she hoped she wouldn't get robbed over and over for everybody to hear."

The night Patricia died, this employee watched her go to her car. She walked right up to her brand-new, bright red Chevrolet Beretta, got in, and drove off. She did not appear frightened. I thought back to the car. The Beretta was not a big vehicle. She would be able to see if someone was hiding in her car. There was nowhere to hide in a car that small.

"The crazy thing is she drove right out of the lot onto Airway Road," the employee said.

"What's odd about that?" I asked.

"The bank is about three doors down in this same shopping center," he said. "She never even drove near it."

It was starting to make sense. Patricia had driven away with the bank bag and the $1,229 it contained. Undoubtedly, she would have reported being robbed again—as she probably had before. But this time it had ended differently.

One of our key suspects was missing. Though we made repeated attempts to locate William Campbell, we couldn't find him. It seemed he had moved away. Not long after Patricia's death, Steven also moved away. Despite our efforts, the investigation stalled.

We had one ally who was never going to give up: Patricia's father. He kept tabs on Steven, including everywhere he moved. Eventually Steven landed in a small town in Virginia.

Almost two years after Patricia's murder, we started playing long shots. We obtained arrest warrants for Steven Anderson and William Campbell. We had more than enough evidence for a warrant, but our case was probably not strong enough to go to trial. We needed a confession, and we hoped that an arrest would give us the leverage to get one.

I called the Virginia State Police, advised them of the warrants, and gave them the address we'd gotten from Patricia's father. The officer I was talking to promised to give that information to the local police.

"You don't sound real hopeful," I said.

"Some of these places down here are pretty backwoods," he said. "They are very territorial. They won't be happy about you big-city cops arresting their friends."

"Not even for murder?" I asked.

"Not even for murder. If they do get them for you, be careful. Remember, these are probably their friends."

Despite this warning, the local police did locate and arrest Anderson and Campbell for us. Once they had them, my partner and I drove down there. Before we left, we checked out a shotgun and an assault rifle from the department armory, nicknamed the "war room."

"Better safe than sorry," my partner said.

"I'm with you," I agreed.

We told the local authorities we would be in town the following afternoon. Just to be safe, we drove through the night to a motel about an hour outside the town. We fortified our room and got some sleep. The next morning, we finished the drive and found the local police station. A small building, it housed both the town jail and a local gas station.

To our surprise, the police chief was cordial and professional. He had prepared a room for us to interview Anderson and Campbell separately.

"Have they made any statements to anyone here?" I asked.

"No, sir," he said. "Not a word."

"Haven't asked for an attorney, refused to answer questions, anything of the sort?"

"No, not a thing."

Good, I thought. *We have a fighting chance.* We spoke with Anderson first.

"How are you doing, Steven?" I asked. "Remember me?"

Steven was done playing the grieving, concerned husband. "What do you want from me?" he asked.

"That's what I want to talk to you about."

"Fuck off. I ain't saying shit."

It was the response I had expected, but I had to try. "Last chance," I told Anderson. He sat motionless in his cell.

Our next stop was Campbell. We introduced ourselves to him. He wasn't particularly friendly either. "Well, you know who I am," Campbell said.

"Yes, we do, and we would like to talk with you," I added.

"Okay," Campbell said as he nodded.

We're still in this, I thought.

As we took him from his cell and walked him to the interview room, I made some quick observations about Campbell. He wasn't very big, and he didn't appear to be very smart. He came along with us like an obedient dog would. Our theory had been that he was the gunman, doing Anderson's bidding, and I knew then that we were probably right. He certainly was not the brains of this—or probably any—operation.

That interview turned out easier than I had expected. After we read him his rights, Campbell signed the form. From his demeanor, I could tell he had been broken long before we arrived. He was tired of being Anderson's gofer but couldn't see a way out. Apparently, I was that way out. Within a few short moments, we were rolling, as Campbell started detailing all of Anderson's criminal enterprises.

They were mostly thefts. Some were fairly elaborate heists. Some were nickel-and-dime deals. Anderson would use him to do the dirty work. I asked about the first robbery of Patricia. As we had expected, there had been no robbery, at least not of Patricia. She'd just turned the money over to Steven, because she was afraid of him. Like Campbell, she felt trapped. But as Patricia gained knowledge about her husband's illegal activities, Steven began to worry that she knew too much. As his paranoia increased, he feared she had a way to get out from under his control—by going to the police.

Steven decided Patricia needed to be eliminated. He told her they would stage another robbery. Patricia would drive to the west side of Dayton with the bank bag, where Campbell would meet her and take the bag. Patricia would then report the robbery to the police. Steven told Patricia to say she had been carjacked by a Black male.

But Campbell received different instructions, and a .38 revolver, from Steven.

Patricia did just as she was told. She drove to the river levy with the bank bag. Campbell met her there and got in her car. After Patricia handed Campbell the bank bag, Campbell emptied the revolver into her chest. Patricia had been an unwitting accomplice in her own murder.

It was as good a confession as I had ever obtained. We had it, or so we thought.

We drove back to Dayton, where prosecutors were already working on a deal with Campbell and his court-appointed attorney. Even though Campbell was the gunman, Steven Anderson was the real target. Campbell would be offered life in prison with a chance for parole in exchange for his testimony against Anderson. It was all coming together quickly now.

Just as quickly, it all fell apart. A few days later, we were called in to the prosecutor's office.

"Bad news," an attorney said as we were ushered into a conference room.

"Did Campbell back out of the deal?" I asked.

"There is no deal," another attorney said.

One of them handed me a piece of paper. It was an arrest report from the town where Anderson and Campbell had been picked up on our warrants.

"This is dated just a few days ago," I said.

"Keep reading."

It was pretty basic stuff. They got the warrant, they found Anderson and Campbell, they arrested them, they read them their rights—and the suspects had asked for a lawyer.

"What?" I said, almost shouting. "I specifically asked if they had asked for a lawyer or refused to answer questions."

"We know, we know," the attorneys said, almost in unison.

"You did everything by the book," one of them continued. "You did it right."

"But it doesn't matter," the other said. "This report says he asked for a lawyer and that prevents you from questioning him, whether you knew about it or not."

"What about the signed rights waiver I went over with him?" I asked.

"Doesn't matter. Campbell's confession is not admissible in court. And without it, we don't have enough to prosecute either Campbell or Anderson."

They explained to me that the defense attorneys said that the arresting officers never filed a report, so they asked them to do one—and this was what the officers filed. There was no way around it. Campbell and Anderson would be set free. I knew they were right, but it still hurt.

I didn't even think the arrest report had been falsified, as some believed. It was a small town and those officers knew this investigation concerned a homicide. Even though the arresting officers had no reason to read Campbell and Anderson their rights, they probably had, just to be safe. But that didn't matter. Both Campbell and Anderson were released.

This investigation cost me a lot of sleep. I would lie awake at night, running it through my head. Could we have done anything differently? Had we done anything wrong? I knew the answers to both questions were a resounding no. It didn't ease the pain of releasing two murderers though.

Patricia's father understood. He understood better than I did. He knew, probably better than anyone else, how empty I felt. Despite his own grief and disappointment, he tried to comfort me.

"Without that confession, we would have never known for sure what had happened to Patricia that night," he once told me.

He was right. Even though Patricia's killers had walked away, at least we'd solved the mystery of her death. We had won the battle, but the murderers had won the war.

Their victory, however, was temporary. Campbell later died of natural causes, long before he saw old age. Divine intervention? Karma? Perhaps. But no one cheats death, not even those who steal life from others. Several years later, Patricia's father died. I just hope Patricia and her father are at peace.

* * *

It wasn't a death notification, but an investigative inquiry from Florida that led me to a suspect's mother—and the answer to one of our cold cases.

Investigators from Florida had called us after they arrested a former Dayton resident for the murder of a local woman. Their suspect had been making a lot of phone calls to a Dayton residence, and they wanted to know if he had made any admissions to whoever lived there. My partner and I were glad to help. You never know when you're going to have to make that type of call yourself. We didn't expect much, just trying to assist some officers we'd never met.

We found ourselves at a run-down residence located near Wolf Creek. An older lady answered the door and let us in. She was the suspect's mother. We told her that our business concerned her son, and that he was accused of killing a woman.

"Yeah, I knew you'd be coming around eventually," she said. "What's it been now, ten years or so?"

I had no idea what she was talking about, but I didn't let it show. "About that many," I said.

As she spoke, I gradually realized what she was talking about. A decade earlier, on the Fourth of July, the body of a young woman had been found floating in Wolf Creek. She was nude and had clearly been beaten to death. It was my case, and it had never been solved.

The young woman had been a prostitute. We had interviewed her pimp boyfriend and even a few of the customers who the pimp was familiar with, but never developed any solid leads. No suspect had been identified. This was not entirely surprising. A prostitute leads a high-risk lifestyle, putting her in contact with total strangers, some of them looking for something quite strange. Those cases were difficult to solve.

The suspect's mother explained that her son had come home with his face scratched and bleeding. He told her that a prostitute had tried to rip him off and he had beaten her to death with a tire iron. As she fought for her life, she scratched his face, so he cut her fingernails. This, in his mind, would prevent any recovery of DNA. After that, he stripped off her clothes and put her body in the creek.

After we'd taken a statement from the mother, we asked about the Florida phone calls.

"Why, yes, he is in Florida now and doing very well," she replied.

We returned to headquarters and checked the file on the Wolf Creek murder. It included a note that the victim's fingernails had been closely cut.

Next, we called our counterparts in Florida. We explained what had happened and told them we would fly down the next day to attempt an interview.

"He'll be ready," they said.

He was ready. The Florida detectives had placed him in one of their interview rooms. I introduced myself, making sure he understood I was from Dayton and had talked with his mother. For some reason, perhaps because I was from his hometown, he acted like I was a long-lost friend. Strange, but within minutes, I had a confession to my Wolf Creek murder. I left the room elated.

"This is a synopsis of our case," one of the Florida detectives said as he handed me some paperwork. "He seems to like you. Would you take a shot at our case?"

Sure, why not? I thought. And he must have liked me, because he quickly delivered his second murder confession of the day. When I told the Florida detectives, we all high-fived each other, then my partner and I headed back home.

Months later, we flew back to testify in his Florida trial. As I approached the witness stand, the defense attorney asked for a recess. The attorney wanted to bar me from testifying about the suspect's confession.

In most cases, prior crimes are inadmissible in trials. The concern is that jurors will assume the defendant is guilty simply because he has a prior history, instead of focusing on the evidence in the trial. This put the defense attorney in a tough spot.

"He can't say he's a homicide detective from Dayton and, what, he just happened to be in Florida obtaining confessions?" he told the judge. "The jury will have to figure out my client is also a suspect in Ohio if you allow this testimony."

"You can't expect me not to use a confession just because it was obtained by a detective from out of state," the prosecutor countered.

"The statement is legally obtained and admissible," the judge said. "However, the jury is likely to figure out the defendant is a suspect in a murder in Ohio when Detective Burke testifies."

The judge was right. I couldn't and wouldn't say that the defendant was a murder suspect in Dayton, but it wasn't going to be hard to figure out. That could prejudice the jury and cause a mistrial. The judge went into his chambers.

A short time later, the judge made a decision. I would testify just as I had planned, with one exception: if asked where I was employed, I was to respond that I was a Florida homicide detective. Other than that, I was instructed to tell the truth, the whole truth, and nothing but the truth, which I did. The defendant was convicted in Florida, and later pleaded guilty in Dayton.

19.
DEAD WITNESSES

TRIALS ARE LONG and grueling. Doing it once is bad enough. But when a conviction is overturned, that usually means a second trial on the exact same case. It's not unheard of to have three trials on the same case, though that's quite rare. You'd think the "reruns" would get easier, but they don't. Instead, the defense has had a practice run, and knows how to improve its case.

It's a common misconception about the court system: Appeals courts do not offer their own verdicts. Appeals courts generally do not consider whether or not a suspect is guilty or innocent. Instead, they review issues raised by the trial itself—did the defendant get a fair trial? Was there an error, or errors? And were those errors egregious enough to deprive the defendant of a fair trial? If the appeals court finds that there was a reversible error, it will vacate the conviction and send the case back to the trial court to do it again.

In my career, I have testified in hundreds of trials, often as the state's representative, working closely with the prosecutors. At times, there was a second trial. But I have only had to try the same case three times, coincidentally, on three occasions. One occurred while I was in my new job in Warren County and the other two happened when I was in Dayton. The Billy Vance homicide was one of them.

"Multiple shooting on Iola with one dead at the scene," dispatch advised. It was just before midnight on February 3, 1996. We headed out.

Like many of the city's older neighborhoods, Iola Avenue houses are a mixed bag of residents. There are elderly folks who have lived there for decades, keeping up their homes while watching the neighborhood collapse around them. Drug dealers and addicts occupy the other structures, often destabilizing the same blocks where the longtime residents live.

This has to be a dope house, I thought while driving to Iola. Sure enough, as I pulled up, a uniformed officer approached me.

"It's a weed house," he said. "Owner's been executed, and another one is on the way to the hospital."

"Any witnesses?" I asked.

"There were other people here," he said. "We're trying to round them up now."

I examined the scene. There was a large amount of blood on the porch just outside the front door.

"That's the one at the hospital," the uniformed officer said.

I nodded. The front door was open and had no visible damage. "No forced entry," I said.

"That's a good sign," my partner added.

"Yeah, they probably let them in because they knew them," I said.

I walked through the structure, which was a standard-issue dope house. Sparsely furnished, but not in bad shape. There was the mandatory big-screen TV and video game console.

"I think you have to have the TV and games before you're allowed to sell drugs," I said.

"Every dope house is the same," my partner said.

We found the aforementioned Billy Vance in the family room. Vance, also known as "Billy Blast," was a twenty-five-year-old Black male, lying facedown on the floor by a bloody pillow. He'd clearly been shot in the back of the head.

"Looks like he was executed," I said. "This was more than a robbery. This was a statement."

Detectives from the drug squad arrived and provided us with some insight and a possible motive. Vance was known as Billy Blast because of the high-quality marijuana he sold. Word on the street was that his product was the best, and that didn't sit well with the local drug lord. I knew exactly who that was: Keith DeWitt, a notorious hoodlum since he was a teenager, ran the dope trade in this end of town. Years earlier, DeWitt had beaten a triple shooting at another drug house in a different jurisdiction. Two of the victims had died, but the third survived and testified that DeWitt had been one of the robbers. Though two of his henchmen went to prison for those crimes, DeWitt beat the rap through an alibi defense, giving him almost legendary status among the city's criminal elements.

If Vance had been cutting into DeWitt's profits while not cutting him in on the action—as the drug detectives suspected—there was no doubt of what DeWitt was capable of. It made sense.

Vance's brother James Townsend, who lived next door, had arrived at the scene. I went to talk with him. Townsend explained that, during the shootings, one of Vance's acquaintances had fled to Townsend's place. Townsend then ran next door, where he found his brother dying on the floor. When he asked Vance who had shot him, all Vance could do was make a *T* sound.

Next, Townsend went to the porch, where our second victim lay bleeding. James Brown, thirty-three, had been shot in the back. When Townsend asked him who was responsible, Brown could only say, "Turtle and Keith DeWitt's boys." Our drug guys were correct.

We quickly picked up DeWitt, who just happened to be in the area. Not surprisingly, he denied any involvement in the shootings. We didn't have enough evidence to hold him, and he was released shortly thereafter.

It was a few days before we were able to interview James Brown. The bullet had severed his spine, leaving him permanently paralyzed. Prior to that interview, we constructed three photo spreads. We never show a victim or witness a single photo and ask, "Is that him?" It would be too unreliable.

When we build a photo spread, we start with a file photo of our suspect. Every time someone is arrested, a photo is taken and added to our database. Usually, we do have something to work with—since murderers are rarely first-time offenders. We next run a computer search on our suspect's parameters—such as race, sex, height, weight, hair color, and hairstyle. The computer would then print out a full-color sheet with a picture of our suspect and five similar pictures.

When we met with Brown, we showed him three different spreads, one for each suspect: DeWitt, Jeffrey Stevens, also known as "Turtle," and Andre Sinkfield, long known as DeWitt's right-hand man. Brown stated that he knew DeWitt and DeWitt wasn't there that night. But he identified Stevens and Sinkfield as the gunmen, then told us what had happened.

Brown, Vance, and two other men who were friends of Vance were in the house when the phone rang. One of the other men picked it up and had a short conversation. Shortly later, there was a knock on the door. The man who had taken the phone call answered the door and let two men in: Sinkfield and Stevens.

"What's up, Turtle Man?" Vance asked. Stevens announced it was a robbery and ordered everyone to the ground. Three of the four complied and gave up their cash and wallets. The one who didn't was the one who had taken the phone call and let the gunmen in the house. That was obviously not a coincidence.

Next, Sinkfield and Stevens placed pillows on the three victims' heads. Stevens then placed his gun against the pillow on Vance's head. He pulled the trigger. Nothing. The gun had misfired.

Stevens exchanged guns with Sinkfield and fired a bullet into the back of Vance's head. Brown was going to be next. Figuring he had nothing to lose, Brown rushed the gunmen and headed for the door. This gave the other victim time to flee and run next door. Brown made it to the porch before he was shot in the back. The two gunmen then fled into the darkness.

Though we obviously suspected that the fourth "victim" was involved—the man on the inside—we were never able to develop any hard proof to back our suspicions. Therefore, he was never charged. But Stevens and Sinkfield were arrested and charged with several counts, including the aggravated murder of Vance.

The two were tried separately. Stevens went first, was convicted, then sentenced to more years than he could likely live. He did supply one more moment of drama, courtesy of a jail clerical order that allowed him to be released just as he was waiting to be transported to prison. After a frantic search, Stevens was quickly captured again, then transported to prison, where he is quietly marking time. His first parole hearing will be the month of his ninety-ninth birthday.

Though Stevens disappeared quickly after one trial, Sinkfield just kept coming back. Sinkfield was smart, an experienced, lifelong criminal. Facing a murder trial didn't intimidate him. In fact, Sinkfield planned an alibi defense using the same strategy that allowed his best friend, Keith DeWitt, to beat a similar case years earlier.

Though we did not have a confession, we *did* have good evidence. Brown had positively identified Sinkfield and he was a strong witness. We could link Stevens to Sinkfield. And we could link Sinkfield to DeWitt—they'd been friends since childhood and DeWitt's family considered him to be almost kin.

We had a motive. And we had the backing of Vance's family, which meant a lot. Sometimes, a victim's family will purposely distance themselves from the case. But Vance's family wanted justice and they were a strong support team for our witness. Frankly, we needed the help.

That was our weak link: the witnesses. As mentioned in prior chapters, when you're looking at witnesses to a dope-house murder, you don't find a lot of nuns or choirboys. Our witnesses were all drug addicts. That's not surprising, since the acquaintances of our suspects and our victims tended to be drug users, sellers, or both.

We were also not surprised that the man who answered the phone and the door refused to cooperate with us. The other victim, the one who had fled without getting shot, first refused to look at Sinkfield's photo spread, but later testified that Sinkfield was one of the robbers. Sinkfield's alibi witnesses were, of course, uncooperative with us. Stevens had no incentive to help us. We knew it would be an interesting trial.

I was the first witness. During my testimony, the prosecutor asked me if I knew Andre Sinkfield.

"Yes, I do."

"How did you first meet Sinkfield?" the prosecutor asked.

"When he tried to kill three Dayton police officers," I said. That got everyone's attention. And it was true.

My first contact with Andre Sinkfield was in February 1989, as our drug unit was serving a search warrant on a Gard Avenue drug house. After identifying themselves as police officers, they forced entry through the front door. Andre Sinkfield was inside. As the officers entered the house, Sinkfield pointed a handgun at them. The officers fired, striking him in the leg, and Sinkfield surrendered.

The search warrant produced more than narcotics. We found a Desert Eagle .44 Magnum handgun and a Dayton police–issue bulletproof vest. The vest had been shot. Sinkfield would later admit to firing the gun at the vest to see if it would really stop a bullet. We never found out how Sinkfield had obtained one of our vests.

In September 1989, Sinkfield pleaded guilty to drug and weapons violations as well as three counts of attempted manslaughter. He was sentenced to ten years in prison but released after only six. He'd been on the street only a short while before the Vance homicide.

This was not the kind of information that the defense attorney wanted the jury to hear. He objected, which resulted in a brief conference away from the eyes and ears of the jury. Prosecutors argued that those convictions were on the record. The defense argued that it could prejudice the jury against Sinkfield. Ultimately, the judge sustained the objection, told the jury to disregard my statement, and allowed the trial to continue.

One by one, our witnesses took the stand. They were not polished, but their stories made sense. James Brown, now in a wheelchair, was powerful. He had no trouble identifying Sinkfield as one of the gunmen. Likewise, Vance's brother provided strong testimony. Our case was better than we'd thought.

There's an old homicide-squad adage that you never know what a street rogue is going to say on the stand, but this time, our witnesses came through.

The defense tried to implicate another friend of Stevens as the second gunman. They also produced a number of alibi witnesses. Their witnesses, just like ours, were mostly street people. The difference was that they were not credible. The jury convicted Sinkfield and the judge sentenced him to life plus many more years. It was over, or so we thought.

The defense filed an appeal concerning the information about Sinkfield's prior conviction. The appeals court ruled that, while my statement about Sinkfield trying to kill police officers was accurate, it shouldn't be allowed. They ruled that the judge was correct in telling the jury to disregard the statement and allowing the trial to proceed. However, in closing arguments, the prosecutor had mentioned the statement. The same statement the jury had been told to disregard. And that was deemed inappropriate. Andre Sinkfield would get a second trial.

Retrials are always problematic. We would have to seek out our witnesses again and keep tabs on them. We would need to know where we could find them when it was their turn to testify again. We would need to review hundreds of pages of testimony from the first trial to refresh our memory and prevent any discrepancies. It was a lot of work.

Sadly, prior to the second trial, my partner on this case passed away. He had retired from DPD and taken a position as a coroner's investigator. Only a few months into this new phase, he suffered a brain aneurysm and died. This led to some necessary theater at the second trial.

Witness testimony is, obviously, part of the trial record. Witnesses that are re-called during a retrial can be questioned about prior testimony if it conflicts with what they are currently saying. But they must testify again. However, if a witness dies, as my partner did, we are allowed to reenact the testimony in any subsequent trial, using the transcripts—though nothing can deviate from that script.

For the second trial, my current partner took the witness stand. The judge identified him and advised the jury that he would be playing the role of my deceased partner. The prosecutor and defense attorney, likewise, would read their parts from the transcript of the previous trial. It all went smoothly. Sinkfield's prior convictions went unmentioned, and the jury convicted him. Again, we thought it was over. Again, we were wrong.

The appeals court, once again, sent the case back, this time on a different issue. In the second trial, the defense had wanted to call a witness, but the judge excluded him. The witness would supposedly have rebutted our rebuttal witness. The judge had allowed defense witnesses to rebut our testimony. And we were given the opportunity to rebut their rebuttal. The judge believed enough was enough and that the jury had sufficient information to make an informed decision about whom to believe. The appeals court found that ruling to be improper.

There would be a third trial. It became a running joke. "Every Christmas we retry Andre Sinkfield," my partner would say. Unfortunately, he was right. The third trial, however, would be quite different from the prior two.

We started locating our witnesses, and to our surprise, we found a lot of them in cemeteries. It had only been two years since the first trial, but dope addicts have a shortened life expectancy. James Brown was still alive and well, as was Vance's brother. Most of our other witnesses, however, were dead. Some had become homicide victims themselves. Others had died accidently, generally from overdoses. There was no evidence that anyone from Sinkfield's or Stevens's family had harmed them. In fact, the defendants would have been better off with live witnesses, who can change their stories. Dead witnesses cannot.

As we entered the third trial, I was confident. After all, I knew what most of our witnesses were going to say. It was in the transcripts. Sgt. Gary White, our supervisor and my partner on this case, would testify several times as several people, portraying numerous dead witnesses. Then he portrayed my partner who had died. Then he testified one more time.

"In a rare occurrence, Sergeant White will be testifying as himself," the judge said.

In the end, the third time was smoother.

"I'm beginning to like dead witnesses," I told Sergeant White. "At least there aren't any surprises."

"I'm just glad it's over," he replied.

"Amen," I added.

And it was over, again. That third jury convicted Sinkfield. Three times, a jury of twelve had convicted Sinkfield. Think about that: thirty-six people had found him guilty.

There were more appeals concerning the credibility of prosecution witnesses, but Sinkfield's run was over. In November 2001, almost six years after the slaying of Billy Blast, the appeals court ruled to uphold Sinkfield's third (and final) conviction.

"We find that there was some testimony that was so incredible that it defied belief," the judges wrote. "Unfortunately, much of the incredible testimony was elicited from defense witnesses."

Sinkfield will remain in Ohio prisons for many more decades. Our dead witnesses saved the day. We won.

20.
THEY ARE DAMN GOOD

THE BONDS BETWEEN police officers are strong. Call it a brotherhood, or a sisterhood, or a personhood, whatever you like: police officers view each other as family, even if they don't know one another. This is true even if they come from other parts of the United States. In September 2000, we would learn that those bonds cross national borders, even oceans.

Back in the 1990s, Bosnia was at war. I knew little about Bosnia, other than it had been part of Yugoslavia. With the end of the communist domination of Eastern Europe, the Balkans seemed to have blown up. Ancient ethnic conflicts surfaced as Yugoslavia collapsed. Like most Americans, I barely understood anything about the situation—including who the players were. I didn't know a Serb from a Croat from a Bosnian. But the war ended in—you guessed it—good old Dayton, Ohio.

One of region's largest employers is Wright-Patterson Air Force Base. Home of the Air Force Materiel Command, the base sits just outside of Dayton's city limits. The National Museum of the United States Air Force draws in hundreds of thousands of visitors annually. The base also houses the Hope Hotel, where the negotiations that ended the Bosnian conflict took place. The resulting agreement was called the Dayton Peace Accord.

This led to other partnerships and a permanent relationship between Dayton and that southeastern European country we knew so little about. That September, our interim police chief called my partner and me into his office and told us that police officials from Bosnia and Herzegovina—that's the country's full name—wanted to send two of their top death investigators to visit.

"Good," I said. "We can use the help."

"No, no, no," the chief laughed. "They want to live with you guys and learn from you for several weeks."

"They could probably show us a thing or two," my partner said. I nodded in agreement. God only knows what they'd seen during the war.

"Well?" the chief asked.

My partner and I looked at each other and nodded. "We're in," my partner said.

"I figured you would be," the chief said, grinning. "They'll be arriving at Dayton International Airport in a few hours."

"What if we had said no?" I asked. The chief broke into laughter.

"Please," he said. "I know you two too well."

We met our new Bosnian partners, Enis and Samir, at the airport. We were pleased to find they could speak English, as neither of us knew a word of any other language. Enis and Samir were not completely fluent, but they were moderately conversational, and we would adapt to them quickly. We introduced ourselves and split up, each of us taking a new Bosnian friend home. I took Enis. My partner took Samir.

I found that my new partner was a veteran detective. He and Samir were assigned to the investigation of war crimes, including thousands of deaths. As we got to know each other that first night, Enis spoke of the atrocities. He described mass graves holding hundreds of decomposing bodies. It was hard to imagine. We talked long into the night, mostly about our jobs, quickly finding there were many more similarities than differences. We got a few hours of sleep, then headed in for our first day at work together.

We had been asked to assist the city of Xenia, which is about twenty minutes east of Dayton. The seat of Greene County, Xenia has had an unfortunate history of tornadoes. A category F5 twister—with winds exceeding 260 miles per hour—devastated the town in 1974, killing more than 30 and leaving thousands homeless. In 1989, an F2 hit, injuring several people, but no one was killed. In all, Xenia has been struck by twenty tornados since 1884.

The latest tornado hit right before our Bosnian friends arrived. Its trail of destruction killed one and injured more than one hundred. As we pulled into the city's most devastated area, Enis was visibly amazed.

"A bomb?" he asked.

"Wind," I said. "Strong wind."

"What do you mean, 'wind'?"

I did my best to explain what a tornado was and how it did this much damage. Enis and Samir were amazed. They explained how Bosnia is surrounded by mountains and sits in a bowl.

"We have unexploded land mines," Enis said. "We have no wind."

We all laughed. *Maybe we could show these guys a thing or two*, I thought. We helped out at the scene, mostly just coordinating with all the agencies involved, and headed home.

During the three weeks Enis and Samir stayed with us, we had five homicide callouts. I was amazed at how similar our investigative techniques were. Enis would look at the scene for the same clues I was looking for as Samir pondered questions to ask witnesses.

"We could use you guys full-time," my partner said.

"We would love to stay, but Bosnia is our home," Enis said.

I also wished they could stay. I liked them both, but Enis and I had more in common. It was as if I'd met the Bosnian version of myself. I would miss him when he left.

Of those five callouts, one stood out. We would always remember it, and so would Enis and Samir, in part for the degree of slaughter that stunned even our war-experienced friends.

We got the call on September 16, 2000: multiple deaths in the city's Pheasant Hill neighborhood. This was an unusual location. Pheasant Hill is a nicer area, with newly built subdivisions, just south of neighboring Huber Heights. It was called "Cop Land" because many city police officers lived there. At the time, I did. Back then, the city required its employees to live in the city limits. Dayton public schools had many of the challenges familiar to poorer urban districts. If you didn't want to send your children to the public schools, your choices were to homeschool or to send them to a private school.

Some tried to get around the rule by secretly living outside the city. Dayton would—and did—hire private detectives to trail employees suspected of living outside the city's borders. If you were caught, you could be fired.

Pheasant Hill was different, a historical fluke of governmental boundaries. It was part of Dayton, but not part of the city's school district. Instead, children who lived there went to Huber Heights schools. Nearly every cop with kids eventually moved to Cop Land.

I looked at Enis. "We could walk to this one," I said. "It's just a few blocks away."

Our scene was in a row of condominiums. Yellow tape was everywhere. I approached the first officer I saw. He pointed out the condo where the bloodshed had occurred.

"How many dead?" I asked.

"Two inside and a little girl taken to the hospital who doesn't look good," he said. "And two small children abducted."

"It would seem we are about to get busy," Enis said.

"It looks that way, my friend, and not in a good way," I said.

Inside the condo, we met another officer. He explained that two dead were in the basement. The other victim, a thirteen-year-old girl, had been found in an upstairs bedroom. There was plenty of blood everywhere, he warned us. We decided to start in the basement.

We climbed down the staircase and peered around a corner. There, we saw the body of a white woman, identified as Martha Madewell. A few weeks shy of her thirty-eighth birthday, Martha lived there with her family. She was on her back, spread-eagle and partially clothed. The officer was right—there was blood all around her body.

"She looks like she's been hit with an ax," another detective said—with good reason, because it would turn out she had been.

Another detective showed me a digital photo of a twelve-pound maul. (A maul is a heavy ax.)

"Where is this from?" I asked.

"Upstairs behind the bathroom door," he said.

We were all in agreement. This was probably our weapon. Next, we looked at Madewell, who had several wounds in the back of her head. Those wounds appeared to match a heavy blunt instrument like the maul. We also noted how her body had been positioned in a blatantly sexual pose.

"She didn't just end up on the floor like this," I said.

"The killer put her here," Enis said. "Is it possible he had sex with her?"

"Anything is possible," I said. "We'll know soon enough." But I suspected Ennis was right.

The next victim was on a couch, just a short distance from Madewell. Nathan Marshall, forty, did not live there. We would later learn that he had been married to Madewell in the past. Apparently, they'd recently gotten back together. Marshall had been struck several times in the face and chest. Again, the maul appeared to be the likely weapon.

"He split his face in two," I said.

"What about the blood?" Enis asked. I had been teaching him about blood-spatter interpretation.

"All of the blood that shows movement is isolated to the couch area, where the male victim is," I said. "When blood leaves the body under force, it shows movement. You can see how the blood is moving upward from the male victim."

"What about the blood that is higher and over to the right?" Enis asked.

"Castoff," I said, adding that, as the maul struck the victims, it picked up blood. When the killer raised the maul to strike again, some of that blood is cast off onto the wall.

"Look at what isn't in the pattern," I told Enis. "There is an area here on the wall just above our male victim that has no blood. We call that a 'void' or 'absence' in the pattern."

"Ah, that's where she was when she was killed," Enis said.

"Exactly."

Reading the blood, we theorized that Madewell had been lying by the victim on the couch when she was attacked. She had probably been on her side, with her face down. The killer probably stood beside the couch, but near their feet. The victims' wounds fit our theory. She had been hacked in the back of the head and he had been hit in the front. After the attack, the killer rolled her off the couch and positioned her on the floor.

The pattern was different in the girl's room. There was blood spatter and castoff on the wall near her bed.

"This blood is in different areas, and there are well-defined areas all along the wall." I showed Enis. "What do you think?"

"They are moving," Enis said.

"Exactly. She put up a fight."

It appeared that Madewell and Marshall had been attacked first, as they slept. Next, the killer came upstairs. But something had woken up Jesica Young, Madewell's daughter. Maybe it was the earlier commotion. But Jesica had fought hard for her life.

At that point, another detective called me from the hospital, where Jessica was still fighting for her life.

"ER doctor thinks she may have been shot in the head with a shotgun," he said.

"What? No way."

"That's what they're saying."

That couldn't be. An accurate shotgun blast to the back of the head would have killed her immediately. If she'd been grazed, the pellets would have caused damage to parts of the room. It seemed more likely that she'd been hit with the maul, causing massive injuries that even experienced doctors couldn't recognize.

"If she's been shot with a shotgun, we should see it here on the wall, and we don't," I said. "They have to be wrong."

Minutes later, the detective called me back. "Disregard," he said. "No shotgun blast."

"What happened?" I asked.

"They looked at the X-ray of her head and thought they saw shotgun pellets," he said. "Doyle, she has braces. She was hit so many times with that maul that it broke the metal braces into tiny pieces. On the X-ray it looked like shotgun pellets."

"Damn."

"There is no way she is going to make it," he said softly.

"I know," I said. Sure enough, Jesica died a few days later.

Jesica had been one of Madewell's four children, all of whom had lived in the house. Another one of the children was her seventeen-year-old brother. One of my fellow detectives was interviewing him. The boy told us that he'd been awakened by thumping noises. As he wandered from his bedroom into the hallway, he found his mother's former husband, fifty-two-year-old Larry Gapen. Jesica's brother told us that Gapen gave no explanation as to why he was there. Gapen took Martha's two youngest children, an eight-year-old girl and a seven-year-old boy, with him. The boy then found the bodies of his parents, as well as his dying sister.

"He kills three and leaves three alive," I said when we were away from the boy.

"The young children are hostages, insurance of a sort," Enis said.

"Yeah, I can see that. But why not kill this kid?" I asked.

"He just killed three people with a heavy ax," Enis said.

"I see where you're going."

"He had already put the ax behind the bathroom door when he ran into the boy here," Enis continued.

"And he was too exhausted to fight him," I said.

"And then he ran," Enis said.

"Hey, I thought we were training you guys," I joked.

"You are, you are," Enis said, laughing.

A broadcast was made for Gapen's arrest. It included descriptions of Gapen and his car, plus information about his two young hostages. While every cop in the city was looking for Gapen, I was researching his background. It was very telling.

Larry Gapen and Martha Madewell had been married for seven years. Gapen brought two children to the marriage. Martha brought four. Ultimately, things didn't work out. Larry had moved out of the house the prior year and the two signed a separation agreement in June. Their divorce had been finalized just two days before the attack.

I delved further and found more troubling information. In July, Gapen had been indicted for the abduction of Madewell, stemming from an incident in which he'd tied her up to force her to talk with him. The charge was still pending, and Gapen had been placed on electronic home detention. He'd been fitted with an electronic ankle bracelet, which acted as a sort of invisible fence for humans. If he cut off the bracelet or left his house, an alarm indicator would notify authorities.

"Are we sure this guy isn't home?" I asked.

"First place we looked," another detective said.

I called the home-detention office. They checked Gapen's activity record, but it seemed like they were taking a long time for what should be a routine inquiry.

"Well, what do you have?" I asked impatiently.

The phone was dead silent. "What is it?" I asked again.

The voice on the other end of the phone finally spoke. "There was a glitch in the system," the man said. "Gapen hasn't been home for some time. The alert system wasn't triggered."

"At least we know when he left his house," I told Enis.

"Too much electronics," Enis said. "Better to build more jails."

"I couldn't agree more," I said.

At that point, another detective entered the office and informed us that police had found Gapen and the two younger children at a donut shop north of Dayton. The children had been unharmed, Gapen was in custody, and uniformed officers were bringing him to us.

When we entered the interview room, we found a short, balding, nondescript man waiting for us. Nothing about Larry Gapen stood out. He sat there defiantly, as if nothing had happened. One of my partners read him his rights. Gapen said he understood. But he refused to talk with us, then uttered the magic phrase: "I have a lawyer."

We knew what that meant. The interview was over. Or was it? As we were leaving the room, Gapen asked us about the little children he had abducted. He wanted to know if they were okay. Yes, that's strange. But in doing this, Gapen had reinitiated contact with us. We were back in. My partner asked Gapen if there was something we needed to know. Quickly, just seconds after refusing to talk with us, Gapen launched into a full confession.

He'd entered the condo through an unlocked back door, then found Madewell and Marshall, her new boyfriend, asleep on the basement couch. He beat them both to death with the heavy maul he had brought with him. As he'd caught them off guard, there'd been no struggle, no noise. Those first two attacks went unnoticed by the four children sleeping in other parts of the house.

Gapen wasn't done with his ex-wife though. Just as Enis had anticipated, Gapen raped Madewell's dead body. When he was finished, he took Madewell's purse and the maul and went upstairs. The first person he found was Jesica, who was awake. He beat her repeatedly with the maul, then he left her bedroom.

Gapen placed the maul behind the bathroom door, then retrieved the two younger children. That was when the seventeen-year-old boy confronted him. Tired, and now unarmed, Gapen turned and fled the condo with the younger children. It was exactly as Enis and I had surmised.

"That's as good as I have ever seen," Enis said after we left the interview room. He was right. The confession was powerful. It would stand up to any challenges in court.

We were still finishing up work on this case when Enis and Samir returned to Bosnia. We promised to keep them informed on the cases they'd assisted on, particularly the Gapen case.

We entered Gapen's trial with a strong case. We had his confession. Jesica's brother had identified Gapen as being in the condo at the time of the slayings. Madewell's purse was found inside Gapen's car. The electronic home-detention log showed that Gapen left his house just before the attacks. Plus, Gapen's DNA had been found on Martha's body.

This was a death penalty case, with Gapen facing multiple aggravated murder counts. The jury easily convicted him of the crimes, but as always with a death penalty case, there is a second phase: the decision of life in prison or death. On that issue, the jury deliberated for three days. Before they came back, I called Enis in Bosnia and put him on speaker.

"Three days," I said. "Feels more like three years."

"They will vote for him to die," Enis reassured us by phone.

"At least for Jesica," one of my partners added.

I knew what he meant. He wasn't trivializing the other murders. But Madewell and Marshall had been caught unaware. They may have never known they were under attack. Jesica was a thirteen-year-old girl, fully conscious as she fought for her life against her former stepfather. She'd suffered horribly.

"If he is not worthy of your death penalty, then no one is," Enis said.

We were still talking with Enis when the bailiff called us. The jury had reached a decision. We returned to the courtroom.

The bailiff read the verdicts. It was painful listening. For each of the aggravated murder counts relating to Madewell and Marshall, the sentence would be life with no parole. For the counts relating to Jesica Young, the sentence would also be life with no parole—except for one.

"'In the sole remaining count, the aggravated murder of Jesica Young with prior calculation and design, we the jury recommend death,'" the bailiff read.

It was hard not to smile. Gapen was sentenced to die. He remains on death row today.

I called Enis.

"We got him, brother," I said. "They gave him the death penalty on one of Jessica's counts."

"As they should," Enis said.

"This was your case too."

"I am proud to have been part of your team."

"We were honored to have you," I replied. In my mind I could see Enis on the other end of the line smiling. I hoped Jesica was smiling as well.

In the short time we had with our Bosnian brothers, we'd worked some pretty horrific cases together. We had bonded and remain friends today. Though we haven't seen each other, we remain in contact.

"You must come to Bosnia and let me be your host," Enis would say.

"That whole land-mine thing scares me," I would reply.

I have yet to travel to Bosnia, though the offer is sincere and still stands. Perhaps I will someday.

Prior to returning home, Enis and Samir were interviewed by the Dayton news media. Enis was asked to describe his thoughts about the homicide squad.

"They are damn good," Enis said.

So are you, my friend.

21.
FROM THE DEVIL IN HELL

BACK IN THE 1960s, my grandmother lived on Green Street near downtown Dayton. The neighborhood, now known as the Oregon District, was an older one, with homes that date back to the 1820s. Her house, a run-down half of a double, was damp and musty. The roof leaked and the floors were creaky. Eventually, my grandmother moved in with us and sold her interest in the home for a few thousand dollars.

She wouldn't recognize the old neighborhood, which was placed on the National Register of Historic Places in 1974. Those old houses, so shoddy back then, have been restored and now command top dollar. The district's main commercial artery is the portion of East Fifth Street that runs from the edge of downtown to Wayne Avenue. That, too, has changed. The intersection of Fifth and Wayne used to be called "Filth and Wine." Now that four-block section is teeming with trendy shops, art galleries, cozy offices, and multiple bars. We always referred to it as a poor-man's Bourbon Street, and that remains a fair assessment.

In 1994, one of those bars was Sloopy's, which sat at the corner of Fifth and Wayne. It was a large bar with a dance floor, covering the first floor of the corner building. Apartments were for lease in the upper floors.

The Oregon District shops and bars do a steady business. On Halloween, the district is sealed off from vehicular traffic and thousands of people party in the street. For the bars, it is the year's busiest and most profitable night. St. Patrick's Day is a close second. The mornings after those holidays tend to be very quiet.

March 19, 1994, was no exception. Sloopy's had two good nights. March 17 was a Thursday, so the festivities continued into Friday. That Saturday morning, two men were at the bar, cleaning up. One was Frank Ferraro, who was part owner of the bar. The other was Robert Knapke, a casual laborer who would float across the district's bars, doing odd jobs as needed. The bar was, at that time, closed.

Our attention was elsewhere. The Ku Klux Klan had obtained a permit to hold a rally at the city's Courthouse Square, just a few blocks from Oregon. Anticipating trouble, city workers had erected tall chain-link fences around the square. Metal detectors were in place, and our special-weapons-and-tactics team was on rooftops, surveying the scene below. Hundreds of uniformed officers were present for crowd control. Most detectives and off-duty officers had been mobilized for this event. My partner and I had been given a pass on this one. You had to leave someone available in case there was a homicide. Good thing they did.

When Ferraro didn't return home and didn't answer the bar's phone, his wife became concerned. Late afternoon, she drove down to the bar and saw his truck parked out front. The bar's side door, leading into the office area, sat open. Sensing that wasn't right, she called the police. Officers arrived to find the bodies of both men inside. They had been beaten to death.

When dispatch called, I wasn't surprised. "Someone get killed at the KKK rally?" I asked.

"No, only a handful of spectators showed up," the dispatcher said. "It'll be over soon. You've got a bigger problem, though."

"Hit me."

"Two workers found inside Sloopy's beaten to death."

"That's a big place," I said. "Who all do you have coming?"

"Right now, just you and your partner. I'll find you an E-crew. Good luck."

"No problem," I said, already thinking of how complex that scene would be.

Uniformed crews had roped off the area around the building. "Just about everything is inside," one told me.

As expected, the scene was immense. Our victims were in two separate areas of the business. There were also a number of potential items of evidence that we'd have to look at, scattered through the bar. Though it was daunting, I wasn't too concerned. My partner was fairly new to homicide, but he was a veteran detective and highly skilled. We had worked together on the robbery squad and I trusted him.

"Looks like it's just us," he said.

"Yeah, this is a big one for just two of us," I said. "But we'll be fine."

As my partner nodded in agreement, my phone rang. "It's dispatch," I said. "Must be an update on our E-crew's ETA."

My partner watched as I talked on the phone. He couldn't hear the dispatcher, obviously, but he could hear me as I said, "You have got to be kidding me."

"No E-crew?" he asked when I hung up.

"No, there's an E-crew en route to both locations."

"What do you mean, 'both locations'?"

"Double homicide on Germantown Street at the mini-mart," I said. "Two employees shot in an apparent robbery."

Thankfully, the Klan rally was breaking up. Dispatch would soon be sending more help to each location. But for now, we were on our own. Two detectives, two scenes, four bodies.

"Well, we're just getting started here," my partner said. "Which one do you want?"

"I'll defer to you. I don't care either way."

"Well, the carryout on Germantown has got to be a hell of a lot smaller scene than this one," he said, smiling. "I'll take the carryout."

"I've always hated you," I said, returning the smile.

"Have a blessed day," he said as he left for Germantown Street. I started my scene investigation. The E-crew tech arrived soon after.

I found Knapke lying facedown on the kitchen floor. He'd been struck several times in the back of the head with a blunt instrument. It looked like he had been walking along normally when he was attacked.

"He was taken by surprise," I said.

"He had to be comfortable with the suspect in order to casually walk in front of him," my E-crew tech said.

"I agree, but look how he's lying," I said.

"He went straight down."

"Exactly. No signs of a struggle," I said.

"And there isn't any sign of forced entry on the door."

"He knew his killer," I said.

Knapke's body was closer to the open door than Ferraro, whose body I found in a restroom. Knapke probably unwittingly opened the door for his killer. Maybe someone else was coming in to help with cleanup? Or maybe our killer knew this would be a good day to rob a bar of this size—just after the second busiest day of the year. There was also the added distraction of the KKK rally. News reports made it clear that the rally was going to be a big concern for the police department. Between the rally, which drew onlookers, and the post-holiday quiet, there was almost no one in the Oregon District that morning.

We knew this wasn't random. The killer had to get into the bar. He counted on being allowed in, meaning he knew the operation and he probably knew at least one of the victims. My first thoughts were that the suspect would be a current or former employee. As we continued the investigation, that theory would ultimately change.

Frank Ferraro was also facedown on the floor, with multiple wounds in the back of the head. But there was a difference. I was certain Knapke had been caught off guard. Not Ferraro. He had been ordered to his final resting place, which was in a bathroom in a different part of the bar. He was far away from Knapke or the open door. A laundry bag covered the back of his head, and he lay upon a jacket, which had been spread across the floor by one of the stalls. Not where you're going to voluntarily lie down.

"Looks like he ordered this one in here and forced him to lie on the floor," I said.

While examining the restroom, we found something behind the toilet tank closest to Ferraro. It was Ferraro's wallet.

"Makes sense," I told the E-crew tech. "Our killer surprises him, tells him he won't hurt him if he does what he says."

"Lets him take off his jacket and spread it on the floor to lie on," the tech said.

"He expected to live. That's why he hid his wallet."

One victim caught by surprise. Another who had time to consider what was happening, perhaps to experience a moment of hope. I don't know which is worse.

"And he had time to hide it while our killer went in the corner here to get the laundry bag," the tech said.

Continuing through the bar, we found a cigarette machine that had been pried open. The money had been removed.

"How much money could be in there?" I asked.

"Clearly, you don't smoke. It's big money."

"That took some time," I said. "He must have known no one else would be coming in for a while."

In the office area, we found our murder weapon: a bloody hammer had been tossed under a desk. Later, a forensic pathologist would determine that this hammer was consistent with the wounds on the bodies.

An officer notified me that the bar manager had just arrived, so I went to talk with him. To protect the scene's integrity, we would not allow him to enter the building, but I did bring him several photos taken inside. I wanted to know how far along in their cleanup duties our two victims had gotten, to help assist us in determining the time of death.

I showed him photos of stools carefully placed on the bar, mop buckets in hallways, and the office. The manager took it all in. Ferraro's wife had already told us the two men had started cleanup at about 5 a.m.

"Since they started at five, how far along are they?" I asked.

"Probably five or six hours," he said. That put us at 10 a.m. or 11 a.m. Late morning.

Then the manager gave us an unexpected and much-needed bonus, handing me back the office photo.

"Our safe is gone," he said, pointing to an empty spot on the floor. "It sits right here." He described it as a midsized gray fire safe.

"Is it too heavy for one man to carry?" I asked.

"No, but it would be easier to use one of our dollies," he said.

"How many dollies do you have?"

"Three. They are all the same. Just your standard aluminum two-wheeled dollies."

I knew what he meant. I had walked through the scene several times and I remembered seeing the dollies. I just couldn't remember how many. I went back inside and told the tech about the missing safe. As he concentrated on that area, I went to count dollies. I found two, then returned outside to the manager.

I needed one more thing: a list of current and former employees. At least one victim knew the killer well enough to let him in. The killer knew there would only be two people there and that after he killed them, no one else would be coming for some time. He knew he had plenty of time to pry open the cigarette machine. He knew there was a safe in the office and he knew he would have the use of a dolly. *It had to be an employee*, I thought. *We could narrow this down quickly with the list of employees.*

Though the manager agreed to get me that list, he quickly relieved me of my assumption. Our suspect pool would be much vaster than just those on the Sloopy's payroll, he said. The reason was that the Oregon bar owners helped one another due to a mutual threat: suburban bars, where parking was plentiful and people felt safer.

"To keep customers in the Oregon, we all work together," he said. "Even though we're competing against each other, it's better for everyone if we keep customers happy, and keep them here. They may be at my bar tonight and someone else's tomorrow, but as long as they stay here in the Oregon, we have a chance."

Perhaps you were running out of change, or a certain brand of beer. The unwritten Oregon code dictated that another bar helped you out. Because of this alliance, every bar in the district had employees who had been to Sloopy's, including some who had been in the office.

"If another bar needed change, we would take them right to the safe," he said. "And they would do the same for us."

I thanked him and sent him home. I was sure my theory was still valid, though it included more potential suspects now.

The murders at Sloopy's and the Germantown carryout were hot news topics. We had two double homicides in one day, plus a KKK rally. But we knew early on that none of these events were related. The carryout suspects were three young men—whom we did eventually identify and arrest—armed with handguns. They didn't fit the Sloopy's scene. Our suspect there knew his victims and his target location. He was cold and calculating. The carryout suspects were neither.

My case stayed in the news for days, with items in every newscast. That creates a lot of pressure, but it can also be helpful. It keeps the public interested, and the calls poured in. It seemed as if everyone wanted this one solved. Of particular interest was that one name kept coming in on the tip line: Edmund E. Emerick III, a twenty-nine-year-old white male.

Most of the Emerick tips were vague. He had worked at an Oregon District bar, close to Sloopy's. He needed money. He had pried open a cigarette machine in the past. He had broken into a safe before. He knew the location of the Sloopy's safe because he'd been in the office before. Tipsters also described Emerick as a very physically abusive person.

These were all good clues, none of which would solve the case by themselves, but which pointed in what seemed to be a correct direction. The closer I looked, the more intriguing Emerick appeared.

The bar he worked at had also employed Knapke, so Knapke probably would have known him. He fit our profile almost completely. But Emerick was not the only person to match the profile. We needed harder evidence.

As part of the investigation, we did a neighborhood canvass of the apartments above Sloopy's, asking residents what they recalled and where they were on the day of the murders. Most weren't even home at the time. None of the residents remembered anything unusual. But we found a visitor who did.

"Do you live here, ma'am?" I asked a woman who was outside the building.

"No, just visiting a friend," she said. But when I asked her about the day in question, she said something had happened around 11 a.m. that had scared her. At the time, she was helping her friend move in to one of the apartments. They were using the entrance in the back of the building. The district was so deserted, it felt eerie.

"Then as I turned around, he was right there," she said.

"Who?" I asked.

"This white guy," she said. "He looked just as surprised to see me. He must have come out of Sloopy's. There was nowhere else he could have been."

"Would you be able to recognize this man again?"

"Yes, he was right in front of me."

I showed her a photo spread. "That's him right there," she said, pointing at a photo of Edmund Emerick.

Uniformed officers found our next witness, a homeless man named Ray Miracle, who had been panhandling in Oregon on March 19. Miracle was interesting. Homeless by choice—believe it or not—he was very intelligent. Tired of what he considered the straight life, he'd given up a traditional lifestyle because he wanted to. He told them he'd seen a man he knew only as "Eddie" outside the bar the morning of the murders.

"Hardly anybody out that day in the Oregon," Miracle said. "I saw Eddie at Sloopy's and hit him up for some money. Surprisingly, he gave me a twenty-dollar bill and hurried off. He usually won't give you shit."

"How do you know Eddie?" I asked.

"He used to run one of the bars."

I showed Miracle a photo spread. He pointed at Emerick's photo and said, "That's him. That's Eddie."

The investigative work continued for what seemed like forever. On April 3, officers arrested Emerick—not for the murders, but for some outstanding traffic warrants. This gave us the chance to talk to him, on our terms.

I met Emerick for the first time that day. He was smart. You could tell. He was sizing me up the same way I was sizing him up. My partner and I read him his rights, and he said he understood. Then I asked him about the day of the murders. An innocent man would be shocked. But Emerick was obviously ready for that question—too ready.

Though March 19 had been over two weeks earlier, Emerick knew his every movement for that day, including the times. That isn't natural. I couldn't tell you in that kind of detail what I did two days ago, let alone two weeks ago. This was a prepared alibi. He told us that he'd visited his father around 11 a.m. From there, he went to a convenience store on the city's south side. Next, he visited a Laundromat. It was all too perfect.

Emerick must have known, almost immediately, that his prepared alibi had hurt him. Once he was back in his cell, he called out to the jailers and told them we had beaten him. He showed them a black eye, which we certainly did not give him.

"This guy must have punched himself," I told my partner.

"Means he's worried about what he told us."

We were already checking out the alibi, stopping first to visit Emerick's father. He confirmed that his son had been there that day but was unsure of the time. That didn't help us, but it didn't help Emerick, either.

Next stop was the carryout, which was more interesting. The clerk on duty had also worked the day of the murders. I didn't expect him to remember anything. Why would he? They sold a lot of beer there. But he did remember the transaction. The clerk said that a man matching Emerick's description had bought a six-pack of beer.

"Why do you remember that?" I asked.

"Because he told me to," the clerk said. "He bought the six-pack, looked right at me, and told me to make sure I remembered what he looked like, what time it was, and that he was here."

"Yeah, that's a little unusual," I said. "Do you know this guy?"

"Nope."

"Would you recognize him if you saw him again?"

"Yeah, sure."

I presented him the photo spread. "That's him right there," he said, pointing to Emerick.

The Laundromat was in the same part of town. Eventually, we found the clerk who had been working on March 19. What she told us was even better than what we had learned at the carryout.

She clearly remembered the transaction with Emerick. She even had his name on the log. She didn't know him, but she easily identified him from the photo spread.

"I remember it because he was picking up an enormous amount of laundry, but he parked a long way away," she said. "He had so much laundry he could barely fit it in his car. In fact, he had to leave his two-wheel dolly here."

"What?" I asked.

"He had a dolly in his car he had to leave behind in order to fit his laundry in the car."

Emerick had left the dolly behind. Unfortunately, it was gone now, but we did have the laundry clerk's testimony. And we were closer to proving Emerick was our killer. Someone had been a little too clever with his prepared alibi.

Several days later, a local news reporter called me. "I've got a letter you need to see," he said. "It's got a weird return address."

"What is it?"

"It's from 'the Devil, in Hell.'"

When I examined the letter, I saw that it was carefully worded and handwritten. The writer claimed to be a Black man upset about the KKK rally and said he had killed the two men at Sloopy's in retaliation.

The reporter and I both knew the letter was not from "the Devil." Nor was it from a Black man. But we both felt it was from the murderer. I was certain Emerick had sent it.

"Damn, this guy never stops," I said.

It was true. This letter was clearly meant to send us in the wrong direction. It didn't. I took the letter and tagged it as evidence, then sent it to the FBI for a handwriting analysis.

The case was slow, but we had momentum on our side. A week later, we learned that a safe was found near a hardware store not far from the Laundromat and carryout. Sure enough, it was the missing Sloopy's safe.

"Nothing is ever a coincidence," I said.

"I agree," my partner said.

Analysts at the crime lab found even more forensic evidence from the safe, which had been scraped against a painted object. One rule of forensic evidence is that when two objects touch, both objects transfer their individual properties to each other.

"It's red paint with a clear-coat top," the lab tech told me.

"Car paint?" I asked.

"Exactly," the tech said.

"So, there should be gray safe paint on the car that this safe came out of?"

"No doubt about it."

I knew Emerick had a small red car. I obtained a search warrant, then had it towed to the lab.

My E-crew tech went through the entire vehicle.

"Got something by the sill plate in the doorjamb," he said.

I moved quickly around the car to his position. "Is that gray paint?" I asked.

"Looks like it to me."

The lab easily matched up the paint samples. The safe from Sloopy's had been scraped against Emerick's car.

In the hatchback area of the car I found a ski mask, gloves, and a tire iron. I thought back to the pried cigarette machine. "Could you use a tire iron to pry open a metal cigarette machine?" I asked, half-jokingly.

"Duh, yeah," the tech said as he came around to look. Then he added, "Oh yeah, we're taking that."

The results of our lab work were coming in. The blood samples we had taken from the scene had been compared to Emerick's. It was a wash. The results neither implicated nor exonerated Emerick. The other evidence, however, was beginning to add up.

The FBI found that it was "extremely likely" that Emerick had written the letter, even though he had tried to disguise his handwriting.

At the crime lab, the toolmark examiner had made plastic casts of the pry marks on the cigarette machine. He then created pry marks in soft lead with Emerick's tire iron and cast those in plastic. Using a microscope, he compared the two sets of casts. They matched. Emerick's tire iron had been used to pry open the Sloopy's cigarette machine.

After more than five months of work, we were ready to pick up Edmund Emerick, but this time it wouldn't be for traffic offenses. I obtained the arrest warrant, then gathered up the squad and some uniformed officers. As we pulled up to Emerick's house, we saw him peering through the window. We quickly surrounded the house, then entered slowly. We carefully searched every room. No Emerick.

"He couldn't have gotten out," I said.

"He's here, he's here," one of my partners said. "Let's be careful."

He was right. We had searched the house but not all the hiding places. We looked through closets more closely now. We searched the attic. We searched the basement. Still no Emerick. Then it happened. My partner put his finger to his lips to say, "Quiet," then pointed to a trapdoor that led to an old root cellar. Not uncommon in these older homes, though we'd missed it the first time. One, two, three: I pulled open the door as my partner pointed his light and his glock into the cellar.

"Get your hands in the air and come out slowly," my partner commanded. Emerick slowly appeared. We had him. Emerick was smarter this time around. He refused to talk to us. We booked him into jail.

"We'll never know the real story," I said. I was wrong.

Emerick would not talk to us, but he did talk to his cellmate, who was both appalled and frightened by what Emerick had told him. He told us that the two of them had been talking about their charges. The cellmate was in for passing a bad check. Emerick said he was in for a double homicide, which definitely got the cellmate's attention.

To his surprise, Emerick laid out the whole case. He said he needed money, and he knew Sloopy's should have a lot of money right after St. Patrick's Day. *I'll bet he was disappointed when he opened the safe*, I thought. By that point, we knew Ferraro had deposited the night's haul in the bank earlier that morning.

Emerick said he knew Knapke and told him he needed to speak with Ferraro, so Knapke let him in. As we suspected, Emerick picked up a hammer and killed Knapke first. As Emerick went around the corner, Ferraro was just coming down the hallway. Emerick ordered Ferraro into the restroom—again, exactly as we'd suspected. He then killed Ferraro, pried open the cigarette machine, and stole the safe, placing it in his car. Next, he went on his neighborhood tour, creating his alibi. The cellmate even said Emerick was concerned about the woman who saw him behind Sloopy's. That was particularly interesting, since there had been no media reports about a female witness. There was no way this inmate could have invented that part of the story.

"Jailhouse" confessions are certainly looked at closely in court, and with good reason. Obviously, we would have preferred that Emerick had confessed to a law-abiding citizen. But all criminals are not the same, and the cellmate was horrified by Emerick's story. The story he gave us perfectly matched our forensic and witness evidence—evidence known only to us and to the killer. There is no way that the cellmate invented this story and placed it in Emerick's mouth. The cellmate was credible, and he made a great witness.

Before the trial, we saw the usual motions to suppress, though one clearly stood out. Even though Emerick had not confessed when we interviewed him, he knew that his prepared alibi was very damaging to him. He needed that statement to be suppressed. So Emerick testified that we had placed him in a chair in the interview room, then handcuffed both of his hands to the chair arms. He was defenseless when we beat him, blackening his eye, he said.

"Very interesting," the prosecutor said. "With both arms handcuffed, how did you sign the rights waiver?"

Good question. Emerick had no good answer and the motion was overruled, allowing us to use the statement about the prepared alibi during the trial.

The trial started in 1996, two years after the murders, and lasted several weeks. Defense experts challenged all of our forensic evidence. That didn't work. Defense attorneys challenged all of our witnesses, who prevailed, as they were extremely credible. The woman who saw Emerick at the rear of Sloopy's had no reason to lie. Nor did our homeless witness, Ray Miracle. Our cellmate testified to what Emerick had told him, and those were things that only the killer would have known. The jury convicted Emerick on every count. The judge sentenced him to life in prison with no chance for parole.

Since that time, Emerick has filed numerous appeals, without much luck. Emerick has never admitted to his crimes and still professes his innocence. When Emerick finally does meet the Devil in Hell, he has a lot of explaining to do.

22.
GATOR

CHRISTMAS 2001 FELT like Christmas. It was cold outside. A light but noticeable layer of snow covered the ground. *I love this time of the year*, I thought, recognizing that I was probably jinxing myself. Sure enough, my cell phone and my pager went off simultaneously. I answered the phone.

"Merry Christmas," the dispatcher said.

"Merry Christmas to you," I said. "Are you calling just to wish me a Merry Christmas because I've been such a good boy this year?"

"Yeah, right. Got one on the east end."

"Okay, send me the address. I'll be on my way in just a second."

"You got it, and really, Merry Christmas, man."

"You too," I said. I ended the call, grabbed my badge, and strapped on my glock. Next, I went to say goodbye to my family.

My kids were older now. They'd grown up watching me leave on callouts, even on holidays. It wasn't unexpected. Still, it was difficult.

"Love you guys," I said as I hugged them. "See you soon."
"Love you too," they said. "Be careful."

Be careful. I thought about that for a moment while I brushed the snow off my unmarked police car. How many other kids tell their parents to be careful? How many other careers are there where your kids don't know if you're coming back?

Everyone on the homicide squad had been involved in tense, life-threatening situations. That's what made us so close: We knew how quickly you could get killed doing this job, and none of us were ready to die. We didn't live in fear, but we weren't foolish, either. We were as careful as we could be. But homicide was a high-risk assignment, and our families knew that. The holiday season didn't change that fact.

Our scene was on the city's east end. As I pulled up, I was greeted by some uniformed officers, who wished me a Merry Christmas.

"Same to you guys," I said. "You could have just sent me a Christmas card, you know."

"Yeah, but we figured we're here, we've got a homicide," one said. "Let's invite Doyle to the party."

We all laughed. "And here we are," I said.

"Wouldn't be Christmas without a homicide," another officer said.

"You got that right," I said.

I was outside of a two-story single-family home. Moderate in size, it was a typical for the east end. The neighborhood was full of older white people who had lived there for decades. This was the home of Thomas King, sixty-one, and his wife, Brenda. She was out of town, visiting relatives. His body was inside.

Thomas King lay on the floor of a small kitchen/dining room area. There was blood on the wall beside him. I looked at the pattern.

"All of the blood is going upward," I said.

"Flat on his back and defenseless," said my partner, who had joined me.

Thomas King's torso was covered with stab wounds, and a bloody kitchen knife lay beside him. His face had been battered beyond recognition. Then I noticed a bloody shoe print on King's clothing. The print was quite large, and the crime lab would later determine it was made by a men's size-twelve lug-sole combat-style boot.

"Stabbed and stomped to death," I said. "He doesn't even look human." It was gruesome. Even his face had been stomped on. There was blood everywhere.

"Look at his foot," my partner said.

I had never seen anything quite like it. The foot was a gangrenous black and had a large open sore on the side. The toes went in all different directions. It looked like something out of a Frankenstein movie.

"That would explain the crutches over here," I said. We would later learn that King had survived an industrial accident several years earlier. Doctors were able to "save" his foot. *That's up for debate*, I thought when told that. Nevertheless, the foot was the reason King had not traveled with his wife. I didn't blame him. It looked painful.

The back door, which had a chain latch and the usual cheap plastic door lock, sat open. I noted that there was no damage.

"My ten-year-old could defeat these locks," our E-crew tech said.

"Yeah, but they aren't defeated," I said. There was no sign that anyone had tampered with the lock.

"He let the killer in," my partner said.

King's stab wounds appeared to have been made with a single-edge knife. A double-edge knife is sharp on both sides, which would leave a sharp incision on both sides of the wound.

A single-edged knife would leave a clean incision on one side of the wound, with a squared edge on the opposite side, where the knife's dull side went in. Sure enough, the knife next to King was a single-edged. More interestingly, the knife matched a set in the kitchen.

"Very smart," my partner said. Just as Edmund Emerick had done at Sloopy's, the killer here had taken a weapon from the scene, used it, and left it behind. There was nothing to tie the killer to that knife. If it had been taken from his own home, we could match it there. If he took it with him, we could match the wounds, or maybe even the remnants of the blood, even if he'd tried to wash it off. We might even catch him holding the knife. There was no chance of that happening here.

King's family helped us determine what items were missing from the home. A thirteen-inch color television had been taken from the kitchen area. A large portable radio was missing from the living room, and a nineteen-inch television had been removed from the bedroom.

"Not a lot to kill a man over," I said.

"It was enough for someone," my partner said.

We sent out a quick broadcast about the homicide, listing the missing items, the knife, and the bloody shoe prints. It wasn't a lot of information, but it ultimately would help solve this case.

The day after Christmas, when most people were reflecting on "peace on earth" or enjoying their presents, we were thinking about Thomas King. We didn't have a suspect yet, but we were certain that King knew his killer well enough to let him into the house. As we discussed the evidence, the phone rang. Sgt. Gary White answered it and had a brief conversation before telling us that there was a double homicide reported in the city's east end.

Arlie and Mae Fugate lived just blocks from the Kings. As we drove to the scene, we were all thinking the same thing.

"Hope we don't have another serial killer at Christmas," one detective said softly.

"Yeah, hope not," another said.

I didn't say anything. I was the last remaining member of the team that had worked the 1992 Christmas Killings, and my thoughts were drifting back to that case.

Like the Kings, the Fugates had lived in a modest two-story home, typical of the neighborhood. A uniformed officer met us at our car.

"Got your intel sheet on the King homicide," he said. "I think your boy struck again."

The scene was remarkably similar to the King homicide. The bodies of Arlie, sixty-eight, and Mae, sixty-nine, lay next to each other on the living room floor. Both looked much older than they were, appearing thin and frail. Both had been beaten and stabbed. Arlie also had the impression of a lug-sole boot on his face, with the same pattern we'd seen on King's clothes. A bloody knife, which we would learn came from the kitchen, lay on the floor beside the Fugates.

"Taken from the scene, used at the scene, left at the scene," I said.

"Who found them?" my partner asked.

"Their son came over when they wouldn't answer the phone," a uniformed officer replied.

"No forced entry, plus they have a working alarm that wasn't activated," our E-crew tech added.

There was also missing property. This time, it was a large jar of change and the couple's wedding rings.

As gruesome as the King scene was, this was even more disturbing. There were two victims, indicating our killer's confidence was growing. A bigger knife had been used, though we didn't know why. Maybe it was what he found in the kitchen. But one thing was certain: our killer was learning and adapting. Despite the missing electronics, the King home had barely been touched. This home had been ransacked. Our killer was growing more brazen. We knew what that meant: he wouldn't stop killing until we stopped him.

A rifle and shotgun hung from a rack on the living room wall. I wondered why the killer didn't take those. Then I knew why.

"He's on foot," I said. My partner asked how I knew that.

"There are plenty of scrappers and junkers walking around the east end," I said. "No one would pay attention to someone carrying a television or a radio."

"And you can put coins and rings in your pocket," my partner said.

"You see where I'm going?" I asked.

"If he had a car, he would have taken these guns," my partner said.

"Even in Dayton, you can't walk down the street with two long guns and not draw attention to yourself," our E-crew tech added.

We chuckled for a brief moment. But we were certain that the killer was on foot, which meant he definitely lived nearby.

"Until we catch him, no one is safe," my partner said. That jarred us back to reality.

We had two scenes with the same killer. I wondered how he chose his victims. Obviously, his preference was older and helpless. But there had to be some other connection—in both cases, our victims let him enter their homes. So, we searched for something that would link them. We checked UPS and FedEx for any common deliveries. We asked cable television companies, utilities, local repair shops, churches, grocery stores. We found no connections. Our victims appeared to have absolutely nothing in common.

"Maybe the killer is the only connection," my partner said.

"Could be," I said, feeling some desperation. "We could use a break."

We were about to get one.

* * *

Late in the afternoon the following day, we were ready to head home. As I was walking out of headquarters, my phone rang. A uniformed officer assigned to the city's east side was on the line. He was almost apologetic.

"Doyle, I hate to bother you, but I may have something for you," the officer said.

"Never a bother," I said. "You know we're open twenty-four hours a day."

That officer had stopped by a local tavern, just as part of a routine check. The bartender told him that a man had recently come into the bar trying to sell a portable color television. The bartender declined to buy it, saying he'd prefer a bigger one. The man left, but returned with a second, larger set about thirty minutes later. The bartender, who knew the man as a hustler and a thief, did not buy either television.

Two television sets. The officer had remembered the intelligence sheet we'd released to uniformed crews.

"I love it," I said. "Stay there. I'm on my way."

The bartender told me that he recognized our mystery television salesman as a prior customer. He didn't know his real name but knew his nickname: Gator. Our suspect was also known to travel on foot, just as we'd surmised. Known to local establishments. The bar was in the same general area as our two homicide scenes. I was very interested in meeting Mr. Gator.

I ran that nickname through our computer system. To my surprise, there were thirty-one Gators. Who knew? One of them caught my attention: Darrell Wayne Ferguson, twenty-eight, who lived with his mother and stepfather right in the heart of the east end, within walking distance from our two scenes.

But there was more. I found an incident report for an aggravated robbery on December 23, two days before Thomas King's body was found. The victim, a double amputee, lived in the general area. He reported that Ferguson had forced his way into his home and then stolen his wallet. As Ferguson left, he told the victim to keep his mouth shut or he would come back and kill him. It was eerily similar to our homicides. We had a frail, defenseless victim who knew his attacker, just as our homicide victims had. *This can't be a coincidence*, I thought.

Ferguson was supposed to be in a court-ordered drug-abuse treatment program in Cincinnati, less than an hour southwest of Dayton. This court order followed a burglary conviction in November 2001, one month before our homicides. I called the treatment center, and after working the phone for a while, I was finally on the line with a clerk who could answer my questions. He confirmed that Gator was a resident at the facility. *Well, there goes a promising lead*, I thought.

"Hold on a moment," the clerk said. "He was given a two-day pass to visit his mother in Dayton."

He explained that the pass was from 9 a.m. on December 21 through noon on December 23. Our homicides didn't start until December 25.

"Hold on," the clerk said. After a pause, he added: "Detective, he never returned. He has not been here since December 21."

I was grateful that the clerk had kept digging. That doesn't always happen. *We certainly have a suspect now*, I thought.

It was December 27. We obtained an arrest warrant for Ferguson. The charge was aggravated robbery and it was in connection with the robbery of the double amputee. The charge didn't matter. It was a reason to bring Ferguson in. Once we had him, we could question him about the homicides. It was late afternoon, and we sent out a broadcast so that officers would know to look for Gator. Then we started searching ourselves.

It's tougher to find suspects in the winter. Not as many people are out on the streets. Plus, this wasn't the type of suspect who had a permanent residence or even a job. You couldn't just walk up to the Gator residence and ring the doorbell. Guys like Gator lived with whoever would take them in. We did have his mother's address, so we started there.

A man answered the door. I introduced myself and asked if Darrell was there. Uniformed officers had already surrounded the house in case he was.

"No, he's not here," the man said. "I'm his stepfather. Is this about the murders?"

I was stunned. Our homicides had been big news across the region. He obviously at least suspected that his stepson had been involved, but he didn't contact us. I hid my anger and disgust.

"Yes, as a matter of fact, it is," I said calmly. "May we come in and talk?"

"Sure," the man said.

We quickly learned that Gator did know our victims—quite well. Ferguson knew the sixty-one-year-old King because Ferguson's mother had been married to King's brother. Arlie and Mae Fugate had been his neighbors at one time. The stepfather also said that Gator had called him a few days earlier, asking him to bring some clean clothes for him. Gator had said he'd gotten blood on his pants. The stepfather declined to help and told Gator not to contact him again.

"So, where do we find him?" I asked.

"He has a girlfriend on East Third Street. When Gator called, I could hear a baby crying in the background, and she has a baby."

Gator's girlfriend lived in a small two-story house. No lights were on when we arrived.

"He may be there," I said.

"Or he may not be," my partner said.

"He's definitely not going to Mom's house anymore," I said. "If we hit this place and he isn't there, he won't come back here, either."

We agreed we'd return the next day and check again. As I drove home, my adrenaline surged as I thought about finding and interviewing Gator. I could hardly wait.

* * *

The following day was quiet. "We're lucky the weather is bad," my partner said as we drove toward Gator's girlfriend's house.

I knew what he meant. The weather had probably kept Gator inside. Surely by now he had sold the rings and the televisions, so he had some money. But not enough to sustain him for long, which meant he would kill again if we didn't find him.

"Hopefully, he's warm and cozy with his girlfriend," I said.

We pulled into the lot of a vacant business across from the house. Everything was shut up nice and tight, just as it had been the night before. Visibility was good during the daylight hours. We could see some movement in the house, but not much more.

"Somebody is home," I said.

"No way of telling who is inside though," my partner said. "I say we hit it," I said.

My partner agreed. "What have we got to lose?" he said.

We called up some patrol officers and headed across the street to the house. We surrounded the structure, but tried to keep out of the view from the windows. My partner and I approached the front door, I knocked with my left hand. My glock was in my right, hidden behind my leg. A woman answered the door.

"Dayton Police Homicide," I said.

"Where's Gator?" my partner asked.

The female opened the door wider to expose the front room. Gator sat on the couch. I recognized him from his mug shot. I raised my glock and ordered him to the ground. Slowly, deliberately, Gator complied. My partner handcuffed him as I kept the gun trained on him. Gator never took his eyes off me, nor I off him.

We placed Gator in the back of a marked cruiser so he could be taken to headquarters for questioning. Inside the house, we found a bag of bloody clothing right next to the couch. We also found a pair of bloodstained lug-sole boots. My partner and I agreed: we would send an E-crew technician and another homicide detective to obtain the paperwork to legally seize the clothing and tag it into evidence. Our focus would be to interview Gator.

Our other detectives were busy, too, contacting Gator's friends. The case was getting stronger. One friend reported that Gator had recently asked him for a ride. When that friend saw blood on Gator's pants, he asked about it. Gator said he'd been in a fight.

A second friend reported making a recent trade with Gator: some rings in exchange for some crack cocaine. That friend pawned the rings. Our detectives found those rings at the pawnshop. Sure enough, they had belonged to the Fugates.

A third friend reported that Gator had visited him around noon on December 27. Gator said he wanted to watch the news, so they did. The friend said that when a story aired about the three homicides, Gator perked up. He bragged about killing all three victims, adding, "They got what they had coming to them." That friend also said that Gator was wearing steel-toed army boots and had blood on his pants.

Gator's girlfriend didn't do him any favors either. She told us that Gator had come to her house late on December 27 and she had watched as he tried to wash blood out of his clothing.

To this day, I'm amazed by a simple fact: so many people knew Gator was the killer, or should have suspected he was, but did nothing. A simple phone call would have been suffi- cient. Until we heard from the bartender, we had no solid sus- pects. Without that bartender, we would surely have had more victims, because Gator wasn't done after the Fugates. Others could have helped prevent further bloodshed but didn't.

When we found Gator in the interview room, he sat there in his underwear. He was a big boy, weighing in at a stocky two hundred and thirty-five pounds. His victims hadn't had a chance.

"You going to get me some clothes?" Gator asked.

"Yeah, we're working on that now," I said. "You know we're taking your clothes for evidence."

"We'll get you some jail clothes," my partner added.

I knew the jail would send over some clothes, but we were in no hurry. Gator was uneasy, sitting there in his underwear, and that was fine with me. Gator Ferguson was exactly the kind of suspect who liked mind games. I wanted to establish imme- diately that he wasn't in charge here.

"We've got a lot to talk about," I began. "First, let's go over your rights."

"I know my rights."

"I'm sure you do, and I'm sure you know that I have to read you your rights."

"Yeah, go ahead."

I went over the rights waiver with Gator. He stated he understood and signed the form. The chess match began.

Gator initially denied any knowledge of the murders. Not uncommon. But we made it clear we weren't going anywhere, and we kept the interview going. After a few hours of Gator's denials, we were getting tired.

"Gator, why would you sit there and lie to me and Detective Burke?" my partner asked.

"I'm not lying. Why do you think I killed those people?"

"I don't know," I shot back. "Why did you kill Mr. King and the Fugates?"

Killers prefer to depersonalize their victims. Instead of using names, they refer to the victims as "them" or "those people." But "those people" had names, and I planned to remind Gator of that over and over again.

"Who?" Gator asked.

"The helpless old people you killed," I said. "Thomas King, Arlie Fugate, and Mae Fugate."

Gator just stared at me. That was fine. I always wanted the suspect's complete attention. We were trying to strike a delicate balance: give Gator enough information to show that we knew he was the killer, without giving him too much. I wanted to hold some of our facts, such as the recovery of the Fugates' rings, in reserve.

"There's blood all over your clothing," my partner said. "Do you think we won't be able to match that to Mr. King and the Fugates?"

"That's my blood from a street fight," Gator said. It was time to turn it up a notch.

"Bullshit," I said. "Do you think we're idiots? Do you think I just started on this job yesterday? Son, I've been bringing in killers like you for almost as long as you've been alive."

Gator just sat there.

"This pisses me off," I said as I stormed out of the room.

I wasn't really angry. I really didn't care about Gator's opinion of me. It was a ploy, and my partner knew exactly what I was doing. So, as Bad Cop left the room, Good Cop started smoothing things over.

"Look, sorry, man," my partner said. "Burke's a little high-strung."

Nice touch, I thought as I listened from outside the room.

"We just want to know what happened," my partner said. "What made you kill Mr. King and the Fugates?"

"I need time to think," Gator said.

"Take your time," my partner said.

We'd been with Gator for several hours. During a break, I told my partner that we needed to move Gator to a holding cell. My partner agreed. If we did obtain a confession, we wanted it to be admissible. Moving Gator out of the small interview room to a larger holding cell would show the court that Gator wasn't under any duress. The holding cell had a toilet, so Gator wouldn't be able to argue that we were preventing him from relieving himself. The cell wouldn't be optimal for interview purposes, but it would have to do.

"You smoke?" I asked as we placed him in the cell.

"No."

"You want something to eat, drink, whatever?" I asked.

"No, I'm good," Gator said. "Thanks, though."

My offers of food, drink, and cigarettes would also help ensure the admission of a confession—if we got one. But I thought we would.

"We're getting closer," I told my partner after we left Gator in the cell.

"We are?" he asked.

I meant it. Gator had thanked me for my offer of food. That was a good sign.

By the time we left the cell, we'd interviewed Gator for nearly six hours. We were tired, but we couldn't give up. We knew we had plenty of evidence against Gator: witness statements, forensics. But you still can't beat a confession. A confession makes all the forensic evidence make sense, linking it in a narrative read in the killer's voice.

I'd been playing the role of the bad cop. It was time to switch personas. I opened the door to check on Gator.

"Come here," Gator said. "I want to talk to you."

I entered the room and sat down.

"I like your ring," Gator said, motioning to my right hand. He was pointing to my gold skull ring, the one with the ruby eyes. The one I'd bought from the pawnshop years earlier.

"Thanks, man," I said. "I like it too."

I held up my right hand so Gator could get a better look at my ring. Gator leaned toward me and quietly asked: "Are you a devil worshipper?"

I didn't even think about it. "Yes, I am," I said. "You?"

"Praise Satan," Gator said.

As far as persona changes go, this one was going to be different. Just for the record, I am not a devil worshipper. But if being one kept Gator talking, then I was perfectly happy to say I was. And, legally speaking, it was perfectly permissible to do so. I brought my partner into the cell.

Gator was clearly more comfortable talking satanist to satanist. What he told us was somewhere between an outright confession and a lie-fession. After he'd given us enough details, we asked to videotape a statement, and he agreed.

Gator told us he'd walked to Thomas King's house. Thomas King let him in.

"After a while I blacked out," Gator said. "When I came to, I saw what I did."

"And remember, you told us you recalled stabbing and stomping on Mr. King," I said.

"Yes," Gator said.

"And the knife that you used?" I asked.

"The knife that I used was from the kitchen."

Gator told us he stole two televisions and a radio. "I sold them on the street and bought some paint and bread," he said.

We knew what he meant. Gator wasn't painting a house. He had bought a can of spray paint to inhale, or "huff," by spraying it into the bread bag. The paint fumes offered a cheap high.

Then Gator uttered the phrase that would ensure his execution: "I tried to put the bread bag on my head and do myself in because I knew what I did was wrong."

I knew what I did was wrong. Those seven words would undercut any insanity defense, any mitigation during the death penalty phase. I hid my glee and Gator continued his confession.

Just as we thought, Gator walked to the Fugates' house, and they recognized their former neighbor and let him in. Gator called the Fugate homicides a "blackout increase" and said, "I did it again." He told of stomping on and stabbing the elderly couple. Gator admitted to taking their wedding rings and a jar of coins. It was a great video confession. We wrapped it up and booked Gator into jail.

Not surprisingly, Gator was indicted on fifteen felony counts, including the aggravated murders of Thomas King and Arlie and Mae Fugate. Those charges carried a potential death sentence.

During the months between the arrest and the trial, our case continued to strengthen. DNA testing matched the blood on Gator's boots to Thomas King and the Fugates. The probability of this blood coming from someone other than our victims was sixty-two million to one.

The crime lab matched Gator's boots to the bloody footprints found at both scenes. Technicians also matched the shoe impression on Arlie's face to the heel of Gator's right boot.

As the trial approached, Gator could see what was happening. He was going to be convicted, and there was a strong possibility that he would be sentenced to death. So, Gator started writing to the court. His letters to the judge were consistent. He admitted killing all three victims and he wanted to be executed.

"What is done is done and if i could bring them back, i wouldn't," Gator wrote in one error-ridden letter. "I have no Remorse for what i did." (sic)

In another passage, Gator wrote: "I is asking you in my right state of mind would you please Find it in good will to give me the Death penalty." (sic)

It seemed everyone felt Gator deserved the death penalty, even Gator. Nearly two years after his arrest, Gator's trial started. I was hopeful that Gator would get his wish.

Gator waived his right to a jury trial. Sometimes defendants do that for tactical reasons, particularly if they're worried a jury could be influenced by particularly gruesome details—such as three older people stomped to death. This meant that a three-judge panel would hear the case. But before the trial started, Gator pleaded guilty to all counts.

So now the judges had to decide if Gator was competent to plead guilty. This is when those seven words from his videotaped interview came back to haunt him. *I knew what I did was wrong.* Each of his competency evaluations cited those words.

The judges found him competent to stand trial, and therefore competent to enter a guilty plea.

But no plea agreement had been made. Prosecutors had not offered Gator anything in exchange for his guilty pleas. So, there would still be a weeklong trial to determine Gator's punishment. The law states that, in accepting a guilty plea in a death penalty case, a three-judge panel must still hear evidence to determine whether the defendant is guilty of murder beyond a reasonable doubt.

Instead of the month-long trial I anticipated, we got a much shorter proceeding. Defense attorneys offered little-to-no cross-examination. We were basically just displaying our evidence to satisfy the judges that Gator was indeed guilty. The judges agreed that he was. Next came the penalty phase.

As expected, the prosecution offered all of the evidence previously admitted as proof that Gator deserved the death penalty. Gator called no witnesses in his defense and he declined to take the witness stand. Instead, Gator elected to read a prepared statement to the judges while the victims' families watched in disbelief.

As Gator walked up to the podium, it was clear he'd lived well in jail. He'd ballooned to two hundred eighty-five pounds. His six-minute statement was sadistic and cruel as he bragged about killing his victims.

"I did it intentionally, and the killings were malicious and hideous acts, just as I intended them to be."

Gator addressed Brenda King, Thomas's widow, and James Cornett, the Fugates' son, by name, telling them that killing their loved ones had given him immense pleasure. He said he hoped that the victims were in hell, in "agonizing pain and torment. They should never rest, only burn for eternity."

This was unbelievable. But Gator wasn't done. He next offered a warning.

"Let's just say that if I was to be freed to go back out in society, I'd pick up where I left off from and take the pleasure of causing destruction," he said. "I will pray night and day as I sit in prison in my own darkness that for every one of you who are here to see justice served, that you and your precious loved ones are driving down the road and the damn car blows up and kills every one of you. May death come over all of you. To my God, and to my family and friends, love. And to my enemies, death. Hail lord Satan. Done."

Oh, you are most certainly done, I thought. Gator was still a coward. He hadn't had the guts to face a cross-examination. Instead, he read a statement so that he could control what was happening and inflict more pain upon his victims' families. But his control was over.

The judges took a brief recess then returned to announce their decision. To no one's surprise, Gator received the death penalty. I could not see how anyone, even the hardiest opponents of capital punishment, could have listened to Gator's statement and felt he deserved to live. Gator deserved death. He caused it, he wanted it, and he had earned it.

I saw Gator once more. Before he was shipped to death row, he had requested an interview with me to clear up some other cases. It was a strange experience, like two old acquaintances talking about the past. For some reason, Gator liked me. I'm not sure why. But strangely, I didn't mind speaking with him, and at times I found it interesting. I didn't respect him, and I sure didn't respect what he'd done, but we had a weird natural rapport. I cannot explain it, but it seemed to extend beyond my playacting as a satanist.

Gator wanted to tell me about the other people he'd killed. I was eager to hear about them. Maybe we could clear some unsolved cases. But Gator was faking. As he spoke, it was clear he was making it up as he went along. The victims were vaguely described as "a white guy" or "a Black girl." The times and locations were similarly vague.

"I think he wanted to boost his numbers in the serial killer ranks," I later told news reporters.

During that last interview, I watched Gator carefully. Here was the self-proclaimed devil-worshipping satanist killer who had garnered national attention. But I didn't see that. All I saw was a big, dumb bully who preyed on the helpless. After it became clear that Gator wasn't offering any information of value, I wrapped up the interview. Gator and I stood and shook hands. As the jailers led him away, Gator turned back.

"I do like that ring," he said.

"Me too," I said. I never saw him again.

Gator got his lethal injection on August 8, 2006. He was the youngest person executed in Ohio in forty-four years.

Looking back, could that have been me? We both grew up in East Dayton, both poor, yet only one of us had gotten on the wrong side of the law. Perhaps, as the saying goes, it was the grace of God—though Gator would have hated that notion, praise Satan and all that.

Here's the difference between Gator Ferguson and the vast majority of people around him, however poor they were. Gator was cruel. He enjoyed hurting people. It gave him pleasure. Though he was a massive person, he picked safer targets: the elderly, the infirm. That makes him a bully, and while all bullies are cowards, that doesn't make him any less treacherous.

It's frightening to think that dangerous people like Gator Ferguson walk the streets among us every day, but it's true. The thought of Gator still haunts me. I still wear my skull ring every day. It reminds me of the evil I've seen, and perhaps more importantly, the evil that I haven't yet seen.

23.
MY BABY'S NOT BURNED

PARKSIDE HOMES WAS one of Dayton's most notorious projects. Though it was smaller than the west side's massive DeSoto Bass, it was large enough. Parkside sat north of downtown. Originally built to offer affordable housing to soldiers returning home from World War II, Parkside had devolved into poverty, marked by plenty of narcotics, violence, and murder.

The rows of two-story brick units looked more like barracks than homes. The roads inside twisted into numerous dead ends, and if you were smart, you paid attention to how to get out. Like many housing projects, Parkside was the kind of place where you always wanted to know how to make a quick exit.

Families lived in Parkside for generations. There were good people living there. There were also the "less than good" and the "actually quite awful." They made you feel sorry for the good folks. While some qualified as low-income families, others seemed to be no-income families. For those, income came from government programs, illegal activity, or both.

Life in Parkside was hard. Every time I was there, I saw plenty of little children. I wondered how many would prevail and find a way out. Sadly, for too many people, the only escape would come from inside a body bag.

On August 30, 2005, just three weeks after she was born, Paris Talley made it out of Parkside.

We got dispatch's call at about eight in the morning. "Going to need the whole squad on this one," the dispatcher said. "Got a dead baby at CMC that came from Parkside."

CMC was the Children's Medical Center. Some of us went there; others, including me, went to Parkside. None of us realized we were embarking on an investigation that would make international news.

Hospital staff told our detectives that Paris had arrived with her mother, twenty-five-year-old China Arnold, and her father, twenty-four-year-old Terrell Talley, who had rushed into the emergency room.

A doctor told our detectives that Paris had suffered burns on most of her body, and that they were not typical. The doctors at CMC were well acquainted with child abuse, including burns. For those too young to talk, we looked for the usual signs. Some children arrived after being dipped in hot water for "punishment." Their burn patterns would include an immersion line and splash marks, along with defensive burns on their hands. Others arrived with pattern burns—which usually indicated someone had tormented them with a hot object, such as a clothes iron, a hot skillet, or a curling iron. You could match the pattern of the burn with that object, just as we'd matched Gator's boot to the impressions on his victims' bodies.

But doctors didn't know what had caused Paris Talley's burns, and neither did we.

"It's a thermal injury, most definitely," one doctor said. "Some sort of dry heat."

An attending nurse, visibly shaken, offered our detectives a gruesome detail: As she was performing CPR on Paris, the nurse's thumb had penetrated the baby's chest wall. It was brittle, as if Paris had been cooked.

Another interesting detail was the mother's reaction. After Paris had been pronounced dead, the doctor and nurse went to speak with the baby's parents. Before they mentioned the burns, China spoke up.

"My baby's not burned," she blurted. "Her skin is just falling off."

When Paris had arrived at the hospital, she'd been wearing a onesie that hid her injuries. Medical staff didn't see the burns until they took off the onesie. So how, the nurse and doctor both wondered, did China know about her baby's injuries? Good question.

Our detectives found China and Terrell, then separated them. Both agreed to be interviewed at headquarters. You never interviewed parents together on cases like this. You always wanted to get an independent statement from each, so that you could compare the two. Then you could see who was telling the truth, and more importantly, who wasn't.

While they were at the hospital, another detective and I went to 415 Hall Avenue, where Paris had lived with her mother. The apartment's layout was the same as every other Parkside unit. There was a kitchen and living area downstairs, with bedrooms and a bathroom upstairs. It was not a large area to deal with. The other detectives had tipped me off to the burns, so as I walked through the residence, I looked for something that could have caused them. Nothing was obvious, though later, I would realize I'd walked past the murder weapon several times.

The first floor was sparsely furnished. In the living area, I saw a couch, a love seat, and a television. A baby car seat was on the floor. Inside the car seat was a towel, a blanket, and a partially full baby bottle. I spotted a bag of crack cocaine on the couch.

The kitchen area was small and typical. There was a clothes dryer, a stove with pots and pans around it, a large microwave oven on the counter, and other generic kitchen items.

The second floor held few surprises, but one was a pink plastic tub sitting on a television. It was obviously out of place. I looked inside and saw cloudy water. On the bottom of the tub, I could see what appeared to be human skin. I jotted down my observations, then left the scene. I was going to observe the autopsy.

Doctor Russell Uptegrove and I looked over Paris's tiny body. Uptegrove showed me how some parts of her body had been severely burned, but others were unharmed. The staff at CMC was correct: these were not typical burn patterns. The thermal injuries on her chest were quite noticeable. They were also clearly defined, with an almost rectangular pattern.

"Could it be a cookie sheet or something like that?" I asked.

"Could be, or a heating pad," Uptegrove said. "Something square or rectangular."

It wasn't much. Autopsies usually offer answers. But I left with few answers and even more questions. I went to head-quarters to see what the parents had to say.

Both were being interviewed as I arrived. I checked on Terrell first. He said that he and China had been out drinking the previous night. His sister watched over Paris and China's three other children, all boys, ages three, six, and seven. During their night out, Terrell and China had argued as to whether he was Paris's father. Terrell told us he knew he was the girl's father, but that China had children by other men. It didn't bother him, he said.

When they got home, the boys were asleep upstairs. Paris was sleeping in her car seat in the living room. China fell asleep on the couch, and around midnight, Terrell left to play video games at another Parkside apartment. He returned around 6 a.m. Everyone was still asleep. Everything seemed normal. Terrell crashed on the couch with China and slept for about an hour before she got up and went upstairs.

At this point, Terrell went to look at his daughter. He saw burn marks on her face. When he touched her, her skin was cold. He called out for China, then the two of them rushed Paris to the hospital.

China was in another interview room. She confirmed that she and Terrell had gone out drinking, and said she was drunk when they got home. She said the other three children were upstairs the whole night, and that Terrell had gone out after she'd passed out on the couch.

She told detectives that she was responsible for the baby's care. She'd seen the red circles on Paris's face and hands but disregarded them. In her statement, she said she'd fallen asleep on the couch with Paris on her chest. Around 2 a.m., she heated up a bottle in a microwave and tried to feed the baby. Paris ate very little, she said.

China said that when she got up, she didn't check on the baby. While she was upstairs, she heard Terrell yelling that Paris wasn't breathing.

China said she didn't know how the baby could have gotten burned. We didn't believe that. China had already admitted that Terrell had been gone most of the night and that the other children had been asleep in another part of the apartment. The baby didn't burn herself. Our detectives kept pressing her. Eventually, she said that she'd been so drunk that she wasn't sure what she did. In a chilling statement, she calmly added: "If I hadn't gotten so drunk, I guess my baby wouldn't have died."

At this point, I began assisting the other detectives because I had information from the scene they didn't. I asked about the crack cocaine on the couch. China said she allowed Terrell to sell drugs from the apartment. I asked about the plastic tub upstairs with skin in it. China replied she had given Paris a bath in it.

Next, I raised information we'd gotten from our canvass of the neighborhood: a neighbor had observed China outside the apartment around 4 a.m., looking around. China denied it.

Next, I asked about her argument with Terrell. She said the argument was about her driving drunk. When confronted with Terrell's version—the argument concerning the baby's paternity—China changed her story. She now admitted to being outside at 4 a.m., waiting for Terrell. *Which meant Terrell was telling the truth about not being there*, I thought. Then she admitted that Terrell was correct about the subject of the argument. It was becoming clear who our liar was, and she wasn't finished. China's next move was to blame Terrell, suggesting the injuries may have occurred when he had her.

"Terrell wasn't even there," another detective said. "Even you said so."

I asked an obvious question: Did she and Terrell have any conversation on the way to the hospital about what may have happened to their child?

"No," China calmly replied. "We didn't talk."

"Terrell hands you your dead, burnt baby and you don't say a word?" I asked. China sat mute. She declined to answer any other questions.

Not smart enough to keep coming up with lies, I thought. To us, her silence was telling. We arrested her for endangering children—it was too early in the investigation to charge her with murder—and booked her into the county jail. The lesser charge would have to suffice for now, buying us time. Other detectives called Children's Services to remove the other children from China's home.

It was a quick start, but there were numerous unanswered questions. The biggest was: How did Paris die?

I returned to China's apartment, hoping to view the scene with a fresh, better-informed perspective. My mind kept returning to the injury on the baby's chest. That pattern resembled a cookie sheet, but I realized it couldn't be. This was an infant, just a few weeks old. She was tiny. Even a small cookie sheet would be far too large. Perhaps China had used a foil tray from a TV dinner, or an oven rack. Perhaps our weapon was a heating pad or a small square skillet.

I walked through the apartment again but found nothing like what I was looking for. But I kept walking past the murder weapon. We all had, every one of us who processed the scene. We just didn't realize it.

Remember "COD MOD TOD"? We had questions on each. Cause of death was not simple, but we knew that Paris died after her body temperature suddenly shot up. The manner of death was obviously homicide. This wasn't an accident, a suicide, or a natural death. But we didn't know how, and we didn't have a good estimate on the time of death. We had no way of knowing how high Paris's temperature had reached. We didn't know where it started, either, so it was difficult to pinpoint the time of death using body core temperature. But the coroner's office could say that the baby had died during the night, a time period in which only one person could be responsible: China Arnold.

It would be months before we would know what our murder weapon was. Doctor Uptegrove examined and reexamined evidence. He also consulted with other pathologists across the country. Then, one day in early May 2006, he summoned us to his office.

By this time, China was out of jail. We couldn't hold her on the endangering charge forever. China had left Parkside and moved to the city's east end. We kept informal tabs on her, but without answers to the case's basic questions, we weren't making any progress.

It's not easy to stun a roomful of homicide detectives, but Doctor Uptegrove did it when he announced he knew what the murder weapon was: the microwave oven in China Arnold's kitchen.

"Are you saying this baby was cooked to death in a microwave?" I asked.

"'Cooked' is probably not the term I would use, but yes, this baby was killed in the microwave," Uptegrove said.

He described his research. He'd only found one similar case, in another state. That child had survived. But its injuries were strikingly similar. Uptegrove had also learned a lot about microwave ovens. Those waves come from a heating unit, which can be on the top, sides, or back of the oven. That can lead to uneven cooking, which is why newer microwaves have a rotating base that spins the food around to even out the heat. This, he said, was why Paris had areas on her body that were severely burned while others were completely spared of injury.

I thought about how many times I had microwaved a frozen dinner or leftovers. Often, part of the dinner would be smoking hot or burnt while some of it remained cool or even frozen. But this was no frozen dinner. This was a living, breathing baby.

By now, I'd been on the squad for more than two decades, working hundreds of homicides. I'd seen more than my share of violence and cruelty, but I'd never seen anything like this. That's why I kept walking past the microwave in China's apartment. I simply never imagined someone could be cruel enough to microwave a baby.

"Was it quick?" I asked.

"Definitely not," Uptegrove said.

On May 18, 2006, we served a search warrant on China's vacant Parkside apartment. Maintenance workers let us in. We hoped, even prayed, that the microwave was still there—and it was, sitting on the countertop. Just to be sure, we compared the photos taken during the initial scene investigation. This appeared to be the same microwave.

"What were the chances?" my partner asked.

"Sometimes we just need a little luck," I said. We sent the microwave off to the lab, then continued with the investigation.

Polygraph examinations are not admissible as evidence in a criminal case. We all knew that. But the "lie detector," as it is known, is still a great investigative tool. On May 26, we asked Terrell to submit to one and he agreed.

A DPD polygraph operator administered the test, starting with a series of questions to determine whether Terrell was suitable for testing. Some people are not. They may be pathological liars, or they may be so drunk or high at the time of the test that the polygraphist can't get a good reading. Terrell was deemed suitable. The next series of questions gauge whether the polygraph operator can determine accurately if the subject is telling the truth. Typically, the subject chooses a random numbered card between one and ten, but does not reveal the number to the operator, who then tells the subject to answer no to every question. The operator asks the same question for each number.

After the operator had asked the ten questions, he consulted the chart, but only for a moment.

"You chose number eight," he said.

Terrell showed the card. It was number eight. The test was valid, and equally important, Terrell knew it.

It was time for the real test.

"Did you see anyone kill Paris?"

"No."

"Did you kill Paris?"

"No."

"Did you cause any of the injuries to Paris?"

"No."

The polygraph operator peered through the charts. "He's telling the truth," he said. Terrell was no angel. But he was also not a murderer.

It would take more weeks, but the crime lab would bring us more good news: They had recovered Paris's DNA from inside the microwave. Lab workers had also constructed a clear plastic box to the oven's exact dimensions, then made a doll that was the same size as Paris. The doll fit perfectly inside the box. As I looked at that doll through the plastic walls, I thought of how Paris must have suffered. It was truly horrifying.

We obtained an arrest warrant for China Arnold on November 27. This was for the aggravated murder of Paris Talley, and it carried death penalty specifications. China and some of her relatives were returning to her new home when we approached. As we arrested her, she asked what for.

"Aggravated murder," my partner answered.

Calmly, coolly, China replied: "What? I didn't kill my baby."

Way too calm, I thought. Not surprised at all. She'd known this day was coming. I was sure of it.

But China was the only calm member of the Arnold family. The others were screaming and running around in circles.

China remained calm in the interview room. Not since Laura Taylor had I observed a young woman so cold and unfeeling. The interview was short, but certainly not sweet. This was a cleanup interview. We wanted a confession, if possible, but would be satisfied with locking China into certain prior statements.

We asked China if she knew what had happened to Paris. No, she said. We asked if she had been the baby's sole caregiver. Yes, she said. She admitted, again, that she had fed the baby at 2 a.m. then gone outside to smoke.

"Terrell wasn't there—you are the one taking care of Paris?" my partner asked.

"I told you, yes," China snapped back.

"We know the burns on Paris are not from water," my partner said.

"Well, all I've got is a microwave, a stove, and a dryer," China said.

How telling, I thought, *that she would mention a microwave.* A team of seasoned investigators had been unable to imagine a microwave oven as a weapon against a helpless baby. So would most normal people. But the killer knew a microwave had been used.

"I don't know what happened," China said.

"Do you deny it happened?" my partner shot back.

"No," China replied.

"You are the only one there?" I asked.

"Yes."

"You are the person who cares for Paris?" I asked.

"Yes."

At that point, I decided to leave the room. China was now alone with my partner, a veteran female detective. Though we'd graduated from the same DPD-Academy class in 1978, we'd never worked together until she came to the squad a few years earlier. I knew she was a sharp detective and a keen interviewer.

I listened to the interview through the closed door.

"Do you have kids?" China asked.

"Yes," my partner said.

"How would you like to be treated like this?" China asked.

"I would want to know what happened," my partner said.

302   DOYLE BURKE AND LOU GRIECO

This caused China to become agitated. "Fuck you, I want an attorney," she said. The interview was over. China did not have the arrest record of a "hardened criminal," but she was hard.

After we booked China into the county jail, my partner said, "I guess we'll never know why she did it."

"Does it matter?" I asked.

"A little," she said. I knew how she felt. After months of investigation, we knew what had happened to Paris and who had done it. But we didn't know why. We didn't need that for a successful prosecution—you can prosecute without a motive—but we still wanted to know. Soon we would.

As she sat in jail awaiting trial, China made several statements to different inmates, including one Linda Williams, who had a sexual relationship with China when they were housed together in a two-person cell. Williams contacted us with an interesting story, which clarified many of our missing details.

According to Williams, China said that she and Terrell had argued all day. She was still angry with him after they returned home, and he left to play video games with a friend. Because China was angry, she put Paris in the microwave, turned it on, and went outside, leaving her baby to suffer alone.

You do have to be careful with jailhouse snitches. But this rang true: China had been outside that night. A neighbor had seen her, and she'd eventually admitted this to us. This was not public knowledge. Williams couldn't be making this up. It had to come from China.

Williams said she asked China how she got Paris in the microwave. "China told me she fit right in," Williams told us.

Williams wanted to know what we all did: Why? So, she asked China, who told her she was angry because Terrell was going to leave her if the baby wasn't his.

I can't say I was surprised. I thought back to the Samuel Moreland case in 1985. I remembered asking my partner,

"How does something like this happen?" And I remembered his reply: "It probably won't get any better when we find out why." Two decades later, those words still resonated. It wasn't that any of us expected there to be a valid reason to microwave an infant. But the motive didn't balance out the horror of the crime. Paris Talley was murdered simply because China Arnold wanted to get even with her boyfriend.

China's first trial started in February 2008. Like Andre Sinkfield, China Arnold would be tried three times. Each time, our evidence was presented to the jury and tested by defense attorneys. We had all of the people we'd interviewed: neighbors, doctors, nurses, cellmates. We had China's own words from our interviews with her. We had the baby's DNA in the microwave. Of course, we had that clear plastic microwave oven mockup with the little doll that represented Paris. It was a powerful piece of evidence, as close to a reenactment as you could get.

We even brought in a microwave expert who explained exactly how China's microwave worked and what it did to Paris. Our experts determined that Paris had been cooked for at least two minutes before she died. Think about that. Look at a clock and watch the second hand travel around for two full rotations and think about a baby cooking in a microwave that long.

The defense's case was much simpler. China, they would say, was way too drunk to know what she was doing. Possibly way too drunk to be able to operate the microwave. Of course, China's blood alcohol content hadn't been tested that night. So, most of their expert testimony about China's state of drunkenness was based on information their expert had gleaned from China.

"Let me get this straight," I said to one of the prosecutors. "This whole theory is based on what a known liar has told them. A liar who, if she was as drunk as they say she was, shouldn't be able to remember how much she drank."

"That pretty much sums it up," the prosecutor said.

The prosecution rested. The defense rested. The jury started deliberating. Then the defense pulled out a *Perry Mason* moment, the kind you see on television shows but rarely in real-life trials. As the jury deliberated, a man contacted the defense attorneys. He told them his son had seen another boy put Paris in the microwave. The defense immediately asked for a mistrial, and the judge granted one.

I was disappointed, but it was far from over. China remained in custody until we could have a second trial. We would then get the chance to explore exactly what, if anything, this new mystery witness had seen.

Round two started in September 2008, with a new jury. Most of the evidence was the same, with a few exceptions. Linda Williams flipped sides, testifying for the defense that she'd lied in the first trial, completely fabricating China's confession. We knew that wasn't true and hoped the jury would see through this.

The mystery boy testified as well. He'd been five when Paris Talley died. He seemed like a sweet kid, but his testimony was ridiculous. Our prosecutor handled him gently. The boy's version of Paris's death made no sense. It contradicted everything we knew about the case and all that the jury had heard from other witnesses. He described a large group of people being in the home, that the death had occurred during daylight hours. We'd also been able to show through follow-up interviews that this boy was nowhere near Parkside when Paris died. It was a shame: someone had put this kid up to this, while blaming another boy for a hideous crime. We didn't know why, but we knew the story was nonsense.

So did the jury. They convicted China of aggravated murder but declined to sentence her to death. Instead, China received a sentence of life in prison without the possibility of parole. It was over, we thought.

The court of appeals changed that, siding with the defense that certain issues surrounding witness testimony had denied Arnold a fair trial.

The third trial started in May 2011, six years since Paris's death. Our case didn't change much. But the defense had. Linda Williams was gone. Neither side wanted her at that point, since she'd lied under oath in at least one of the two prior trials. The mystery boy was gone, too, as well as the aspersions against the other child. This time, the defense tried to paint Terrell as a viable suspect.

It didn't work. The jury convicted China of aggravated murder and, once again, she was sentenced to life in prison without the possibility of parole. There were appeals, but none of them went anywhere.

The thought of killing an infant in a microwave oven rightfully horrifies people. They always ask: How do you do it? How do you see these things and not have nightmares? The short answer is that we do it for the victims, and that's true. But you *do* have nightmares and sleepless nights. I always say this is my chosen career, but this is not my life. I have a great home life, a fantastic wife, wonderful children, terrific friends. I have a vocation, but I also have an escape. You have to.

China Arnold remains in prison today, and likely will until she dies—rightfully so.

China Arnold put a living, breathing baby girl, her baby girl, in a microwave oven and cooked her to death—all because of an argument with her boyfriend. It was unbelievable cruelty for the most banal of reasons. Our quest for justice took six years, but we got there.

24.
YOU DON'T HAVE
TO DO THIS

IT'S A DANGEROUS job. Everybody knows this, though not everyone respects just how dangerous it is. Between 1786 and 2020, according to the National Law Enforcement Officers Memorial Fund, 22,611 American law enforcement officers died in the line of duty. For the 10 years between 2009 and 2019, the average was 162 deaths per year.

Every one of those deaths affects everyone else. This is particularly true of other police officers. When we hear news of a line-of-duty death, we feel it, even if it happened halfway across the country in a town we've never heard of.

For the public, it's a reminder that we're human, and that some of us give the ultimate sacrifice. Hopefully, it's also a reminder of how many more of us have come close. The public can be quite ambivalent about police: you don't like us when we give you a traffic ticket, but you sure as hell want us there when someone's breaking into your house. Thankfully, most of the public is usually appalled at the death of a police officer.

I know this because I knew four Dayton officers who were killed in the line of duty during my time on the job, and in three of those cases, I was one of the investigators. That is the saddest, hardest duty I've ever known.

I am sometimes asked if I value the life of a police officer over that of a civilian. There is no correct answer to that question, but I always answer it and I answer it truthfully: With a question of my own. I don't value one life over another. But that police officer lying there is my brother or sister. Are you affected more by the loss of a loved one or the loss of a complete stranger? It's inevitable that you're going to be more affected by the loss of a family member, and the police is, in many ways, a family.

I was still in uniform when I experienced my first line-of-duty death. On Sunday, October 11, 1981, Dayton Officer Eddie Hobson responded to his last call.

It was a routine call, just a disturbance. Officer Hobson was driving to the scene when a vehicle turned left in front of his cruiser. The ensuing collision pushed the cruiser into a telephone pole. Officer Hobson died at the scene. He'd been on the job for eight months and was survived by his wife and three children.

The other driver fled the scene but was apprehended. He later pleaded guilty to vehicular homicide, a misdemeanor.

I only met Eddie once, briefly, at a recruit party where new officers were introduced to their field training officers. Eddie was one of the recruits, and I was the FTO for one of his academy classmates.

Eddie was eager to start patrolling. He impressed me with his enthusiasm, which was exceeded only by his smile. He seemed proud to be a Dayton officer and we were proud to have him. Eddie struck me as a great asset for the department: an intelligent, vibrant family man who could be a role model for others in the city. We'll never know what he would have accomplished.

While I barely knew Eddie, his death affected me. Other police deaths would affect me even more, far more than I realized was possible.

I worked with a lot of partners and sergeants in my career. I was close to all of them, but probably none more than Sgt. Larry Grossnickle. For the Grossnickle clan, the Dayton Police Department is a family affair. Larry's father, Lyle, retired from the department as a lieutenant. Larry himself spent many years in homicide. In 1996, Lyle and Larry got to see the third generation enter the department, as Larry's son, Jason, graduated from the police academy.

On May 23, a few months into his new career, Jake, as he was known, stopped by homicide to visit his dad. He was on his way to start his shift at the west side's Third District headquarters. We all kidded with him. We'd known Jake since he was a boy. It is no exaggeration to say that the rest of us were like proud uncles and aunts. Then Jake left.

Less than thirty minutes later, an emergency-assistance call went out. "Officers down!" the radio blared.

Two officers had been ambushed while walking into Third District headquarters. They had no way of knowing that a deranged person had just murdered a potato-chip delivery man at a local store—for no apparent motive—then headed to the nearest police station.

The gunman was twenty-four-year-old Maurice Fareed, whose family owned that convenience store. He was working that day when he'd taken the store gun, kept by the register, then shot the delivery man. We still don't know why, and likely never will. But Fareed took his first victim's delivery truck and drove to the Third District. As the officers were walking into work, Fareed ran up behind them and started shooting.

Both officers were hit in the head. One lived—he had turned his head at probably the right moment and the bullet passed through his jaw. He would return to the force. The other officer died. That was Jake Grossnickle, whose tour of duty lasted only three months.

Other officers ran from the building and returned fire, killing Fareed. Minutes after that, those of us on the homicide squad arrived at a chaotic disaster scene. But for Larry Grossnickle, it was a parent's unfathomable loss. As he arrived, he did not know that one of the victims was his son, but officers ran to him, preventing him from approaching the scene.

Larry left to take care of his family. I took care of the scene. Someone had to. Our chief, who knew how close I was to the Grossnickle family, came over to me and nervously patted my shoulder.

"Doyle, you don't have to do this," he said.

"Thanks, Chief, but I do," I said.

He nodded knowingly and walked away.

I cannot express how much I appreciated his concern for me, especially considering the chaos that surrounded us, and the loss that we all felt. But that's what families do: we take care of one another. And that's why I told the chief that I had to continue working this investigation. I had to do this for our DPD family.

At that point in my career, I'd already been the lead investigator on one line-of-duty death. This was my second. It was not a job I relished. Though countless others would assist me, as the investigation winded down, it would be only me peering into the file, looking at the lab sheets, inspecting the photos—all constantly reminding me of our loss. I had to do this. I wouldn't wish it on anyone else.

When officers are involved in a shooting, particularly a fatal one, the case is usually reviewed by a county grand jury to see if charges are appropriate. Fareed, obviously, was dead and would never stand trial. In all, four officers returned fire and justifiably killed Fareed. The grand jury declined to charge any with a criminal act.

Just four years later, we'd deal with another fatal shooting of a police officer, though in this case, death was not instantaneous. Forty-three-year-old Officer Mary Beall would suffer for more than two years before succumbing to her injuries.

On May 15, 2000, Beall (pronounced "Bell") and her partner responded to the report of a man shooting at his girlfriend. Beall could have shot Raham Twitty, who threatened both officers with his gun. Instead, she tried to reason with him—something that's worth remembering the next time you wonder why an officer shoots an armed suspect.

Mary tried to talk Twitty into surrendering peacefully, even laying her gun on the ground first, hoping he would follow her. Instead, Twitty, twenty-one, fired a bullet into her neck, paralyzing her instantly. Other officers then shot Twitty, who was captured and eventually sent to prison.

Mary had only been an officer for three years. She fought valiantly for her life but died on August 25, 2002. She was survived by her three children and her husband, John, also a Dayton police officer.

Mary was able to testify at Twitty's trial. Her assailant was sentenced to seventy-six years in prison, but Twitty didn't make it anywhere near that long. In 2010, he died of natural causes at Lebanon Correctional Institution.

Ironically, I received the call about his death. I'd retired from DPD in 2007 and was now the Chief Investigator for the Warren County Coroner's Office—and that prison was in our county. As I heard the name "Raham Twitty," I was flooded with memories like water from a fire hose. I composed myself, handled the call, and notified my family at DPD.

As noted earlier, Jake Grossnickle was my second line-of-duty death investigation and Mary Beall was the third—and hopefully final.

The first was Officer Steve Whalen.

March 22, 1991, began as any other spring day. It was a Friday, so most people were looking forward to the weekend. There was no warning of the horror that awaited us.

Karl Ray Vultee, thirty-three, had been a successful businessman in Beavercreek, a Dayton suburb located in nearby Greene County. But Vultee's mental state was unraveling. As he sank deeper and deeper into depression and other mental disorders, his business and his marriage failed. By 1991, he was clearly disturbed. Friends and family worried that something needed to be done, and they tried. But according to psychiatrists, Vultee was not dangerous. On March 22, Vultee would prove them wrong.

By this time, Vultee was living in a cheap motel on Dayton's north side. The few items he still owned were kept in a storage locker in Beavercreek. Vultee had withdrawn from everyone. He had withdrawn from life.

That day, Vultee found a steel lock securing the door of his motel room. When he enquired, a clerk explained that Vultee continuously broke the rules of his rental agreement and, as such, had been locked out. Furious, Vultee drove off in his red pickup truck, vowing to return.

Officer Steve Whalen knew nothing of this. Whalen, thirty-eight, and a fifteen-year police veteran, was in the city's east side, starting his shift. Steve and I were good friends. When I was a neighborhood-assistance officer, Steve worked in the same district where I was assigned. He was always willing to help me, and as we became friends, we were surprised to learn we lived just five houses from each other. When I became a police officer, Steve was one of the first to congratulate me. Though I was assigned to a different district and our paths rarely passed on duty, we stayed friends.

Vultee drove to his storage locker and took out the .223-caliber AR-15 rifle he'd stashed there, then returned to the motel. The desk clerk saw Vultee's truck pull into the lot, then watched as Vultee got out, rifle in hand. He calmly, deliberately walked to his room, where he took aim at the lock and fired. Then he returned to his truck and drove to the desk clerk's window.

"I'll kill anyone who tries to stop me," Vultee vowed as he drove away. The clerk called the police.

DPD officers arrived at the motel, surveyed the damage to the door, and noted the spent casings. This was hardly a whodunit. All of Vultee's information was at the front desk on his rental agreement. Though the damage to the door qualified as only a misdemeanor offense, the officers knew this was serious. Vultee had used a rifle to shoot the lock, then vowed to kill anyone who tried to stop him from whatever his next plans were. Those officers gave a detailed broadcast over the police radio, including a description of Vultee and his red truck. The broadcast advised all officers to use caution if they encountered Vultee.

Officer Whalen never heard that broadcast.

Steve was one of our most personable officers and was devoted to serving the community. As such, he frequently attended community meetings. This particular night, Steve had a civilian rider with him. She was interested in police work and Steve was a logical choice to show her what it was like. In those days, if you signed a waiver of liability and had a valid reason to do a ride-along, it would be allowed. That day's events would change that policy.

Steve and his rider attended an east-end community meeting. He advised dispatch of his location and turned his radio down so as not to disrupt the meeting—causing him to miss the vital broadcast about Vultee.

As Steve was at the meeting, Lt. Randy Beane was patrolling the east end, searching for Vultee and his truck. It was now dark, which made the search more difficult. Lieutenant Beane was well liked, a savvy police officer who had once served on the homicide squad.

The meeting adjourned. Steve turned his radio volume back up and he and his civilian rider returned to his cruiser. As they approached the intersection of Xenia and St. Paul Avenues—right in the heart of Steve's beat—they passed Beane, who was in an unmarked cruiser. Vultee's red truck was just in front of Steve's cruiser. Beane saw the truck, motioned to Steve, then made a U-turn so he could back up Steve.

Steve activated his overhead lights and Vultee slowly pulled his truck to a stop.

"Why are we pulling this guy over?" the rider asked.

"I don't know," Steve said. "The lieutenant must have seen him do something."

Steve left his cruiser and approached the truck. Apparently thinking this was just a traffic stop, he approached it as such. Beane was now outside of his car too.

Without warning, Vultee opened fire from his truck, hitting both officers, who each returned fire, to no avail. Beane activated his emergency button, drawing officers from across the city. The first cruiser, carrying a two-person crew, arrived just as Vultee was pulling away. The officer who was driving dropped off his partner to tend to the fallen officers, then began to pursue Vultee.

That first officer surveyed the scene. The civilian rider was uninjured. At the sound of the shots, she had curled up under the cruiser's dashboard. Lieutenant Beane had been shot in the legs but would fully recover.

Steve had been shot in the head. He lay motionless in the street as paramedics arrived. Though Steve was transported to the nearest hospital, where he was pronounced dead, I think we all believe he died at the scene.

The pursuit of Vultee continued down US 35, as more than thirty cruisers joined the chase. Vultee was heading east, back toward Beavercreek, his hometown. When he got there, he pulled into a service station where two Beavercreek police officers were fueling their marked cruisers. Vultee left his rifle in the truck and ran toward the Beavercreek officers, who had no idea what was going on. But seeing the swarm of Dayton cruisers, lights and sirens blaring, they knew it wasn't good.

Dayton is in Montgomery County. Though Beavercreek is only a few miles from Dayton's eastern border, it is in Greene County. The pursuit had started in Montgomery County, and none of the radio traffic had been relayed to Greene County. It was chaos, with officers screaming, "Get down, get down" and "back off" and "get away from him" and "hands in the air" and "freeze." Amazingly, Vultee complied and was taken into custody uninjured.

I wasn't there for any of that. As it usually happens, my involvement started with a call from dispatch. This one was particularly urgent.

"Doyle, we've got two officers shot at Xenia and St. Paul, it's—"

"Say no more," I said. "I'm en route."

"Thanks, man."

He was grateful. I knew I was just one of many, many calls that dispatcher needed to make—to other members of the homicide squad, to internal affairs, to the department's command staff. He would have to repeat those details, over and over again. I would spare him from repeating them to me, as I was responding no matter what.

I found a crowded scene, with two blocks of Xenia Avenue cordoned off by the familiar bright yellow police tape. Lieutenant Beane's unmarked cruiser sat behind Officer Whalen's marked car. I looked at the unmarked first. I spotted divots in the asphalt, caused by Vultee's gunfire, in front of and below the open driver's door. There were bullet holes through the door, which were consistent with the injuries to Lieutenant Beane's legs.

Steve's cruiser had multiple bullet holes to the driver's side door, hood, and windshield. His gun, flashlight, and DPD hat sat in the street by a pool of blood. I looked at the hat. There was a bullet hole right through the cap band. A few moments later, some uniformed officers solemnly approached me with an update: Officer Whalen was dead.

I'd lost a good friend, but there was no time to grieve. Not then. We had work to do. And believe it or not, I was glad of that. Working this case would keep me occupied and distract me from the horror of that loss. I also knew this investigation would carry an awesome responsibility. I wasn't sure if I was prepared for that, but I wanted this case. And I was assigned this case.

At this point, I'd been on the squad for six years. I'd seen a lot. But this was a fellow officer gunned down in the street. Everyone in the department would be watching me. I resolved not to let them down.

In Beavercreek, crews were photographing Vultee's truck, which would be towed to the crime lab in Dayton. The rifle was going there too. Vultee was being transported to Dayton police headquarters. When I was finished at the murder scene, I drove to headquarters to interview the man who had killed my friend.

He was already seated in an interview room when my partner and I arrived. Vultee was a small man who appeared older than his early thirties. I'd expected a hardened criminal, someone easy to hate—and I wanted to hate him. Instead, I was looking at a pathetic person. Vultee wasn't mouthy. He bordered on timid. In a way, that made the whole situation even more sad.

To our surprise, Vultee freely admitted to shooting Officer Whalen, then elaborated on it. That led to a rant about how Officer Whalen, whom he did not know, was a threat to him. Vultee then described a conspiracy against him that linked Steve and the Beavercreek police as well. It was incredible. None of it made any sense, at least not to anyone who wasn't Karl Vultee. After he'd rambled for a while, my partner and I left the interview room.

"Well, it is a confession," my partner said.

"Hell, he might as well have said space aliens were involved," I said.

"Worse than that, I think he believes it."

"I know."

There was no doubt Vultee was unbalanced. But that did not mean that he would be found not guilty by reason of insanity. That's a legal question, not a medical diagnosis. It should be noted that many, many disturbed people are sitting in prisons. They may have genuine mental illnesses or disorders. But they are not insane. To be found not guilty by reason of insanity, one must either not know what they were doing at the time they were doing it or know what they were doing but not realize it was wrong.

Vultee had acted deliberately and with purpose. He had shot two DPD officers, one fatally. He had fled the scene and surrendered at the site he chose. I truly believed his actions showed, regardless of any mental disorder, that he knew what he was doing.

There was plenty of work to be done. But the day after the shootings, my most important task was to meet with the parents of Officer Whalen.

My partner and I drove to the home of Bill and Helen Whalen. They lived in an immaculately kept, modest house in Riverside, a suburb on Dayton's east side, nestled between the city and Beavercreek. Several of Steve's fellow officers were present. There would be a strong police presence for as long as the family wanted it.

I introduced myself. The Whalens were an older couple, looking frail and helpless seated together on the couch. Unsurprisingly, they appeared exhausted from the events of the previous twenty-four hours. I explained how well I'd known their son and that we had been friends.

"I'm so sorry for your loss," I said softly. They knew I meant it. I could tell. I assured them the DPD would take care of everything. Whatever they needed. I also assured them I would get justice for Steve. What else could I say?

"Doyle is one of the best we've got," an officer said.

"Thanks," I said. "I'll do my best."

"We're all counting on you," another officer said. I nodded. By now Vultee's mental state had become common knowledge. All of us knew this was far from over.

Though Ohio law has since changed, back then, the killing of a police officer did not automatically carry an aggravated murder charge. On the lesser charge of murder, the penalty was fifteen years to life. I could not accept that Officer Whalen's killer could possibly be released in fifteen years.

For aggravated murder and a potential penalty of death (or life in prison with no parole), we would need to show that Vultee acted with a purpose and "with prior calculation and design." That meant we would have to show that Vultee had planned his attack on the officers.

I was part of the discussion with the prosecutors. It dragged on. I understood their quandary.

But I knew this case warranted an aggravated murder charge. I reminded them about Vultee's threat to the motel clerk that he would kill anyone who tried to stop him. "Doesn't that show prior calculation and design?" I asked. It was a good point. They agreed. I walked out of the prosecutor's office with a warrant for aggravated murder with death penalty specifications.

To my surprise, there was a large group of DPD officers waiting in the hallway. They gathered around me, patted me on the back, and thanked me for working a most difficult case. "We appreciate it, Doyle," one said.

"I know," I said. "Thanks for being here."

It truly meant a lot to me, but it also reminded me of my responsibility to every last DPD officer. The officers left as I filed the warrant with the clerk of courts.

I was mentally and physically exhausted, too tired to take the stairs like I usually did. I stared straight ahead as I waited for the elevator to come. Just then, Jorge "George" Del Rio, an undercover Dayton detective, came around the corner.

"You okay?" he asked.

"Yeah, I'm fine," I replied, trying to crack a smile. But I wasn't, and apparently it showed. Steve wasn't just a DPD officer. He was my friend. This was a tough one for me.

"You know we're all here for you if you need us," George said.

"I know that, and I appreciate it," I said as I got on the elevator. "I'll get some rest tomorrow."

I didn't know George particularly well. He was a younger guy, relatively new to the force. Perhaps that's why his kindness stood out to me, because I didn't know him well. But I always remembered it, particularly on November 7, 2019, when George's tour of duty ended. Del Rio, still an undercover officer, had represented Dayton police on a US Drug Enforcement

Administration task force for nineteen years. He was shot in the head while executing a federal search warrant at a drug house, becoming the twenty-fifth Dayton officer to die in the line of duty.

* * *

The funeral of a police officer killed in the line of duty is as impressive and moving an event as you will ever experience. Steve's funeral was no exception. The procession of marked cruisers, with overhead lights flashing, stretched for miles. All along the route, people stood in awe. Some saluted, some had signs, some just watched. All were respectful. The procession originated at the University of Dayton Arena and ended a few miles later at a cemetery in a southern suburb of Dayton. I learned later that the last cruiser was exiting the lot at UD just as the first cruiser was arriving at the cemetery.

There were hundreds of cruisers from multiple jurisdictions. Thousands of officers stood at attention in their dress uniforms. A black mourning band was draped across each and every officer's badge out of respect for our fallen comrade. It was a fitting show of respect. I'll never forget it.

In the weeks that followed, Vultee began sending letters from jail to several different people connected to the case, including me. They were the rambling thoughts of a madman. On the envelopes, Vultee would add crude drawings of men with knives or guns, or even holding a severed head. Vultee was crazy. I was no longer even thinking about the death penalty. I just wanted a conviction.

Vultee's trial was to begin in July 1992. But concerns about his sanity loomed over everyone, including the defense team. The man was obviously disturbed. But was he, legally speaking, insane? That could be a close call, and both sides knew it. For us, that meant a cop killer could avoid prison. For the defense, it could mean a death sentence for their client.

Just before the trial was to start, the two sides reached an agreement. Vultee withdrew his pleas of not guilty and not guilty by reason of insanity. He then pleaded guilty to all felony counts, including the aggravated murder of Officer Steve Whalen. The three-judge panel accepted his guilty pleas. That left the penalty phase of the trial, because this was a capital case.

Vultee waived his right to a jury for the penalty phase, so the three-judge panel would view a mini-trial. We called witnesses and displayed evidence supporting why we thought the death penalty was appropriate. The defense called a series of psychologists and psychiatrists to testify about Vultee's mental state.

The three-judge panel came to a unanimous decision: while Vultee was responsible for his actions, he was also mentally ill. The judges declined to impose the death penalty. But Vultee was sentenced to life in prison. His first review for potential release will be in June 2048. If alive, Vultee will be ninety years old then. And there is no guarantee he will be released then. It is truly a life sentence.

I left the courtroom satisfied with the decision of the judges. Vultee was deranged. I knew that from the start. By now, it was obvious to everyone. I felt justice had been served and I think that Steve would have thought so. But I wanted to make sure Bill and Helen Whalen understood.

My mind wandered as I drove to their home. This horror was the result of a chance meeting between Karl Vultee and two police officers. Any deviation—a left turn here, a right turn there—by any of the three and they would never have met. Steve would still be alive. But there is also no guarantee that Vultee wouldn't have killed someone else that night, perhaps another unsuspecting officer. I thought back to some of the close calls I'd experienced. Fate and luck are sometimes on our side. Sometimes they are not. It was the nature of the job, and of life itself. I pulled into the driveway and exited my car.

I'd gotten to know the Whalens since Steve's death. They greeted me warmly. I explained what had occurred, and that it was the best resolution we could have obtained, given the circumstances. They understood. More importantly, they were satisfied.

Bill and Helen became part of my family. We regularly visited each other, and they were included in every holiday and birthday celebration we had. Sadly, Bill passed away a few years later. I was at his side when he died at Hospice of Dayton.

Helen had now lost both of the men in her life. But she was not alone. She had two brothers and their families, who lived in the area. She also had multiple DPD officers who kept in touch with her. Helen had once remarked how Steve would call her every morning to check on her and how she missed those calls. So, I started calling her.

Fate had taken Steve from us. But fate had given me Bill and Helen. It's strange how things work out sometimes. For twenty-five years after Steve's death, calling Helen was part of my daily routine—I spoke with her every day. When she needed hospice care, I arranged it. When she died on October 5, 2017, at the age of ninety, I was standing next to her bed.

25.
CLOSING TIME

ALL CAREERS, LIKE all lives, come to an end. I retired from the Dayton Police Department in 2007. But I wasn't done with death investigation. The new Warren County Coroner was my good friend, Russell Uptegrove, whom you'll remember from the China Arnold case. Russ and I had worked together numerous times and we had a developed a special bond. There are some people you work well with (and maybe some you don't), but there are only a select few where you truly complement each other. When Russ offered me the position of chief investigator, I accepted. It was a good fit, and a good way to transition into the next phase of my life. Just as life goes on, so does death, including violent death—and so I'd be able to continue doing death investigations.

Warren County sits between Dayton and Cincinnati. The northern edge includes some of Dayton's southern suburbs. But as Dayton's metropolitan area expands south and Cincinnati's expands north, southwest Ohio's Interstate 75 corridor is merging into one metropolis. Along the interstate, you'll find towns that are growing exponentially. But the county still holds many rural hollows, places I'd lived reasonably near all of my life yet never had visited. Warren County was a particularly interesting place to be these days, and this would be a great opportunity for me and my family.

I'd had a great run in Dayton, where I'd been on the force for nearly twenty-nine years. The last twenty-two I'd been on the homicide squad. Looking back, I feel fortunate to have worked in what was a golden era of forensic expansion, as new technologies, digital and other, changed how we did business.

I watched forensic scene investigation evolve from Polaroid photos and tape measures to 3D mapping and laser measurements. When I started, the best that blood analysis could give you was the type—if you could even get that. The type would be used to exclude suspects, but not to identify them. Now, DNA evidence can truly identify the suspect beyond a reasonable doubt.

From surveillance cameras at private businesses—there are more of them out there than you can imagine—we can identify suspects even if we're not lucky enough to have human eyewitnesses.

Cellular phones give us a good idea of where our suspects were at any given time. If a suspect states he can't possibly be the murderer because he was in Indiana at the time, and he produces a group of cronies to back up that alibi, it's awfully nice to be able to ask: Then why was your phone pinging to a cellular tower two blocks from the crime scene in Ohio?

Still, technology doesn't change everything. It doesn't alter the basic decency most people have, regardless of race, religion, or social status. Nor does it change the sheer awfulness of that small—but busy—percentage of people who commit most of our crimes and cause so much misery.

Perhaps most critically, technology doesn't eliminate the most important trait of a good homicide detective: the never-give-up work ethic.

When it was time to leave, my wife threw me a retirement party at the Fraternal Order of Police Hall. She had issued a general invitation that any and all were welcome. I was over-whelmed by the response. Every aspect of my professional life showed up. Dayton officers and those from other depart-ments, prosecutors, defense attorneys, news crews, victims' rel-atives, and friends too numerous to list here. Obviously, my now-adult children were there. Thankfully, Helen Whalen was still healthy enough to attend. It wouldn't have been the same without her.

The *Dayton Daily News* ran a front-page story about my career. A local news station did its own story, set to the song "Closing Time," by the group Semisonic. It was all a lot to take in, but it was much appreciated.

"'Bout time we got some good press, huh, Burke?" one of my partners remarked. Yes, there were few "good" stories sur-rounding our job. It just wasn't that type of work.

I stepped away from all my well-wishers and took a moment alone to think back over all the years. Death spares no race, no economic class. White, Black, brown, blue, nobody makes it out alive. Money can buy you everything except life. Even bil-lionaires die. But violent death cheats.

I am frequently asked what my toughest case has been. The answer is simple to me: the next one. I've survived the ones in the past. Who knows what horror tomorrow might bring? The next one may be the worst one. We'll find out.

How do you rank tragedies such as these? You can't and you don't. Every victim is grieved by someone. Some cases are more sensational than others, but even the "routine" homicide is a tragedy. In the time it takes to pull a trigger, shove a knife, or—in the case of China Arnold—program a microwave oven, lives are changed forever. Many lives had been changed in my career, mine included.

The unsolved cases haunt you, both the ones where you're certain who the suspect is but never got the right evidentiary breaks, and the ones that are true mysteries. You know it's impossible to solve every case, but you work your hardest. That's all anyone can do. But I still think about the ones that got away.

I have witnessed humankind at its worst. I have worked cases that were so gruesome, they didn't seem real. I have arrested conscience-free murderers, true sociopaths whose only remorse was that they got caught. Yet I also met good people who tried to do the right thing, be they witnesses or friends or relatives of the deceased. I'm not left with any real regrets about my career choice.

At the time of my retirement, I had investigated more than eight hundred homicides and countless other suspicious deaths. Some I barely recall. Others I remember as if they happened yesterday.

To civilians who have read this book, I hope it helps you better understand death investigation and the men and women who do it each and every day. It is a responsibility entrusted to us that we do not take lightly.

To my brothers and sisters still serving in law enforcement today: stay safe and take care of one another. To those who have retired from service: hold your head high and be proud of the career you chose.

It was my honor to have served as a Dayton police officer. I served with pride. I am still proud today.

At my retirement party, I recognized the familiar face of Anthony Dyer's mother. Anthony was the young boy who had been killed by the Folks Gang a decade earlier. One of Anthony's killers was Dayron Talbott, who had survived Samuel Moreland's rampage a decade before that.

Anthony's mother was still coping with his loss. I expect she always will. It's sometimes said that closure is a myth, and that is probably true. But she had taken the time to stop by and wish me well. I was happy to see her and to know that, despite her grief, she was doing well. We talked briefly, hugged each other, and then she was gone.

That was the best retirement gift I could have ever hoped for. Maybe sometimes we do make a difference. Maybe sometimes we can right a wrong, at least somewhat. I sure hope so.

GRAND PATRONS

Alan T. Kraker
Andrew Farlaino
Ava Housley
Nicole Burke
Cathleen Combs
Christina Stiakakis
David A. Matthews
David Becker
Dennis Hatcher
Doug P. Roderick
Fire48off
Gary L. Engel
Janie Fideler
Jason Antonick
Jeannette Bradshaw
John M. Stevens Jr.
Jonathan M. Westendorf
Judy A. Yahle
Kurt Schwarz
Lauren Simon
Lee Lehman

Lisa Jay
Melissa M. Tkach
Miami Armory Shooting
Michelle Heinrich
Millie Isaacs
Monica Becker
Monnie Bush
Nicholas Behymer
Reil Becker
Richard Bens
Ronald Hess
Russell Uptegrove
Sara E. Newton
Seth Whitlock
Shannon Nuckols Deye
Springboro Biomed
Springboro Shooting Sports
Stephen M. Crews
Susan N. Grieco
Thomas C. Ste Marie
Thomas Schiff
Vincent A. Grieco Jr.
Wanda G. Lai
William H. Bowman

INKSHARES

INKSHARES is a reader-driven publisher and producer based in Oakland, California. Our books are selected not by a group of editors, but by readers worldwide.

While we've published books by established writers like *Big Fish* author Daniel Wallace and *Star Wars: Rogue One* scribe Gary Whitta, our aim remains surfacing and developing the new author voices of tomorrow.

Previously unknown Inkshares authors have received starred reviews and been featured in the *New York Times.* Their books are on the front tables of Barnes & Noble and hundreds of independents nationwide, and many have been licensed by publishers in other major markets. They are also being adapted by Oscar-winning screenwriters at the biggest studios and networks.

Interested in making your own story a reality? Visit Inkshares.com to start your own project or find other great books.

CPSIA information can be obtained
at www.ICGtesting.com
Printed in the USA
LVHW072248290623
751231LV00004B/27